SELF-LEADERSHIP IN SOCIAL WORK
Reflections from practice

Bill McKitterick

First published in Great Britain in 2015 by

Policy Press
University of Bristol
1-9 Old Park Hill
Bristol BS2 8BB
UK
t: +44 (0)117 954 5940
e: pp-info@bristol.ac.uk
www.policypress.co.uk

North American office:
Policy Press
c/o The University of Chicago Press
1427 East 60th Street
Chicago, IL 60637, USA
t: +1 773 702 7700
f: +1 773-702-9756
e:sales@press.uchicago.edu
www.press.uchicago.edu

© Policy Press 2015

British Library Cataloguing in Publication Data
A catalogue record for this book is available from the British Library.

Library of Congress Cataloging-in-Publication Data
A catalog record for this book has been requested.

ISBN 978 1 44731 485 1 paperback

Cover design by Policy Press
Front cover: image kindly supplied by Florin Garoi
Printed and bound in Great Britain by CMP, Poole
The Policy Press uses environmentally responsible print partners

Contents

Acknowledgements   v
Introduction   vi

one   What leadership means in practice in social work   1

two   Leadership vacuum   31

three   Sources of leadership in the profession   55

four   Clarity of purpose in social work practice   73

five   The social worker manager as leader, colleague and   93
           champion

six   Leadership within direct practice   113

seven   Leadership within a multi-disciplinary environment   129

eight   Optimism, filling the vacuum and taking the lead   149

References   171
Index   197

Acknowledgements

Peter Gilbert's seminal book *Leadership, being effective and remaining human* (2005, Russell House Publishing) remains a rare discourse on leadership by practitioners rather than being the exclusive domain of managers. In particular his analysis of its essential aspects and the etymology of the word guided my early thinking. Malcolm Grundy's writing about a vacuum of leadership in another field, *Leadership and oversight* (2011, Mowbray), and Barbara Kellerman's *The end of leadership* (2012, Harper Collins), a critique of the leadership industry and the potential authority of 'followership', have been illuminating and have helped identify the current challenges for social work as part of the wider malaise of the repression of managerialism.

Friends and colleagues in social work have provided both the inspiration and impetus for this book, just as much as the negative forces of organisational self-interest and anti-professionalism in human services. The people I have met and worked with over my time in social work – children, young people, adults, community groups, families and carers – have been both an inspiration and an education in what social work can and should achieve. This is beyond care management, relentless assessments, an exclusive focus on performance indicators and passive implementation of ritualised procedures. They have shown me how social work is about change, the therapeutic imperative and social justice.

Finally I thank members of my family, Jodie, Jenny, Kerry and James, who have endured and contributed to my ruminations about social work and in particular the development of the ideas about leadership in human services explored in this book.

Introduction

The narrative of this book is an analysis of leadership ideas, considered alongside the current vacuum in social work leadership. This is linked to management and administrative support being confused with professional leadership. Social workers need to recognise themselves as experts in their field and act as leaders. They therefore need to be recognised and acknowledged as leaders, a valued part of the collective and participative leadership of an ambitious profession. Part of the current shared challenge is social work's capacity for, and arguably an embrace of, ambiguity, and a lack of clarity of purpose, unless prescribed by others. The self-confident assertion and demonstration of social workers' specific skills, knowledge and evidence base, leadership from within rather than from above or outside, are the most effective challenges to the constraints of a culture of regulation, legal and regulatory definition and managerialism. Ultimately this will ensure a creative, skilful and assertive social work service, firmly rooted in the experience and voices of the people served, rather than a passive administration of welfare and social care. By asserting a far more confident clarity of purpose in direct practice, including social worker managers, working with colleagues and in multi-disciplinary settings, there can be optimism. This leadership belongs to all, and will come from within us all – but it requires confidence, respect and ambition in equal measures.

Leadership is a vital, central, part of being a practising social worker. While many of the UK national initiatives in social work have been from government and carried out as ministerial initiatives or by government-funded bodies, the knowledge, experience and expertise of what constitutes good and effective practice is a responsibility held by every social worker. Terms such as 'competence' and 'capability', used within government or regulatory guidance, can only reflect the internal knowledge, evidence base, expertise and values of social work; they cannot prescribe or restrict them. In making the case for the ownership of leadership from *within* social work, I have combined an analysis of the contemporary challenges with evidence that informs successful ways forward. The constant changes in the architecture of the organisations around social work, the births and deaths of the quangos (quasi-autonomous non-governmental organisations), and the power struggles between organisations and titular positions that would make a claim to exercise leadership, have demonstrated that only social workers as individuals can take responsibility and exercise leadership, both within their practice and with their colleagues. Social workers, in whatever role, can articulate and explain how social work can achieve positive change. This book explores tactics and strategies to provide leadership, within multi-disciplinary teams, around vulnerable children, adults and families, as well as leadership within social work teams and services. In addition, the use of leadership within direct practice, sharing knowledge, skills, insight and drawing on models of empowerment, is explored and demonstrated.

I address the questions of why social work leadership is valuable, what it is, how is it done, and why it is so lacking and undeveloped in the current literature, policy documents and organisational behaviour. This is not a traditional book about generic leadership and management skills. In the current climate of restricted public spending and uncertainties about the extent and future scale of the welfare state, the lack of a coherent leadership of the social work profession 'from the front' or 'from the top' can be pernicious and destructive. In any event, this lack of leadership is chillingly unambitious. Positively, its absence gives each of us the opportunity to take control, to build and to take authority. My aim is to encourage the current generations of social workers to exercise leadership in their own practice, within their service and in their future professional careers, primarily from within. I argue that the current drivers of social work are outside the profession or are managerialist in their approach, slavishly following or second-guessing the current interests of government ministers. I recall, as a member of a group of directors of social services invited to advise ministers, being kicked under the table by a colleague when I pointed out that a potential policy line would be harmful to social work safeguarding services. I was later told that it was more important to 'keep a seat at the ministerial table' than to tell the truth. It may be that, in the future, social work empowered and emboldened by success in self-leadership can combat the current constellation of impenetrable employer, managerial and government organisational self-interests.

This book includes an overview of the current literature and research on leadership, centred on public service and closely related professions. Shared and distinct principles and themes for social work are examined, alongside ideas drawn from general management and from the wider social care arena. This is within the narrative of the current changes in public services, often termed as 'reform' and 'transformations', often forgetting history, failing to make good use of the experience and evidence held within social workers. The impetus to write this book arose from my experience in practice, in the leadership of social work practice and professional development, working in government intervention teams in services following critical inspections, contributing to the social work reform programme in England and in particular, working with social workers early in their careers, with their managers and educators. The book identifies the responsibilities and opportunities for building greater confidence, based on a greater emphasis on evidence-informed practice, through self-leadership and leadership by *all* social workers across the services.

The aims of the book are to:

- build the case for confident, skilled, assertive and knowledgeable self-leadership, from within each social worker;
- challenge the current managerialist agenda in the provision of social work services that is focused on prescribed process, limited delegated discretion and low use of evidence-informed practice;
- critically analyse what lies behind this, the barriers to change and the positive opportunities for transformation;
- provoke reflection and debate, with an emphasis on learning and developing specific qualities and practice skills;
- explore current theories and models of leadership across a wide range of settings, the thinking on a contemporary vacuum in leadership and doubts about the value of leadership education;
- examine the aspirations and impact of the social work reform programme in England following the deaths of Victoria Climbié and Peter Connelly, the Munro review of child protection and the uncertainties about the role of social work in adult social care.

There is currently a substantial and enduring lack of confidence within the profession. There is a failure of leadership at senior level to create and support a strong professional identity, firmly bedded in competent practice. Social work is a purposeful activity to achieve positive change, the 'therapeutic imperative', and social justice, as opposed to the passive administration of social care and welfare. The central thesis of the book is the importance of establishing leadership from within social work itself, based on practice skills and knowledge, as opposed to the managerialist agenda of prescribed process and central direction. The focus is on a reflective analysis of leadership in social work, a practical exploration of the development of leadership skills and styles, firmly based in current social work practice across different service areas.

Setting the scene and making the case for the reclamation of professionalism and ownership of leadership requires an analysis of the challenges faced, the forces behind them and the evidence that informs successful ways forward. The book aims to show how the effectiveness and value of social work can be fulfilled through the development and use of knowledge, evidence, practice skills and professional development. It looks at how social workers, in whatever role, can articulate and explain how social work can make a difference and achieve positive change. It is important to identify the tactics and strategies to provide leadership, individually, within teams and in senior positions.

Can social work and social workers engage and re-engage in collective action to challenge social injustice, including poor or ineffectual services? Can each social worker take or re-take collegiate control of the organisations that claim to represent them, or prescribe how they practise and what they do? These are not questions of individuals in high-profile positions making headline statements; rather, it is the combined activities and thinking of individual social workers, building alternative solutions and clearly articulating what makes services good and effective. This should be both as individual professionals, and collectively, as members of a profession, not driven by ever-increasing guidance, regulation or government intervention.

The leadership skills and approaches required for social work practice are explored. These are integrated with suggestions on the contribution of social work to progressive continuing professional development, drawing on contemporary social work practice skills, research knowledge and the service and public policy context. Consideration is given to how positional leaders, such as supervisors, academic researchers, inspirational figures and senior managers, can be used to develop and promote practice skills and reflective and creative practice. Supporting the development of capabilities in leadership requires the identification of what forms of leadership best suit the individual and the circumstances.

The emphasis is on the particular knowledge and approaches that all social workers can and must successfully use. These are to be exercised in practice, within professional supervision, within teams and with colleagues. This will lay the foundations for rigorous professional development, moving to become senior practitioners and key decision makers within the profession, as assertive, respected and effective leaders. It should also enable social worker managers to reclaim their own professional status and responsibilities. I fear that for many of them this will require learning practice knowledge anew, making space for reflective analysis and a rekindling of the fire in their belly for social justice and purposeful practice. Social workers use leadership in their direct work with the people they serve, developing and sharing insight, developing a shared plan of how social work help will be given, how other services and interventions will assist. Sharing knowledge and the evidence of what works shares authority and power in the solutions to problems. This is a user- and carer-focused approach, democratically sharing the knowledge of evidence-informed practice to achieve greater effectiveness and benefits in the social work service provided, as well as having an impact on the wider public services in which it is located.

Leadership within related professions and services are examined for both shared and distinct principles and themes. This is within the narrative of the current reform and transformations of public services. The leadership of social work and of social work practice is at a critical time – social workers are increasingly located in multi-disciplinary teams, managed by non-social workers, and their roles and responsibilities either more tightly defined, as in child protection and children in care, or more diffusely, as in services for adults. An increasing number of social workers are working in organisations not led by social workers and in independent practice. This book identifies the responsibilities and opportunities for building greater confidence, through self-leadership and leadership by *all* social workers across these services.

Outline of the book

Self-leadership has been under-recognised in social work, leadership often confused with management and reserved to organisations or specific posts, separated from practice and practice wisdom. Drawing on my experience as a practitioner, supervisor, manager and educator, and reflecting on the challenges of reduced expenditure, increasing demands and critical inspections, I can only see a way forward which places all social workers, at whatever stage in their career, as leaders in their direct practice, in their work with colleagues and in their use of knowledge, evidence and experience. Separating professional capabilities in practice, education and management plays down the social worker as *practitioner, professional* and *social scientist* (Croisdale-Appleby, 2014), and inadvertently isolates the manager from evidence-informed practice and the educator from practice.

Chapter One examines the definitions, descriptions and styles of leadership. It addresses how judgement, discretion and choice for each social worker can be fostered and encouraged, as opposed to practice being prescribed and contained as a technical activity. Leadership in other services and professions is considered. In Chapter Two the leadership vacuum is addressed; while there are many organisations and titular positions that may claim leadership in social work, this is often to the detriment of facilitating or supporting expertise, confidence, trust and the development of a profession-owned corpus of knowledge, evidence and wisdom.

Chapters Three and Four focus on the sources of leadership and the imperative for greater clarity about what social work claims and demonstrates it can achieve. The recent history of aspirations and ambitions for greater trust and autonomy have been met by a resistance to collegiate and collective working and defensiveness in those organisations and interests which would lose authority, influence and money if social work became more self-reliant and self-sustaining. Chapter Five turns to the role and responsibility of managers who are social workers, looking at their role as fellow professionals, colleagues rather than directors of technicians or general managers. Leadership in direct practice is considered in Chapter Six. There are two aspects – first, working directly with individuals and families, respecting self-determination, protection and above all working towards the solutions they can identify as effective for themselves, and second, working with colleagues and within teams, sharing insights, knowledge and skills.

The challenge of working in multi-disciplinary teams where line management may not be by a social worker, and working collaboratively with other professionals, is addressed in Chapter Seven. Other professional groups may have greater confidence in their distinct knowledge and skill base, and can appear to have greater autonomy. The communication skills and methods social workers can use from the start of their careers enable the sharing of their knowledge and distinctive perspective, demonstrating their practice skills, the contributions they bring, and explaining their roles and responsibilities.

All social workers use their leadership qualities and skills in these settings, within the discourses of direct practice and in working collaboratively with colleagues. Looking to the future, in developing a greater confidence and clarity of knowledge, skills and evidence-informed practice, the vacuum in leadership can be filled by a more assertive, collective collegiate profession, rather than being legislatively, managerially and procedurally driven. The dependence on government funding and initiatives can be shrugged off, learning from our own practice, knowledge and experience.

ONE

What leadership means in practice in social work

Introduction

In this chapter descriptions of leadership are reviewed and its purpose discussed. What is its value, and what are the benefits of good leadership? Leadership is an integral, core part of both direct professional practice, and how we all work within services and with colleagues. The management of the organisation and of the services where social work is located, while important, depend on assertive, confident and competent professionalism. Without this, social work and social work services are subject to the negative forces of managerialism, the denial of expertise and creativity, with a dominance of technocratic or procedurally driven prescription of what is done and how it is done (Harris and White, 2009, p 149). It is interesting to reflect that this is not a new issue, but has been an increasingly troublesome one for social work. In a different context, Seabrook (2013, p 98) quotes the report from the Poor Law commissioners in 1834:

> ... the object of machinery is to diminish the want, not only of physical, but of moral and intellectual qualities on the part of the workman. In many cases it enables the master to confine him to narrow routine of similar operations, in which the least error or delay is capable of immediate detection. Judgement or intelligence are not required for processes which can be performed only in one mode, and which constant repetition has made mechanical.

It is notable that the English College of Social Work (2014, p 3) begins a description of the distinctive role of social workers with, 'Social workers use a distinctive range of legal and social work knowledge and skills.' Legal knowledge and skills are given precedence over those of social work. In the same document on the role and functions of social workers in England, out of a total of 130 references, 99 are from legislation or case law, 25 from government guidance or government organisations, and only three from social work organisations. This underlines the lack of clarity or certainty on what social work, of itself, can and should demonstrate – this is to deny the body of experience and expertise each social worker brings to their work. The evidence base for effective interventions as active social workers is an integral part of the leadership of practice, which recognises the range of research methods and approaches available across social sciences (Shaw and Norton, 2007; Rubin and Babbie, 2011). According to Featherstone et al (2014, p 73), 'There is a pressing need to develop forms of organisational learning and social work education, which inoculate practitioners against becoming passive vessels into which chunks of knowledge or … policy incantations … may be poured.' We have far to go.

A range of different accounts and definitions of leadership are discussed in this book, including transformational leadership, servant and citizen leadership, and self-leadership and the overall transactional nature of all leadership. The spectrum of traditional leadership accounts, from dictatorial and authoritarian, to servant or citizen, are aligned against the consequent level or degree of discretion and authority permitted or encouraged. This chapter concludes with considering leadership in other services and professions, including education and the health service.

Leadership is an integral part of practice, in direct work and in work with colleagues. While leadership is often linked with the management of an overall service, behaving as competent social workers is not just to follow, but to show the way through knowledge, skills and capability how a good and effective service is to be given. There are institutions and structures that could fulfil leadership roles for the profession, but in my experience they are weak, unambitious, unrepresentative and fragmented. They are not comprehensively rooted in authority drawn from the knowledge and experience built up from within the profession; they are also impermeable, rooted in organisational survival, and almost all dependent on central government or local government employer funding. Their focus and potential positive impact are often diluted by divergent responsibilities across social care and across all services for adults, children and families.

Description and purpose of leadership

It would not be appropriate to start from an assumption that leadership is simply of itself 'a good thing'. The leadership of the profession as a whole has been unconvincing, so dispersed as to be almost invisible, and certainly beyond the influence of most. My own experience representing directors of social services during the planning and re-design of social work education, which led to the new degree and postgraduate qualification in 2003, contributing to the early planning of a college of social work and to several of the other work streams of the Social Work Task Force and Reform Board, has been that the views and experience from practice, while they may be sought, are not in fact heeded. Key decisions are made behind closed doors and reported back for information, not discussion or debate. Nevertheless, the social work sense of purpose, value base and therapeutic traditions have remained remarkably resilient, with some shared sense of veiled pride in its identity.

The origins of the meaning of leadership are rooted in a sense of direction and a way forward. Gilbert (2005, p 4) gives an excellent analysis of the etymology, the meaning of the term 'leadership': 'The Anglo-Saxon *laed* means a path or road, related to the verb *lithan,* to travel or proceed.' Grundy (2011) identifies the meaning from the Old English of 'travelling together', making pathways to a new place. The modern association with management arguably masks or obscures the leadership within everyone, including the people who use social work and their carers. Equally, the push to expect all managers to be leaders risks diverting managers from being effective and supportive administrators. Bennis (1989) actually defines leaders as innovators and managers as administrators! There are models of citizen leadership which are being used in the contributions of people who use social work services, their families and their carers, supporting empowerment, personalisation and a stronger and more assertive voice in how social workers work with and alongside them. (This is discussed later in this chapter, within the section on citizen leadership.)

I believe that the value and benefits of leadership are:

- identifying and maintaining a sense of direction;
- holding true to the purpose of achieving positive change, in undertaking purposeful work. In social work terms this is the 'therapeutic imperative' – if nothing is being achieved, then social work is not being done, or any other kind of work!
- building on what is already known, through progressive learning and using the research evidence base of what works;
- sharing authority including power, experience and expertise. This is a two-way transactional process, learning from and being guided by the people served and their carers, and within professional supervision and organisational structures;
- giving confident, credible and effective support, advice and direction to colleagues. This is particularly critical in working within multi-disciplinary teams and integrated services.

Skills for Care and Development, the UK-wide sector skills body for adult and children's social care, offers, within its National Occupational Standards, a definition of leadership as, 'the ability to provide a model of best practice that is creative, innovative, motivating and flexible and supports people to follow by example and through respect' (2012, p 10). This is a positive, practice-driven description, which emphasises the value and importance of the direct service provided. Interestingly it is directly followed by:

> Management is the ability to lead and organise the effective running of the provision and to meet the overall service needs and those required by legislation, registration and inspection. Effective managers are able to solve problems, balance the needs of all within the provision, to manage competing demands and to cope under stress. (2012, p 10)

This is an interesting distinction as it emphasises the critical and central roles in leadership of best practice, creativity and leading by example. Such leadership is the responsibility of *all* – it is centrally located in practice expertise and knowledge. Those managers who are professionals need to retain and continuously develop their practice knowledge and skills that are specific to their own profession. An alternative distinction is drawn by Kotter (1996), who delineates the activities and processes of management as planning, budgeting, organising human resources, controlling and problem solving, and leadership as setting direction, aligning people, motivating and inspiring. This set of leadership activities are as pertinent to direct social work practice, working with colleagues on a complex case involving several colleagues across professional and organisational boundaries, and in working in teams, as they are for positional leaders occupying senior positions.

Leadership based on practice skills and knowledge provides the key for good and effective services. It requires a strong focus on purpose and outcomes. This is not the same as service performance indicators that are a proxy, designed to enable senior managers, local and national government, auditors and inspectorates to gain a simple overview of how a service is operating compared to others. While these have value, the focus for improving social work services is the quality, the personal experience of the service, and the outcomes for the people served and their carers.

Core of leadership within social work practice
- Practice skills, direct experience and knowledge, 'practice wisdom' (Sheppard, 1995).
- Critical awareness and knowledge of current research evidence, 'what works', the social worker as a social scientist (Croisdale-Appleby, 2014).
- Strong focus on the purpose of the service and the outcomes being sought – what success *is*.

Historically social workers worked in teams with 'team leaders', while later the title was changed to 'team manager' with no real change in responsibilities. The best supervisors and first line mangers remain those who deputise for their team members, who undertake joint work, assert their own professional competence and are proud to maintain their own practice knowledge and skills. Equally, they use supervision to promote the reflective learning of social workers in their team, to assure their progressive professional development, and undertake their management and administrative responsibilities as a support function for the service, not the dominant part of their role or in supervision. They are open in sharing their own professional and practice skills development as colleagues within their teams and using supervision for mutual learning. Their own practice skills and research awareness are just as vital.

Different descriptions of leadership

There is limited consensus as to what constitutes leadership and an enormous literature (see, for example, Marturano and Gosling, 2007). One definition offered by Robinson (2001, p 93) is, 'Leadership is exercised when ideas expressed in talk or action are recognised by others as capable of progressing tasks or problems which are important to them.' This description emphasises the interaction and achieving progress jointly. Fairhurst (2007, p 5) builds on this with an analysis of this account of leadership as *process* which:

- influences and gives meaning in order to advance to a goal;
- is an attribute identified by followers or observers;
- is focused on a process, not on communication;
- identifies leadership as influence, which does not necessarily have to be exercised by one individual.

This recognises the essential *transformational* nature of much leadership, focusing on development and positive change. These ways of looking at leadership have the benefit of moving beyond the 'great' individual and positional leadership, where it is associated with or exercised from a specific role or designated post. The 'transformational' model of leadership (Bass and Alvilio, 1994) emphasises the promotion of the potential of each individual, helping them to stretch beyond expectations.

Core components of transformational leadership
- Identifying the vision and strategic direction.
- Promoting change.
- Motivation for continuous improvement.
- Recognising the potential of each individual and promoting teamworking.
- Trusting and empowering people, and investing in their development.

This can be looked at as a set of actions and behaviours that managers can undertake and promote. It is equally and powerfully applicable to direct practice. It links to the notion of *resonance*, leaders drawing on and drawing out, welcoming the qualities and contribution of others (Boyatzis and McKee, 2005). This is different from traditional accounts of leaders as heroes, directing and based on power. Equally and more importantly, these behaviours can be used by social workers, individually within their team and in the service, in the way they hold on to their own sense of direction and purpose, and how they model and encourage their colleagues and teams to operate.

Practice example

An adult social care team identifies the need to make best use of the skills of the social work members in light of increasing service demands, decreasing budgets and the national policy expectation of promoting personal budgets and personalisation. The social workers are increasingly frustrated by the limited opportunities to use their skills in working with individuals, families and the wider community, bogged down in process-driven care management and formulaic assessments. In discussions within the team, the more experienced social workers initiate a straightforward analysis of the work coming to the team, and identify with the team manager the kinds of referrals that could be looked after by the para-professional staff in the team, those who would benefit most from critical analysis, counselling, family group work, and the community development skills of social workers, and those that could be turned around at source with advice and consultation. This focuses their work on the more complex cases of protection of vulnerable adults, conflicting interests, navigating services for the most complex needs, and working with the local community on developing and maintaining access to ordinary resources for older people and people with disabilities. They also make themselves available for advice, consultation and co-working for the other members of the team. While remaining direct practitioners, they also rise above their designated caseload as a resource and source of expertise to the service as a whole.

The social workers directly helped the team manager in the allocation of work across the team, became more active in providing advice and consultation to their team colleagues and partner agencies, and initiated outreach work with community groups in the area to encourage and support those that could provide informal social care and social inclusion for older people and people with disabilities. They also gathered the experience of the whole team on the challenging policy questions for the local authority in the successful implementation of personal budgets, the appropriate use of the funds, and how to safeguard the interests of those who received them. This enabled the team manager to work with senior colleagues on the resolution of these challenges, and consequently made it much easier to increase the take-up of creative personal budgets. In addition, the social workers and the team manager, as part of their shared continuing professional development, joined their local university post-qualifying awards programme, and used the access to knowledge and research skills to investigate the effectiveness of their own services, as well as that of the social care services used.

This transformation came from the initiative and enthusiasm of the social workers in the team. They and their team manager worked together as professional colleagues, not simply as the manager and the managed. They were driven by their own social work values of promoting choice and self-determination, with the opportunities of personal budgets and their desire to make the best use of their professional training and skills. Equally, by working through others, they increased the overall expertise of the team, and in seeking the expertise of the local university, they not only progressed their own professional development, but also initiated relevant service evaluation to increase the long-term effectiveness of the service. Notably this transformation did not originate from performance targets on the proportion of people receiving personal budgets for their own care, or simply following government guidance on care management procedures.

Earlier thinking about leadership looked at styles and the transactional nature of leadership. The emphasis was on striking a balance between a focus on strategic direction and tasks, giving appropriate attention to relationships, and adapting the overall leadership style to particular circumstances. This is evident in traditional, military and large business models with responsibility, power and authority vested in designated individuals. These models arguably relegate as *followers* those who provide a direct and sensitive service, those who need to analyse very complex information, to make judgements, and who share power with those they serve. The danger for social work services is the suppression of creativity, the expectation of slavish adherence to process, procedures and legal guidance. These all, of course, have value, but they are supports or reference points, in providing a good, flexible and sensitive service. They are a means to the end, not the end in itself. They do not of themselves define what a good or effective service is.

Practice example

It is striking that many enquiries after child protection tragedies refer to legal advice taken by social workers, on whether the threshold for legal proceedings had been met or not. There is rarely evidence of social workers themselves being clear about what they wished to present to a court in seeking to protect a child and the court being asked to make the decision. The legal 'advice' to social workers can take precedence over the judgements of a social worker, screening, gatekeeping and acting as the case decision maker. This encourages a passive adherence to the advice of another profession and self-denigration of the competence of social workers. This feeds the adoption of passive roles of care management and care coordination, where the focus is on gathering information and judgements from others, waiting for managers, panels or case conferences to make decisions on what is to be done. Greater focus is required on professional judgement and valuing of the individual expertise of social workers, as envisaged in the Munro review of child protection (2011), and indirectly in the work of Narey (2011) on adoption. Notably each of these English national social work initiatives was commissioned by politicians, not from within the profession or the service.

The child sexual exploitation scandals, notably more recently in Rotherham (see Jay, 2014), illustrate how public service bodies and formal systems of working together can fail to successfully address or prevent serious abuse of children and young people: 'children as young as 11 were deemed to be having consensual sexual intercourse when in fact they were being raped and abused by adults' (Jay, 2014, p 67). While recommendations for improved joint agency arrangements and working procedures have their value, what can be lacking are the routes or working methods for social workers to address their apparent powerlessness to protect children. There is a lack of opportunity for social workers to openly share their knowledge and experience, except through formalised, internal and essentially private working systems. This has progressively stood in the way of social work developing its own expertise *and* raising its voice about the intolerable injustice of the abuse.

Servant and citizen leadership

The role of employing organisations can be looked at as the place from where social workers provide a service, the people who receive this service as the prime, ultimate beneficiaries. There can be a radical inversion of hierarchical authority and power. The tasks of administration and management are essentially facilitating and support functions, rather than direction and central control. The person seeking or receiving a service remains in control, and is the primary source of direction and the arbiter of acceptable solutions. This tradition is alive and vibrant in the social work language, the values of empowerment, social justice and self-determination being firmly rooted. However, it is often not in evidence in the workplace or in how social workers experience the oversight and defining of their roles:

> Citizen leadership is about 'leading together'. It is a model of collaborative working between people who use services, informal carers and paid workers. Citizen leaders want empowered staff and one of their criticisms of social work services is how disempowered social workers have become. (Newman, 2009, p 7)

Later in this book, Chapter Four explores the challenges of personalisation and the provision of personal budgets, and the difficulties the social work profession has had in adopting these into practice with any enthusiasm, despite being logical social policy extensions of the professional value base. This suggests that the managerial agenda of centralised budget decisions and trying to eliminate risk, as opposed to sharing risk and self-determination, have taken precedence and dominated social work practice.

The social control and 'tough love' aspects of social work services ultimately share many common objectives with the people served. The person with periodic episodes of troublesome mental illness often accepts retrospectively the necessity for compulsory admission to hospital, particularly if the care and treatment in the future is focused on minimising the repeat of coercion, and is provided by a familiar, empathetic, skilled and dedicated professional. There is less acceptance if the compulsion is undertaken by people who are unknown and who do not follow through in recovery. Assessing and managing risk in mental health services can be greatly enhanced by openly and skilfully involving people who use services and their carers (see Langan and Lindow, 2004). To fail to respect their self-knowledge and guidance as an integral part of the provision of an effective and safe service risks successful recovery and the provision of acceptable care and support. The person using mental services, as well as their family, can show the way forward – they are a vital and integral part of the leadership process and journey.

In child protection, most parents share the objective of a safe and secure future for their child. Parents who are asked at the conclusion of a child protection plan speak positively about how social workers have directly helped them, and how respectfully they have been treated in case discussions and planning of the appropriate services to enable them to protect their children. Parents cite practical advice and guidance from the social worker, the opportunities to share their worries and frustrations, to gain insight and to learn new skills. There is inevitably conflict, aggression, resistance to change and bitterness; however, professionally, social workers need to remember and learn from the families and children who have been protected in order to build the practice knowledge and wisdom about what works. A proportion of families or individual family members can be highly resistant to change (see Littlechild, 2008), compliance can be disguised or the level of aggression so high that any aspiration to relationship-based practice can seem unattainable. Nevertheless, determination, unflinching courage, co-working and rigorous reflective and analytical supervision can win through (see Ferguson, 2011). Featherstone et al (2014, p 135) explore current changes in political discourse about families experiencing problems: 'the changing positioning of families away from having rights and responsibilities in supporting their children, to ... the identifying and targeting of a category of families as resistant and failing'. To adopt punitive language or rhetoric denies the challenges so many families face, including denial of social justice and easy access to good public services. It also places an enormous barrier between the social worker and the people they seek to help.

Safeguarding and protecting vulnerable adults has been a more recent development in social work practice and public policy, and in the development of confident and competent social work skills. There has been caution in escalating all potential risks to the overwhelming numbers that have developed in child protection services, and confusion about the meaning of 'mental capacity' in relation to a vulnerable person's acceptance of abusive behaviour. Mental capacity risks being regarded as something a person has or does not, with a failure to recognise gradations, variation over time and in specific situations (Ash, 2013). Social work needs to identify the positive interventions it can make, to ensure the resource is targeted to best effect, and support the development of good overall safeguarding practice. The danger is that it is only defined in policy and legal terms (SCIE, 2011), rather than building on direct practice experience and research in social work practice.

Leader as a gardener

The Christian tradition, particularly sharply focused in reformation and revolutionary Europe in the 16th and 17nth centuries, used a number of graphic images of leadership within churches. One is the model of a leader as the gardener, drawing on the stories of God in the Garden of Eden and Jesus in his appearance to Mary Magdalene in the Garden of Gethsemane as a gardener after his resurrection. The artist Albrecht Dürer portrayed him in an engraving in 1510 carrying a spade, clothed as an ordinary man. A gardener, as a leader, is the guardian and ceaseless worker maintaining the perfection of the Garden of Eden. A gardener both maintains and seeks to enhance the perfection of nature, to work with nature, and at the same time removes weeds (and prunes excess growth!). This image of a leader and leadership addresses the paradox, the ambiguity of social work in nurturing and in control. The work of a social worker, like a gardener, is firmly located in hard, methodical, dirty, skilled, knowledgeable and essentially humble work.

This model is taken up by Huzzard and Spoelstra (2011) – the leader as gardener, tending the flowers and ensuring that the fertilizer is working. Sharman (2007) uses the image of a leader in commercial organisations as a head gardener, focusing on the strengths of the individual, helping them develop themselves, rather than being developed by others. The leader nurtures and seeks to provide the right environment where the individual can flourish. This is another articulation of 'transformational' leadership. The fight for universal citizenship in revolutionary England invoked teachings to legitimise the rights of the poor and the redistribution of property (Hill, 1993), representing God as the highwayman in the words of ballads and in the writings of Leveller preachers who used the spiritual leadership of the Bible for justice, challenge and change. This is the use of a body of knowledge, literature and shared tradition as a source of authority and self-expression, which resonates with the social justice and empowerment traditions of social work that can be used in direct practice and in roles within organisations. Servant leadership (Greenleaf, 2002) is explored in Chapter Five, looking at the cross-over with participative styles of leadership.

Citizen leadership

Citizen leadership is used in the work of the Scottish Consortium for Learning Disability (SCLD) User and Carer Forum (2008). The Forum defined citizen leadership as 'an activity, it happens when citizens have power and influence and responsibility to make decisions. Citizen Leadership happens when individuals have some control over their own services. It also happens when citizens take action for the benefit of other citizens' (p 7). This is central to the values of social work and most professions working in human services. The inclusion of carers is of particular importance in working positively and inclusively with whole families and social networks. The relationship and family group working skills of social workers are key parts of empowerment and respect for individuals. The social work as servant leader in this context is a facilitator, mediator, therapist, counsellor and advocate working *for* the person who uses services, or a prospective user of services, and their carers.

The Forum developed a model of leadership that can equally be applied by social workers in their own practice, in how skills are mobilised and used from the knowledge of people who use services and their carers (van Zwanenberg, 2010). SCLD (2008), in their exploration of the characteristics of citizen leadership, include influencing and enabling others to make a contribution, helping to make this happen, recognising the leadership potential of everyone and recognising that people's leadership potential can only be fulfilled through opportunities for development. It enables people to have more control over their own services, through working in partnership with those services both for the benefit of other people who use services as well as for the individual.

This articulates what is familiar to social work, forming a useful tool to critique our own practice and behaviour, an expression of citizen centred-ness (Lister, 1998). Equally, it can be used as a prism through which to view how social workers work with colleagues and their own leadership of social work itself.

Listening to children and young people, allowing their voices to be heard and heeded in practice, is not always evident. The wider responsibilities to other family members, the pressure on time and perhaps lack of skills in relating to them can be explanations but do not excuse. Principles of citizen and servant leadership apply to people of all ages. Young people taking part in a research study on safeguarding by the Children's Commissioner for England (2009) said that it is 'not only important to feel protected but they also needed to feel cared about. All of the young people felt that social workers could improve how they engaged with and listened ... all felt that they were not being fully listened to, respected or trusted, and that there was a lack of empathy from their social worker and an absence of dialogue.' (p 7). This is a clear exposition of the relationship-based practice of social work addressed later in this book. There is an additional telling insight in the same report for social work practice and for employers; it highlights the invidious position in which social workers are placed in explaining agency decisions that they may well not agree with. As an invaluable, although chilling confrontation and critique, such research findings are to be used as a source of citizen leadership, where children and young people who have given generously of their time and thoughts show the way to improve how they are served. This is true of citizen leadership. The next step is to show how they will be followed.

Although self-leadership and 'followership' are addressed later, it is useful to pause at this stage and address how these children and young people can be followed in order to address these major challenges. Within social work teams experienced colleagues can share how they have built up their own practical resources, skills and practice wisdom (Sheppard, 1995) in communication and building relationships. When social workers have appointments to meet with individual children and young people, their colleagues can treat this as sacred and reserved time, and cover for any emergencies or other work pressures that could interfere with this vital work. Where social workers have not, in their professional qualifying training, had experience and education in direct work with children and young people, this should be a central part of their personal development plan (Ryan and Walker, 2007; Lefevre, 2013). In any event, this should be part of regular refresher training. Direct work with children and young people is central to all social work practice, and cannot be delegated or off-loaded on to others because of time, or even lack of skill. At a wider level of leadership it is vital to use this and other examples of key practice skill deficits to continue to press for a prescribed assessed practice curriculum within qualifying professional training. The current lack of clarity on core skills, absent in the *Professional capabilities framework* (Social Work Reform Board, 2010; College of Social Work, 2013b), coupled with a naive expectation that social workers can pick up such skills early in their career after qualifying, is at the heart of the inconsistency and leadership deficit in the profession. It also helps to explain the perceived gap between university teaching and practice demands. Listening to people receiving social work services as citizens is to be shown the way, in this example by children and young people.

Self-leadership and leadership with peers

The sense of purpose and direction in the work comes largely from within the individual social worker, in the commitment to provide a good, skilled and effective service. Qualifying professional training and rigorous, validated and career-long continuous professional development, including partnership university post-qualifying awards, underpin this. This is progressively internalised in knowledge, enhanced intuition and practice skills. The relationship-based nature of social work, together with the complexity and ambiguities of the territory of the work, demands personal strength and resilience. While it is possible to administer social care, be it in services for adults or children and families, as a procedure-driven process through call centres and formulaic and legalistic instructions, the art and science of social work practice demands a highly personalised, emotionally aware and sophisticated interaction with individuals and families. When this is located in the managerialist culture, a focus on performance targets, finite public budgets, ambiguous social policies and the wider demands of local government, the sense of direction and purposeful social work practice of necessity comes from within the individual. It may be that the nascent College of Social Work in England, if re-established as an ambitious and truly collegiate organisation, with wholly independent funding, might provide a wider sense of professional community. Despite being recommended by the Social Work Task Force (2009, p 45) as an 'independent voice for social work and for the profession', with a £5 million government start-up grant, it remains largely dependent on central and employer funding, and lacks a fully elected leadership, with a low individual membership and low levels of member contributions to its work. At present there remains a multiplicity of organisations and structures that oversee, instruct and try to prescribe social work. In this vacuum, the risk is that organisations responsible for providing a social work service retreat to the law and government guidance to stipulate in prescription what is to be done and how it is to be done. The space and opportunity for individual judgement is restricted, and creativity and responsiveness to individual needs is restrained or even prevented.

The concept of *self-leadership* looks beyond leadership through position or role. It recognises the responsibility of everyone to take charge collectively and individually, in creating and maintaining direction, and to be motivated to work effectively (Mantz and Neck, 2009). It is linked to *emotional intelligence*, the understanding of the emotions of ourselves and of others, and the process of actively using them. The process is viewed as seeing emotions, understanding them, using them and managing them (Goleman, 1998). It is part of empathy, recognising and valuing the experience and emotions of others, insight in understanding our own emotions and reactions, and making thoughtful and purposeful use of all of this (Morrison, 2008). It is central to the social work relationship in reflection, sharing and in positive communication skills (Ingram, 2013). It is linked to the related ideas about *mindfulness*, the skills of giving attention to what is occurring in the immediate present, while at the same time having an objective and strategic view of situations (Dolman and Bond, 2011). It is developing the faculty of being at the same time both tactical *and* strategic, it enables engagement in what is present, what requires work now, what is directly useful to those around, and at the same time, having a wider, longer-term perspective, learning for the future and maintaining a strategic sense of direction. It is also an aspect of resilience: 'being resilient is an on-going process or personal quest for self-knowledge' (Grant and Kinman, 2013, p 358; see also Beddoe et al, 2014).

While the focus on self-awareness and awareness of others is core to much of social work education, there is also a strong linkage to social workers managing themselves. Part of this is taking responsibility for one's own well-being, beyond what may reasonably be expected from a professional supervisor and manager. Barker, Martin and Zournazi (2008) identify how developing skills in managing one's own emotions can enable activists to be more effective in achieving the changes they are seeking, especially when they address this within their teams and with colleagues. They write with a focus on activists for social change, who, like social workers, share the same potential traps of being focused on the negative, being overwhelmed by apparently insuperable problems and by disillusionment. They argue for the skilful development of a focus on optimism or joy, using the term 'joyful activism'. What a wonderful thought and approach to bring into the workplace and into practice! It is a form of cognitive self-management of mood and feelings, a facet of reflection and reflexivity within which remembering and celebrating successes and the expressions of appreciation received can be assured. My own experience in local authority social services has been of substantially more letters received of thanks and appreciation of the work of individuals and the service than complaints. Faced with some intractable problems, often of great magnitude, it is possible to focus on negative experiences and forget our original sense of purpose and vocation to achieve positive change.

The perception of the need for leadership, and the role and responsibilities of leaders is, to a large extent, subjective, dependent on the position of the observer. Their expectations will be inextricably linked to their experience, their perceptions of their own power and authority, and their own ambition to exercise choice and independence of thought. Self-leadership '... is a methodology for creating choices, and therefore a greater flexibility and independence of thought. It creates the options of responsibility and accountability whilst improving wellbeing and resilience' (Holroyd and Brown, 2011, p 69).

Five essential aspects of leadership are identified by Gilbert (2005), and can be translated into the practical tasks of exercising self-leadership.

Table 1.1: Five essential aspects of leadership

Essential aspects of leadership[1]	Self-leadership task in social work practice	Self-leadership task in working with colleagues
Integrity, authenticity and trustworthy-ness	Empathy, open sharing of all information, reliability, honouring commitments	Sharing expertise and experience, providing support and direct help
An explicit value base	Using practice evidence, promoting independence, balancing the wishes and needs of the most vulnerable, those with no voice, carers and the wider community	Modelling professional standards and values. Sharing and discussing professional and practice dilemmas
Providing and maintaining direction	Clarity on what is being worked towards, as opposed to process and procedure, the 'therapeutic imperative'. Analysis and reflection followed by synthesis, action and review	Clarity on role and purpose of the work, promoting an evidence base of what works
Inspiring and empowering	Sharing knowledge, practice wisdom and information. Exploring insight and promoting choice	Encouraging less experienced colleagues, sharing knowledge and resources
Delivery	Providing a direct service as a social worker, assuring the appropriate delivery of services by others. Rising above the banality of the hollow model of care management	Being available to help at times of pressure, to assist in complex and stressful work, being an active member of the team and sharing work

[1] Source: Essential aspects of leadership from Gilbert (2005, p 5)

The central thesis of this book is that leadership is the responsibility of *all* social workers, not just for people in designated posts. Indeed, many social workers in senior roles risk showing greater concern about their management position and behave as if they have lost or discarded their professional identity, discarded their skills and failed to keep abreast of current knowledge and research. The exercise of leadership and the use of leadership skills begins from the very start of a social worker's career, and continues throughout.

Practice examples

A parent of a young child who has an abusive partner will need to explore the risks to that child with their social worker, how they could protect them, and explore how the risks can be reduced or eliminated. The skilled social worker is sharing knowledge, working with feelings, helping to develop insight and helping the parent assert themself and learn new skills. The focus is on a sharing of knowledge and empowerment. The passive social worker screens for the level of risk, and if it seems high, refers to a meeting with other professionals that will decide what needs to be done. In such circumstances the social worker's role becomes one of coordinating the work of others, rarely providing a direct service themself. The active social worker leads the parent in their work to safeguard the child, and leads the agency in identifying and providing the range of other direct help the family needs.

The parents of a young adult with learning difficulties, who are finding it difficult to continue to provide full-time care, need more than an offer of respite care or direct payments. They need a knowledgeable and insightful social worker who recognises the combination of long-term grief, regret and perhaps guilt at needing to share care, and their fears for the long-term future. They need an understanding of the wider impact on the family, relationships and other children. These are skills akin to therapy and counselling. To enter families without this capability is to deny the depths of emotions and the complexities the families face. The social worker is both to be led by the family's personal experience, needs and solutions of choice and leads from their shared insights and knowledge of effective service options.

Spectrum of traditional leadership theories and styles

Styles of leadership can be characterised or ranked by the level of negotiation or choice the leader expects of or allows their followers. In social work this has been described as 'opening some discretionary space' (Briskman, 2013, p 54). A similar analysis can be made for the amount of autonomy, discretion, individual judgement and level of creativity permitted. This is at the heart of the Munro review of child protection (2010) that challenged how the discretion and professional judgements of social workers are under-valued and under-used. At this stage it is unclear if these ambitions can be realised if professional training and greater use of evidence-based skilled direct intervention with families are not advanced.

A dictatorial or authoritarian leadership style can be strong on charisma and inspiration. There is likely to be little discussion about objectives or the means by which they are to be achieved. The pitfalls of a simple and isolated policy edict, for example, to increase the number and speed of adoptions of children in public care, backed by prescriptive processes and procedures, are plain to see. Much of the delays in adoption decisions are not caused by resistant social workers or local authority directors of children's services – the causes are rooted in minimal social worker discretion, 'bloated' (Narey, 2011) paperwork and processes, decisions made in a multitude of meetings, panels and court hearings. There is only limited scope for a social worker to drive the process forward, to force the pace, to exercise judgement and discretion, or to be creative. The professionalism of the social worker is constrained by the minutiae of process, enshrined in the policies of government, which, at the same time, scream for greater speed and greater numbers. This is not a suggestion that adoption decisions should be taken more lightly, but a battle cry for people to give social workers more respect and trust. Equally, the profession has to demonstrate its trustworthiness by better professional training, supervision, practice skills and greater use of research knowledge. There is a bind, however – social workers are seen not to be very good at their job, so the rules, prescriptions and oversight are increased, discretion is reduced and outputs reduce. Creativity and flexibility are discouraged or rejected. A 'pace-setting' or 'transactional' leadership style would be to ask the questions of the professionals and to increase their knowledge and skills. Social workers as citizens or servant leaders would already have identified the blockages, campaigned to have them cleared, and authoritatively demonstrated how this could be achieved. The absence of this has led to social work being exposed to blame and greater management by targets, process and spasmodic policy edict.

Table 1.2: Models of leadership

Model of leadership	Scope for negotiation and choice	Level of discretion
Dictatorial or authoritarian	Close to nil	Limited by tight procedures and systems, bound by pre-existing rules
Pace-setting	Overall objectives, outcomes measured and performance indicators are not negotiable, but creativity is encouraged to achieve them	Discretion is permitted if it enables the defined, given, objectives to be met
Transformational	Discussion about the 'what' and the 'how to provide' the best service is encouraged	Progressively discretion and greater professional autonomy is achieved
Citizen or servant	High	Shared recognition of the principles, decision making and discretion applied close to the person using the social work service

Discretion and autonomy

Table 1.2 shows the contrast between the traditional theories of leadership, focused on the characteristics and behaviour of leaders, moving through the contemporary models that focus on process and interaction, highlighting the opportunities and benefits of locating leadership in practice.

Early research messages from the national pilot of social work practice (Stanley et al, 2012, p 33; see also SCIE and University of Bristol, 2013) indicate that the greater autonomy for staff in the 'arm's-length' or independent social work service organisations 'allowed more streamlined decision making than was possible in a bureaucratic local authority which left more time available for face-to-face work with children and young people, family and carers and freedom to work creatively'. Frontline staff felt they had greater opportunities for participating in decision making, innovative practice was encouraged, supervision had a greater priority, and they felt more confident in challenging practice decisions. While these are a relatively small number of national pilots over a limited number of sites, it does give an indication of how greater discretion can be given and autonomy encouraged alongside indications of better outcomes for adults, children and young people.

In the fields of law and regulation there has been a growing recognition that discretion is inevitably applied and is needed due to the complexity of individual situations and to avoid unintended consequences of well-intentioned rules. Dworkin (1977), an American philosopher, used the image of a ring doughnut, the dough as the set of rules, regulations and laws, and the hole in the middle as the discretion to be applied by the judiciary, public officials and regulators. This model or image has continued to be developed. Discretion is seen as the 'space' between rules and within rules, where people working in regulated services, which includes, of course, much social work practice, can make choices (Black, 2002). Dworkin's doughnut model contrasts the constrained discretion where people are bound by pre-existing and binding rules and the capacity or space for greater discretion where rules cannot be applied in a mechanical way. The authoritarian leadership style would expect little discretion to be applied; the hole in the middle of the doughnut would be small and the surrounding dough thick (see Figure 1.1). Transformational leadership would expect and encourage the degree of autonomy and discretion to be increased as the social worker becomes more experienced, demonstrates increased capability and uses a wider range of practice research evidence and a diversity of proven therapeutic interventions. The dough ring of the doughnut would be thinner and the hole in the middle larger (see Figure 1.2).

If the relevant laws and any central or local government regulation are seen as a framework and context, which intellectually and in practice are internalised as principles, the space between and within them are the ways to provide a creative, responsive, personal and truly professional service. Part of the development of skills in self-leadership is demonstrating how this can be done successfully and to good effect. Conversely, if there is a failure to internalise the principles, to develop specific skills and to demonstrate good outcomes for the people served and their carers, social workers cannot expect to escape top-down regulation and prescription.

The concept of *organisational citizenship* has been explored by some writers as a way of describing the sense of common purpose that organisations, their leaders and managers seek to achieve. A culture built on mission statements and all staff being encouraged to feel they have a valued voice is seen as a 'mimic' of citizenship in its original

Figure 1.1: 'Dworkin doughnut' of discretion – authoritatian leadership

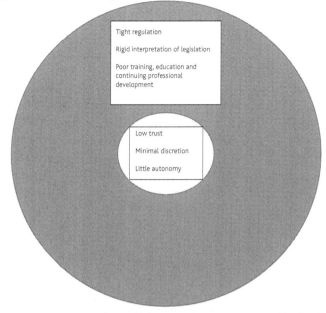

Tight regulation

Rigid interpretation of legislation

Poor training, education and continuing professional development

Low trust

Minimal discretion

Little autonomy

Figure 1.2: 'Dworkin doughnut' of discretion – transformational leadership

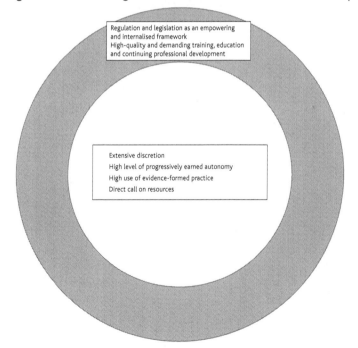

Regulation and legislation as an empowering and internalised framework
High-quality and demanding training, education and continuing professional development

Extensive discretion
High level of progressively earned autonomy
High use of evidence-formed practice
Direct call on resources

meaning of membership of the state. There is a potential paradox in an organisation and staff having a common interest in shared objectives, and the risk of something akin to false class consciousness: 'The paradox is that some senses of belonging that might be real and fulfilling to some people strike others as vacuous propaganda' (Parker, 2002, p 60). If the focus of a social worker's accountability and direction is closely aligned to their professional responsibilities and skills, then such false presentation of purpose can be avoided. Where the wider and conflicting objectives of large organisations such as local authorities are deemed to be more important, or are treated as more powerful, they risk subsuming and submerging the sense of purpose, and ultimately the quality and effectiveness of the social work service.

Pause for a wider view

At this point I would like to pause and look more widely at an eclectic range or descriptions of leadership. Much study and writing about leadership has been focused on large organisations, which have fairly narrow objectives in their overall strategic direction. There is very little on how specialist or expert work and its concomitant knowledge and skill base are maintained, developed and sustained.

According to the 'Just William' school of leadership (Crompton, 1927):

> The Outlaws were just passing the house of Mr Markson, their fearsome headmaster. William remarked somewhat rashly, "I'm not scared of 'Old Markie'." The Outlaws dared William to enter "Old Markie's" house. They all knew he was still in his study at school marking papers. "Go on then," said Ginger, "just go into his house and take something, just to prove you are not frightened of him."
>
> William's blood was up "Alright I'll show you." William climbed in through a conveniently open window and came out carrying his booty, although William did not know it, an extremely valuable green Chinese figure of a god. They gazed at him speechless. William had once again consolidated his position as leader.

This is the passive school of leadership, to follow a leader who shows verve, nerve and panache in achieving the visible challenge of a remote and intimidating source of power and oppression, without any chance of a wider defeat or of achieving change. The elation is short-lived, but it may be possible in this period of positive feelings and transient sense of power to use this confidence to develop and hone strategies and skills to achieve real exercise of power, to achieve change.

As another example, the title of leader of an orchestra is held by a violinist, sitting at the front desk, under the nose of the conductor. Their role is maintaining the esprit de corps of the orchestra, calming the natural exuberance of the brass section, coordinating the tuning of the instruments before a performance and potentially being a spokesperson for the whole group in the face of difficult conductors and general managers. They owe their leadership to their ability as a violinist, so gaining their authority is positional rather than by election. They, however, like everyone else, are subject to the will of the conductor during a performance. They lead through their position, the earned respect of their colleagues and most important of all, as a skilled professional in the making of music.

By way of a third example, in the 17th century both the revolution that led to the Dutch Republic and the victory of Oliver Cromwell in the English Civil War were aided by a major change in how armies worked.

> The essence of this military revolution was the reliance on 'the free way' as against 'the formal,' a recognition of the fact that free men consciously motivated by a belief in their cause could get the better of mere professionals simply by superior morale and discipline. Cromwell's troopers, originally, were picked men, well drilled, well equipped, well horsed, well paid. (Hill, 1970, p 76)

In this context the term 'professional' means mercenary. This is a description of successful leadership that focuses on the personal motivation of those who are led *and* how well they are provided with the means to do their job.

It is also worth considering 'leaderless-ness': not all human activity requires a titular or positional leader. Collective and shared responsibility, the sharing and collaborative searching for solutions and knowledge, are effective ways of building a shared authority and shared power. This is familiar territory for social work, both in working relationships and particularly in work with those with the least power and social workers striving for their empowerment. The shared traditions with community development, subject to periodic fashion, emphasise the importance of engagement, collective empowerment and building of a vision, delivering services that are local and self-governed (Hadley and McGrath, 1984; Hoggett and Hambleton, 1987; Smale et al, 1988). In case studies in the environmentalist movement, 'leaderlessness is seen as a strength, and part of the overall philosophy of self-organisation and individual and collective empowerment' (Purkis, 2001, p 176). The challenge in any radical movement for change and the sharing of power is always to avoid simply replicating the power structures as opposition, unintentionally sharing the same characteristics as the original opponent. The trick is to share power, just as leadership can be shared and dispersed rather than located in institutions or individuals. If what is being sought to lead is of value, then sharing and empowerment are strengths, not weaknesses. According to Jones (2012, p 77), 'Informal leaders also have influence and power which is not based on organisational status but on their experience, behaviour and personality.... Leadership is often more about enabling and encouragement, coaching and consultation, than about bossing and directing.'

Academic research into success in Formula One car racing showed in an analysis of almost 16,000 races over the last 60 years that expert leaders, who had started as drivers or mechanics, achieved far greater success in senior leadership positions than general managers. Their teams won up to twice as many races (Goodall and Pogrebna, 2012). Closer to social work, Goodall and her research colleagues, using both qualitative and quantitative data, found a clear association between the success of hospitals led by experts compared to those run by general managers. Her thesis is that in organisations that rely on expert knowledge, expert leaders in that field are required (Goodall, 2011). A social work organisation that has a leader who has practised as a social worker and respects the expertise of social workers will, as a consequence, respect the practice, knowledge and expertise of good social workers. The organisation will be well placed to promote continuing professional development in research knowledge and in progressive practice skills.

Leadership in other services and professions

It is helpful to look across to other services and organisations for their perspectives on leadership. Grundy (2011) identifies the leadership role of bishops, for example, as gathering, shaping and articulating a vision that most will own because they recognise it as containing *their own* voice. This outward-looking and inclusive leadership, he argues, means that it is found to be credible and acceptable. Social work, it can be contended, needs to own its own voice and vision, which is its sense of purpose, knowledge and skill base. All have a responsibility to articulate this clearly and with no compromise. Without exercising this, the expression of its own authority and purpose, it is open to use or abuse as the provision of public officials to be used for any purpose defined in regulation, or at best, just part of a general, homogeneous workforce, rather like some would see teachers, the police or the prison service. Grundy (2011, p 112) goes on to promote the need for church leadership to 'respect diversity and adopt a permissive style', despite any perceptions we have of the authoritarian and centralised style of leadership in the established church! There are strong echoes here in the aspirations of Munro (2011) in promoting greater discretion and judgement.

There is an interesting literature developed in the leadership of services for early childhood (see, for example, Kagan and Hallmark, 2001; Rodd, 2005; Jones and Pound, 2008). Part of the discussions about how leadership has a distinct form and kind of applicability in this setting is focused on the predominance of women in the workforce, the collaborative ways of working together with groups of children and within teams. Particular attention is given to the positive leadership role in working with parents, as partners, to share knowledge and ways of interacting with children. There are some similarities for teams of social workers, but also some critical differences. The gender issue is present, although far less in the higher levels of management and designated senior positions. Also, social workers work largely alone, with individuals and family groups. Nevertheless, the insights on the leadership role with parents and families overall are valuable, both in practice as an individual or in co-working with colleagues. In leadership within practice, social workers can model modes of communication, build mutual insight into the problems and challenges faced by people who use their services, and share knowledge and problem-solving skills.

Within schools there has been a steady growth in a culture and practice of teachers learning together, both in their practice as teachers and in their own shared professional development. There is recognition that all the school staff have a role to play, '... enrolled in the mission of the school. It starts with them, it largely falls on their shoulders; it is the staff who enrol the children, the parents and the community. In the past too many head teachers and leadership teams have thought they could bring about change by themselves in spite of the staff' (Riddell, 2003, p 111).

Riddell identifies eight key components of leadership within schools:

- shared custodianship of the school's vision;
- developing learning systems;
- helping staff develop meaning in the work they are engaged in;
- creating capacity;
- helping create coherence;
- choosing priorities for the school;
- developing an organisation suffused with reflective processes;
- making the time to make effective change.

While the language of the learning organisation is well known within the social work profession and to the managers and leaders, it remains hard to make the space and maintain investment in continuing professional development and accredited post-qualifying education (Senge, 1990; Gould and Baldwin, 2004). The emphasis on reflective processes and reflection is equally familiar, but nevertheless, many social workers do not have access to this within the ordinary discipline of good professional supervision. Sergiovanni (1990) identified three factors that are crucial to leadership within schools:

- empowerment, with the sharing of responsibility and accountability;
- enablement, promoting team and individual growth and development;
- enhancement, drawing leader and follower roles together to increase commitment and performance.

In the National Health Service (NHS) there are a number of strands or sources of leadership: the hierarchical structures of political and general management, the royal medical colleges and centrally designed and directed change programmes. The NHS has developed a clinical leadership competency framework (NHS Institute for Innovation and Improvement and the Academy of Medical Royal Colleges, 2009). It uses a shared leadership model (Bradford and Cohen, 2008) that seeks and welcomes the acts of leadership from everyone, and the focus is on the achievements of a group, service or team. It explicitly moves away from traditional charismatic and hierarchical models. This is interesting in the perceptions and experiences of the health service being driven simultaneously by managerialism and professional hierarchies. In part, this can arguably be explained by the authority, strength and power of the professions being so great that they are willing to share some of this; paradoxically, at the same time, this culture is being challenged and changed. The *Healthcare leadership model* of the NHS Leadership Academy (2014) emphasises the leadership roles and responsibilities of all.

The context is a multi-professional service, much care and treatment being provided by teams. Most of the professions providing the direct services have a far stronger tradition of evidence-based practice and formalised continuing professional development than social work. While much social care is provided by teams of people in different roles, and much social work is provided alongside professionals in other organisations, there is no explicit authority in the social worker's role; much influence is by negotiation, competence and confidence. These are powers or skills of influence – they are the ones the social worker has to develop as part of their leadership within multi-agency and multi-disciplinary work.

The NHS has been focused on change and innovation, in the midst of continuous structural turbulence, and so much of its leadership thinking has been focused on this. It is arguable that much of the use of the word 'leadership' in the NHS has been about managing change. The focus remains on promoting shared leadership (Darzi, 2008), empowering professional staff to lead change, enhancing professionalism and a strong focus on improving the quality of education, reformed in partnership with the professions. While there is a rhetorical tone in this language, the reality is that individual professionals and the professions overall are in a far more influential position in the NHS than social workers in social work and social care or teachers in education and schools. The focus on change, transformation, reorganisation and reform can relegate maintaining and developing practice knowledge and skills to a second-order, second-class activity. If senior leadership and management attention is too focused on organisational and structural mutations, then individual professional social workers, in whatever role and position in organisations, have the responsibility to work individually and collectively to maintain, sustain and progress the direction of social work through the seas of change.

TWO

Leadership vacuum

Introduction

There has been an historic reticence and ambivalence within social work about claiming professional status, elitism, and indeed, knowledge and evidence-informed practice. This has been exploited by public policy makers and managers who have feared first, social work's social justice heritage, second, who seek the efficient administration of rationed social welfare, and third, who look to social work to undertake a degree of social control. Social work is capable of living with and mediating these ambiguities, but the analysis of how social work is led and managed demonstrates that this is not evident in the current structural or organisational landscape. In this chapter the impact of social work being constrained as a 'state-mediated' profession (Johnson, 1972), with restricted discretionary space (Briskman, 2013), is explored. It has not proved possible to collectively resist the imposition of managerialism and the limitations of the performance indicator culture. Enterprise and change are not driven from within social work itself, but arise from government ministers' initiatives on issues such as adoption (Narey, 2011), social work education (Croisdale-Appleby, 2014; Narey, 2014) and service failure (Social Work Task Force, 2009; Munro, 2010, 2011; Social Work Reform Board, 2012).

There is a strong argument to be made and won – to seek, engage and promote the personal, professional experience of social workers. This is distinct from the views, aspirations and prejudices of managers, organisational interests and policy makers. This chapter explores the diversion of social workers who become managers to a focus on managerialism, externalised defined targets and measures as opposed to their own responsibilities to develop their own practice knowledge, practice wisdom and evidence-informed case and service decision making.

The current location of cohesive leadership for social work across institutions or specific roles is not clear. The roles recently created in England of Chief Social Worker for Adults in the Department of Health and Chief Social Worker for Children and Families in the Department of Education are embedded in the civil service. This is an important potential focus for government policy. The role of principal social worker created in most local authority children's and adult services, and in a growing number of other organisations has taken a wide variety of forms and sets of responsibilities. Leadership may be wholly absent, except within the individual, personal actions and practice of each determined social worker, ambitious for the impact, the effectiveness of their practice, their listening, engagement and interaction. State-funded bodies come and go (Bilton, 2010); experienced practitioners become managers and are defined in that new role, with expectations of management behaviour, value base and day-to-day activities, rather than as expert and competent practitioners. Nevertheless, they are directly responsible for the development of the specialist knowledge and skills of those they manage. They are cast as responsible for the quality and effectiveness of the social work service, through the design and continuous improvement, in the light of the best research evidence and the mediation of any national policy guidance. They often make many of the most critical decisions in complex cases, through their contribution to case reviews, panel decisions and in allocating scarce financial resources.

The development of a strong culture of self-leadership within social work has been held back by an internal ambivalence about professional elitism, resistance by employers and policy makers to an assertive professionalism, internal resistance to research and evidence-based practice and inconsistent standards in qualifying education identified by the Social Work Task Force (2009), the review commissioned by the Secretary of State for Education, Michael Gove (Narey, 2014) and the review commissioned by the Department of Health Minister of State, Norman Lamb (Croisdale-Appleby, 2014). It is striking that none of these reviews were initiated from within social work, although all three listened to and largely heeded social workers. None contain great surprises; none have led to any profession-initiated collective action.

Public policy context

The contemporary context of public services includes the challenge for efficiencies, masking real reductions in services. Target-driven managerialism is inherently in opposition to professional judgement and discretion. Coats and Passmore (2008, p 13) describe the development of:

> ... a healthy respect for professional judgement without allowing professionals to hold the trump card when it comes to service design or the identification of publicly valuable outcomes. In other words, public value offers grounds to challenge professional judgement and avoid 'producer capture', whilst recognising that 'professionalism' is a characteristic to be cherished.

Is the professionalism of social work cherished by the state, the court of public opinion or the organisations that fund and regulate social work and social workers?

In national political and public policy debates the size and responsibility of the state continues to be questioned. Holding on to the characterisation of leadership as *showing the way* and the focus on leadership in social work as *coming from within*, the responsibility belongs to all, whatever their role or organisational position. It is not a responsibility that can be allocated or devolved to individuals in a particular position, still less to organisations, and even less to employers. The location of social work within state-funded services does not absolve those social workers in direct practice and in supervisory, managerial and educational positions from developing and holding on to the full range of practice skills and knowledge in psychosocial interventions, including promoting social change and social justice. While an employer or specific role may not specifically value or seek to directly gain the benefit of all these capabilities of a social worker, a strong personal commitment to these remains an asset for the people who the individual social worker and the social work service are serving. For the employer or manager, this may be an irritant or a bonus.

The vacuum in social work leadership has its roots in a lack of confidence and consensus in practice skills and knowledge within social work. Even more perniciously, this is shared in the perceptions of government and other funding bodies. And there is resistance within institutions and interests that are potentially threatened by a confident social work.

This has particular toxicity when the challenge of social justice is maintained alongside the individualisation of problems and needs. The uncomfortable messages from promoting social justice include highlighting the problems caused by structural inequalities, lack of respect and lack of value. Protecting and safeguarding children has as much to do with income, health, employment for parents, good housing and an education that values all children and young people as much as individual pathology, family relationships and lifestyle choices. Enabling older people and people with disabilities to have a full, active and fulfilling life requires a continuing battle to demonstrate that the same expectations of equity in health and re-ablement or recovery outcomes are available for all. The period in old age when people enjoy independence and a full social life could be increased to the standards in comparable European countries where social isolation is lower and the years of poor health prior to death are lower (Bazalgette et al, 2012). Healthy life expectancy is increasing more slowly than life expectancy in the UK; consequently, older people can currently expect an increasing number of years in poor health. Older people do not need to live in secure, secluded institutions or in social isolation and exclusion in such large numbers any more than do people with learning difficulties.

The space occupied by the vacuum in leadership belongs to social work, not to managers or managerialism, not to shifting government policies, and not to interests that seek to exclude or resist the inherent optimistic challenge for change in social work. The ambitions for positive change, the 'therapeutic imperative' (McKitterick, 2012a) and for social justice, beyond the individual case, however hard or contested, are core to social work as an 'ethical career' (SWAN, 2004), committed to positive challenge and making a difference, not the administration of passive welfare for the most disadvantaged and dependent.

The exercise of discretion and judgement can be central to public sector staff, including social workers, characterised by Lipsky (1980) as 'street-level bureaucrats'. The freedom to be flexible and creative is necessary to provide a personal and responsive service faced with complex needs and distress. The evolution of a performance-measured public service, with an emphasis on what can be measured, rather than identifying outcomes that are of value to the service funders and better still the people being served, gives rise to a dissonance that can subvert more complex, responsive services, tailored to personalised needs. There is a striking juxtaposition here for the 'personalisation' agenda, which can be interpreted (see Ferguson, 2007) as a form of consumerism, simplifying care as a commodity, and distancing the collective welfare state from both the provision and responsibility for publically or privately funded care. Alternatively, the social work heritage of choice, self-direction and empowerment would suggest we should welcome it!

> The intangible character of outcomes means that measures are always dependent on constructs that attempt to generate proxies or substitutes for the outcome. (Cutler and Waine, 1997, p 37)

Performance indicators are just that, they indicate as a proxy for the whole picture. When used alone they are of limited value and can distort practice and divert from good practice. Simply measuring delayed discharges from hospital can mask respecting the choices of older people, rush people into long-term care, and avoid ambitious medical recovery and the regaining of independence. Counting the days taken to complete a formulaic assessment of the needs or the risks for children can ignore the timely provision of direct work and help. The number of days becomes more important than the quality and efficacy of the service provided during those days. As these indicators become the preoccupation of managers, they infect and take over reflective supervision. Critical analysis becomes an irrelevance. Performance measures are non-negotiable and become the dominant business. Ownership and sharing aspirations for maximising independence and choice for older people, protecting children and helping families where there are risks of harm or neglect are in danger of not being sustained or even internalised as they are not perceived to be the core business of managers and the employing organisation.

Examples of externally driven agendas

Comparing adoption rates of children in care and the speed of adoption placements between local authorities and nationally over time has value, however confused the government interest, at times influenced by a wish to provide children to adults who want to adopt. This can risk taking precedence over seeking positive outcomes for children and young people who can no longer live with their birth parents. The conflicting and intertwined rights of children and birth families, coupled with a lack of trust in the skills and judgements of social workers, has caused an accretion of bloated procedures, less to do with promoting and ensuring good practice, and more to do with legal processes and government guidance. It is notable that while local authorities and social work got the public blame for adoption delays and perceived low adoption rates, it took a ministerial adviser, who is not a social worker, to force change. Martin Narey, a passionate advocate for the most disadvantaged children and young people, who has seen the results of blighted childhoods and has successfully run third sector children's services, heard the frustrations of social workers, and has pushed to open government and judicial doors to address these issues (DfE, 2011b). It is striking that social work itself did not take this initiative, especially as social work had been taking the blame for years. Why not? Is there an innate sense of powerlessness? Where is the space for discourse? The research and practice evidence was well known, the frustrations for practitioners were experienced every day, and the delays for children were known to be harmful. On the other hand, social work has had notable achievements in this area – the success of adoption as an alternative to long-term care, particularly for 'hard-to-place' and older children, alongside other routes to permanence, including kinship care and foster care. If this could all be achieved, largely unsung, why could the same not be achieved for delays and obstructions in legal and procedural process?

In the UK adoption initiatives come from government. The Houghton Committee in 1972 and the Adoption and Permanence Taskforce in 2000 did include key social worker members; however, there is little evidence that the initiative or impetus for action came from within the profession. The current initiatives are an approach consistent with the previous political administration:

New Labour is sceptical of the claim that welfare professionals, motivated by a public service ethics, can be relied upon to develop high quality, cost effective services without external monitoring. From this perspective, a modern welfare state will only operate effectively if central government sets rigorous targets and establishes audit and inspection regimes. (Page, 2007, pp 109-10)

It is an example of a service being changed, reformed, modernised and effectively managed by national government ministers. The knowledge and experience of social workers, backed by rigorous research undertaken by social work academics, is strong (Sellick et al, 2004; Triseliotis et al, 2005; Selwyn et al, 2006). Why did it require party political initiatives at national government level to improve services rather than individual and collective initiatives from social workers? Did these academic research champions have no voice, purchase or influence within the profession? The answer is surely 'yes'. This is surely a critique of social work and the credible authority and assertiveness of social workers, and is a failure of all organisations that might currently claim to represent social work, the service or the profession.

The Seebohm Implementation Action Group, an initiative of the Association of Child Care Officers and the Child Poverty Action Group (CPAG) in 1969, later joined by other organisations (Younghusband, 1978), showed a refreshing and inspiring example of energetic and committed individuals taking forward a government-sponsored initiative, making it their own. The Children Act 1989, which has stood the test of time, was the result of consistent advocacy for reform by social workers, social work academics and the professional body, the British Association of Social Workers (BASW), working closely together and with both main political parties, in a spirit of consensus. Times had changed for the Social Work Task Force and Munro reports, when policy implementation seems only to be managed by government, with salaried organisational nominees, rather than from the initiative and personal time commitment from within the membership of social work organisations.

Child protection performance indicators focus on the measurable, what can be rendered into numbers and timescales. This has distorted practice, with assessment categories and the completion of computer-based prescribed formats taking precedence, with little expectation of analysis or reflection (Wastell and White, 2010). The legal definition of a child protection referral to a social worker, where the local authority has reasonable cause to suspect that a child is suffering or is likely to suffer significant harm (Children Act 1989), becomes, in office speak, 'a Section 47', with a timescale of days to complete a prescribed computer-based assessment, rather than a child who needs to be known to be safe before the social worker and their professional supervisor go to their respective beds that night. The sheer scale of the numbers of families, children and young people referred 'into children's social care' (DfE, 2014a) overwhelms the personal sense of responsibility of the social worker, in whatever role and level of responsibility, to act towards any child as if they were their own. The legal duties rest with the local authority, and the sense of personal accountability in both the social worker and their immediate line manager is diverted to performance indicators and prescribed process. The sense of personal responsibility, or public accountability, for a wrong judgement are artificially located, diverted into judgements of poor achievement shown in performance indicators or an inquiry *after* a tragedy.

In this environment the personal is 'alienated', in Hegelian terms (Hegel, 1977). It is estranged from the original vocation and recognition of itself. In being expected to be an operative, the social worker becomes a technician, a clerk, an administrator. The human self of the social worker is alienated from their perception of themselves, perceiving no opportunity for change, to influence or to be creative. Part of this is due to the location of so much social work within local authorities, where the embedded professions of finance and law hold sway, and even the new disciplines of human resources and health and safety have more authority and power. The merging of general management and case decision-making roles, and the more diffuse responsibilities for social care, dilute the intrinsic focus of social work. The determination of how the job is done is defined almost exclusively by government-funded organisations and civil servants, to the exclusion of collective and collaborative work by social workers themselves. Briskman (2013) and Halfpenny (2011) suggest that the increased proceduralisation of practice increases the imbalance of power between social workers and the individuals they are working with, because both have to adhere to the prescribed procedures, with limited space for discretion and choice. In recovering their own self, the ambitions in their vocation, self-leadership can be recaptured at the levels of individual thinking, personal initiative or working collectively with allies. This requires tenacity, boundless optimism, time outside paid work, and courage.

The consequences, intended or not, of an emphasis on performance management by proxy indicators, as opposed to real measures of outcomes, can include tunnel vision, a narrow focus, fixation on measures and service ossification (Smith, 1995). Managers of social work services and supervisors of practice can attend to that which can be measured easily. The pursuit of short-term targets can be at the expense of broader strategic objectives, misrepresenting and manipulating the data for external audiences, including inspectorates and funders. The challenge for social workers, be they in direct practice or in a managerial position, is to use the performance data available and to *add* to it. For example, the wide open door to referrals to social care within local authority children's services leads to mass screening, mass basic assessments and limited direct services. In 2013/14 nearly 660,000 children and young people were referred, most requiring some form of formal assessments (DfE, 2014a). The sources of these referrals include 28% from within local authority services and 24% from the police. The energetic self-leadership within a team of social workers will actively and collectively review its application of the thresholds, how speedily and effectively it responds to the most pressing cases, review patterns of re-referrals and 'near-misses'. Patterns of referrals from partner agencies such as schools, police or health professionals can be analysed, and proactive outreach and consultation offered to reduce the referrals in and increase direct social work intervention. This peer review can lead to improvements in practice in the service provided to children and families, and contribute to the continuing professional development of all team members, however experienced or senior. It is an example of "*quiet challenges*" by social workers working in and against managerialism for more critical forms of practice that seek to engage with furthering service users' interests' (White, 2009, p 129; emphasis added).

Social work with adults

The relatively recent legacy in social work practice which has over-emphasised assessment at the expense of direct therapeutic work to achieve change, has had a debilitating effect on practice skills and sense of purpose. However, the terminology of 'social diagnosis' was widely used in earlier times (Richmond, 1917; Sainsbury, 1970), although ridiculed by Wootton (1959) as a pretentious emulation of medicine. In English local authority adult social care services in 2010/11 there were about 1.8 million assessments of the needs of individuals and reviews of social care services, half undertaken by social workers and other professional staff (Audit Commission, 2012). In children's social care services the number of assessments of children in need and those subject to a child protection plan continues to grow year on year, an increase in referrals of 10.8% in 2013/14. While the specific responsibilities to deploy social workers to undertake assessments of children and young people who may be in need or who may require protection is spelled out in the Children Act 1989, and re-affirmed in the revised child protection procedures (DfE, 2013), there is no such prescription in services for adults. The revision of the rules and requirements for social work education of 1995 (CCETSW) led to the development of the idea of specialist skill and career 'pathways', which, for adult services (Stevens et al, 1996), was dominated by care management, largely silent on specific social work interventions, suggesting a generalist role in social care. There were later greater ambitions and expectations. A general statement, 'Complex assessments need the specialist knowledge and skills only qualified and experienced social workers can provide', comes from the Audit Commission (2012, p 3). Kerr and colleagues at the Social Work Research Centre at the University of Stirling identified:

> Effective social work with older people should focus on intensive care management with those who have complex, fluctuating and/or rapidly changing needs. Pressure to manage budgets and establish eligibility must not reduce social workers' capacity to engage with the older person and use the full repertoire of their skills in a holistic way. (Kerr et al, 2005, p 5)

In England, the College of Social Work (2012, p 5), perhaps in a 'back to the future' mode, as well as using the thoroughly contemporary terminology of a 'business case', stated:

Social work with adults, carers and families then, is having to re-invent itself. Social workers in adult social care cannot rely on the old verities of care management and must demonstrate their value.... Assessment, planning and review are evolving but will remain intrinsic to social work, and there will be new opportunities in community development, safeguarding, prevention and early intervention, and interpersonal support, all of which our members are eager to embrace.

Entering the managerial world with a business case for social work requires a focus on effectiveness in government social policy terms, enhancing quality of life, delaying and reducing the need for care and support, ensuring people have a positive experience of care, and safeguarding vulnerable people (DH, 2013). All of this is consistent with social work's potential knowledge, skill base and values in social justice. However, it would be naive to assume that without enormous energy and tenacity to carve out and maintain the space for relationship-based working, alongside building a credible evidence base on effectiveness, a focus on positive change can be achieved. The challenge is the current exclusion and limited quality of life experienced by so many adults who use adult social care services. The trick in leading social work practice from within, be it in terms of strategy or tactics, is to be ahead of the managerialist agenda, to stridently articulate what it strives to achieve, both within job and employment role and as individual professionals, beyond the immediate workplace.

Scandals and tragedies in services for adults have a lesser impact on social work than those in children's services, perhaps because expectations are lower or the responsibilities of social workers are less defined. The Winterbourne View Hospital scandal (Flynn, 2012) identified two key roles for social workers, as care coordinators and safeguarding. A substantial minority of the patients at the privately run, but publically funded, hospital had a care coordinator, under the terms of the statutory Care Programme Approach (CPA), who was a social worker. There were 40 safeguarding referrals to local authority adult social care services in 43 months, including 27 allegations of staff-to-patient harm. The review identified key missing elements in the social work response, a lack of professional challenge, deference to the police and insufficient curiosity and vigilance. The response in both government policy and local authority resolve has been largely focused on re-commissioning services for people with learning disabilities with complex care and treatment needs more locally and in more open community settings. An expectation came later for a national review of all people with learning disabilities inpatient in specialist hospitals (LGA, 2013). The national census report (HSCIC, 2014) showed that on admission, 77.9 per cent of people living in these hospitals were subject to detention under the Mental Health Act 1983. For such a large majority to have had the active service of a social worker at the point of admission and yet apparently been abandoned to long-term care calls into question any sense of enduring interest or commitment. It indicates the role of a social worker as an approved mental health professional (AMHP) has been undertaken for an administrative event, rather than an enduring and active service.

It is entirely appropriate to strive again with the approach of more local and community settings that had followed the earlier national scandals in hospitals for people with learning disabilities, such as Ely Hospital (DH, 1969), Farleigh Hospital (DH, 1971), South Ockendon Hospital (DH 1974) and Normansfield (DH, 1978). It is telling that it took a media initiative to re-ignite enthusiasm, not a remembered history within social work. I worked in Normansfield Hospital for periods from 1968 to 1971 while a student. Like Winterbourne View, relatives were stopped from being allowed to go to the wards, and family visits took place in a designated visitor area. The features of isolation from the community and mainstream services in secluded, and often secure specialist services are well known to foster abuse and neglect, with staff isolated from external training and access to a wider professional network. Why did we not remember the lessons of these historic abuses?

The old long-stay hospitals developed a social work service to reduce this isolation and encourage family involvement (Morris, 1969). If social workers 'are highly trained and have the skills and knowledge to ensure the protection of vulnerable people' (College of Social Work, 2012, p 16), what has happened to blunt these skills, and why was the social work service withdrawn from people living in secure settings? What happened to the confidence in 'professional challenge', the 'concerned curiosity and vigilance' and the bringing of 'a more challenging filter and lens to the task of safeguarding' (Flynn, 2012, pp 130, 131)? Lessons have yet to be wholly learned by all professionals (Plomin, 2013), and the focus of most agencies remains on systems rather than on individual professional practice and individual responsibility.

The national government policy response to the Winterbourne View Hospital was a pledge that within 18 months all people living inappropriately in assessment and treatment units would be moved back into the community (DH, 2012). However, that target, albeit ambitious, was missed. By March 2014, less than 10 per cent had moved, and more people were moving in to the units than out of them (Parton, 2014). Arguably an approach grounded in the practice and commitment of local social workers and community health staff would achieve more than a focus on commissioners and government edict.

Silence in challenging and not seeing elder abuse has been highlighted by Ash (2013). She identifies a narrowing of vision and the development of a 'cognitive shield' in what is a potentially complex area of work with individuals who may be being abused or neglected, who are highly dependent on immediate carers who may be potential abusers. If the person lives in their own home, reliant on the abuser as their principle carer, with no alternative forms of care and accommodation that do not entail loss of familiar care and independence, they are potentially trapped. This suggests that reflective analytical professional supervision in this area of social work is not well developed. National data on referrals of abuse of vulnerable adults (HSCIC, 2014) shows that the source of harm was a social care worker in 32 per cent of cases and a partner or other family member (23 per cent). The scope for relationship-based practice is constrained in much social work with older people by the emphasis on care management; consequently, the skills and expertise in communication, working with family relationships and in building trust, can be less evident or developed in practice. This makes it harder not only to identify elder abuse, but equally important, to address it in the ambivalent and ambiguous relationship between an older person and their potential abuser who is their carer.

Clearly the over-emphasis on care management in social work with adults has been a factor, emphasising assessment and review, with a focus on others providing direct services. There has been limited attention on the social work service and on direct social work intervention. This has probably been exacerbated by multi-disciplinary teams where social workers are far less clear or focused on their own specific skills and knowledge (see Chapter Seven). In the field of services for people with learning difficulties, health and education professionals have developed specialist expertise. Despite the responsibility for funding and commissioning specialist services for people with complex and challenging needs being shared by the health service and local authority social care, the lack of specialist practice expertise can make it hard to judge the efficacy of externally provided services, both at the point of placement and at review. This is further complicated by the potential loss of primary responsibility when a service is jointly funded. For all the longstanding organisation of multi-disciplinary teams, and the more recent 'pooling' of budgets instituted to demonstrate a shared responsibility for potentially high-cost services, there has not been clarity on the personal responsibility of a single or defined team of lead professionals, with the confidence, knowledge, tenacity and authority to ensure all is well, and that good services are being provided. This is a function or activity that stands above and beyond commissioning and purchasing.

Challenge of social work education, knowledge and continuing professional development

Social work education has had a mixed history in its place within higher education. It started in universities before the First World War (Younghusband, 1978), and by the 1950s, the majority of social work education was still located in universities (Younghusband, 1959). By the 1970s a majority of social workers had started their education and training after a first degree or a graduate course. However, the demands of a large expansion in social work posts, and an emphasis on professional training for all social workers which grew steadily after the Seebohm Report (1968), was met by non-graduate qualifying programmes until the requirement for all qualifying training to be at graduate or Master's level from 2003.

Reviewing and reflecting on the destination of the optimistic conclusions of the Social Work Task Force (2009) and the final work plan of the Social Work Reform Board in England (2012), the bulk of the work has been effectively delegated to employers and the Local Government Association. This includes a career framework, the assessed and supported first year of employment after qualification and registration, standards for professional supervision, the provision and oversight of continuing professional development, and progression in the *Professional capabilities framework*. The further development of the content of the framework was passed to the College of Social Work, which is now largely funded by government and employers. The ambitions for a qualifying professional qualification at Master's level and further learning opportunities leading to higher education awards have fallen by the wayside, despite a strong tradition of such learning being in place since the 1970s. This is not the only example of the Task Force and Reform Board presiding over a reduction in standards, or even more perniciously, being outmanoeuvred by employer, managerial and civil service interests in restricting and restraining the potential authority or power of social work and social workers. This suggests a fear for their own authority and power or simply a loss of impetus or interest, as the key board members moved on to other work, coupled with a complex programme of implementation instituted with diverse accountabilities.

The plan for a second stage of registration, dependent on structured further professional development and objective assessment after the first year in practice, were discarded. The cost and the technical challenge of implementing two categories of registration were the reasons given, although other occupations have more than one category in the same regulator's registration. The special continuing professional development, with an assessment of capability for the first year after qualifying, initially entitled newly qualified social worker (NQSW), and initiated in 2008, later re-titled the assessed and supported year in employment (ASYE) in 2012, remains an initiative, dependent on government funding, rather than being incorporated into ordinary, internalised standards and practice, owned and routinely implemented by social work and social workers. The evaluation of the first three years showed that the most successful arrangements for evidencing the outcomes and achievement at the end of the first year after registration involved using the records of learning and practice, the university and employer partnership post-qualifying award, progression and pay (Carpenter et al, 2012). This learning and these standards needs ambitious champions across and within the whole social work workforce, rather than the inconsistent interest and action of employers (Host Policy Research, 2013; Wiseman and Davies, 2013).

While social work has commendably turned its face against seeking professional elite status in a principled way, there remains authority available from the direct account of the people it serves, and in its position as an intermediary to access scarce social care services. There is authority in leadership from evidence-informed practice and practice wisdom (Sheppard, 1995; O'Sullivan, 2005; Tsui, 2008). It is not clear why social work and social workers have not sought the authority to lead themselves, or alternatively, have failed in their attempts. The vacuum in leadership is characterised in an enduring perception of lack of esteem (Younghusband, 1959, p 207) and in sense of purpose, described as 'a crisis in professional identity' and 'the lack of professional recognition' (Asquith et al, 2005, p 4). The determined optimism of 'a new engaged practice' and 'an ethical career' (Jones et al, 2004) demonstrates an enduring commitment within members of the profession to take responsibility for its own efficacy and public benefit. This is notable when contrasted with the external, government or employer-led institutions that emphasise the administration of wider social care services, assessment for limited resources and management of risk.

There are currents and forces within social work and external to it that have hindered the development of a strong culture of self-leadership. Internally, the anti-professional tradition in social work has been strong, linked to a rejection of the elitism of more traditional occupations, portrayed as conspiracy against the laity (Shaw, 1911) and the strong principles of social justice. Standing alongside the person served, working in collaboration on identifying and seeking solutions, while now puffed in government policies on personalisation, are core working methods. Cooperative approaches, negotiated agreements and discursive relationships have been historically defining features of practice (Jordan, 1983).

Second, there is a longstanding and enduring agnosticism, bordering on outright atheism (Jordan with Jordan, 2000), paradoxically linked to the Labour Party's 'Third Way', part of the enduring neoliberal thrust of central direction for both the value or benefit of evidence-informed practice. The paradox is that a more established and promoted evidence base for social work practice would be a strong riposte to resist the prescriptive processes faced by social workers found to be so dispiriting and disempowering. There are the propagandists and enthusiasts, the determined advocates (Sheldon and Chilvers, 2000; Macdonald, 2001; Newman et al, 2005; Blewett and Boaz, 2010; Forrester and Harwin, 2011), who all recognise the challenges of evaluative research, and are confident that this can achieve credible evidence to improve service outcomes.

In the field of child protection, Featherstone et al (2014, p 73) argue that research skills need to be at the centre of education and service organisational culture:

> Social workers and managers need to draw on published research studies to help them understand children's and families' needs, matters of safety and risk and to plan their interventions.
>
> Social workers and managers need to develop research skills, such as observation, synthesis of information and analysis so that they can "increase the sum of knowledge" about a particular family's circumstances.
>
> Social workers and managers need to use research skills to examine their responses and as a check on the essential but fallible intuitive judgements.

All this requires enthusiastic enquiry and energetic continuing professional development beyond passively awaiting training courses and government guidance.

Furthermore, confidence in the rigour of social work education has a very real impact, not only on the credibility of practitioners, but also on their own confidence in the value and benefits of the service they provide. The Social Work Task Force (2009, p 16) 'heard from many sources that the initial education and training is not yet reliable enough in meeting its primary objective, which must be to prepare students for the demands of frontline practice'. This has been re-emphasised five years later in the government-commissioned reviews of social work education by Narey (2014) and Croisdale-Appleby (2014).

This is not the place for a discussion of the prior educational achievements of the university student intake for social work education and training; suffice to say that widening access to higher education requires investment in the overall educational inputs at universities in order to ensure the less prepared undergraduates can fully benefit from and enjoy their time at university. Both the quality of the higher education provided *and* the quality of the practice learning are critical for the production of people who are confident in their own roles, skills base and competence in practice. The oversight of the quality and content of university education has not always been rigorous, and inconsistencies were identified by the Social Work Task Force (2009).

There is no evidence that this has yet been addressed by government, regulators or even more insidiously, by the profession itself.

Key elements of the reformed social work training of 2002 (DH, 2002) included the requirement for a statutory practice placement (Holmes et al, 2013), widely ignored by universities and by all the regulatory systems. The study of human growth and development was also required, yet Ward et al (2010, p 4) found that 'interviews with social workers revealed that child development had only been a small part of qualifying training, often quickly forgotten'. Shortcomings such as these not only leave a proportion of social work graduates unprepared or at least ill-prepared for practice, and a significant proportion severely disadvantaged in the employment market; my own experience in mentoring such social workers is that they are virtually unemployable as social workers unless they have the good fortune to gain these skills and the knowledge in non-professional roles after their university training. These are issues that are wholly within the power and capacity of social work to successfully address, in providing sufficient, appropriate practice learning, and in the education curriculum, designed and overseen within professional, employer and university partnerships. The risks of growing employer-based routes to social work qualification are not only the same shortage of good practice learning opportunities, but also a focus on quick-fix technician training in uncertain practice methods, and the loss of educational opportunity to prepare for a career in professional social work and leadership in practice. The development of a consensus for a more formal curriculum, both in terms of academic study and in practice learning, will be a way of resisting the forces that seek to reduce the capacity and knowledge base of social work, to a technical, procedurally driven occupation.

Taking the lead

The scope to be proactive, to take a lead at case and team level, is there, given tenacity, energy and confidence. These challenges are akin to the term 'tempered radical' used to describe corporate professionals assertively seeking to achieve positive change. Six attributes are identified in such leaders (see Meyerson, 1995):

- speak their own truths even when they are afraid;
- have strong support networks;

- are biased towards action, even if only small actions;
- have clarity on their own most important goals;
- promote experimentation; and
- engage in reflective discussions with their colleagues.

This includes the elements of the proactive approach advanced by Thompson and Thompson (2008):

- having your say;
- using all opportunities to make a contribution;
- challenge when necessary;
- seeking out like-minded people to form alliances;
- developing a collective voice; and
- using all available channels to make those representations and challenges, rather than succumbing to low morale.

In terms of a shared discourse within social work, common goals are drawn from the foundation of social justice, hearing and heeding the voices of the people receiving social work services and their carers. Professions have been categorised by Johnson (1972) in an analysis of their power, as *collegiate, patronage*, where power has been externally given, and *mediated*, where it is negotiated and conditional. The source of power within the profession and professional activity is viewed as dependent on its independence and ownership. Social work at this time in the UK does not have any organisation that exercises collective, collaborative or collegiate action. The use of the description of professions as *collegiate*, where the power comes from collective and collaborative action, is significant in the context of the English College of Social Work, which, despite its title, has turned away from open elections and open collaborative work with its membership, and is largely state and employer-funded. Although fully open elections are planned to take place in the future, this is too little too late, since the structures and working methods of the organisation will have been consolidated. Johnson's analysis categorises social work as one of the 'state-mediated professions'. Cousins (1987, p 97, referenced by Harris and White, 2009, p 131) identified such professions as those which 'do not resist the extension of state power for they have no choice but to be public employees. On the contrary they generally welcome the extension of state power, for it is the only source of such power as they themselves possess; indeed these occupational groups owe their very existence to the power of the state.' However, if the power of social work is accepted as dependent on state consent, not only is the social justice element made conditional, but the content and the way of working are also prescribed. It is a paradox that social work, which had so much of its origins in the voluntary and charity sector being incorporated into the welfare state, has submerged its independence, its own direction and its own determination.

White (2009, p 131) identifies that if social work accepts its position as a state-mediated profession, its ends are established by the state. Citing Derber (1983), it is 'ideologically subordinated' by the state and the ends are determined by the state, and the 'means' are subject to only 'technical autonomy'. This is writ large in the English College of Social Work's *Roles and functions of social workers in England* (2014), which is almost totally reliant on government and legal prescription. This can only be read as that organisation placing itself as subordinate to the state, reflecting its origins and continuing funding dependency. This flies in the face of the social work profession having had its own professional organisations and training in universities since the first decade of the 20th century (Younghusband, 1978). Nevertheless, if the 'ends' of social work are articulated in a direct way, which reflects day-to-day work and responsibilities, the risks of subordination are radically lessened. Examples of these 'ends', which pre-date the welfare state, include ensuring vulnerable children are safe from harm, securing high-quality family care for children who can no longer live with their birth families, achieving good education for children who are in public care, enabling older people to live independently with a high quality of life, helping people with mental health problems to achieve and maintain recovery, and ensuring people with learning difficulties who have high care needs are well cared for and are socially included. The language is straightforward and the 'ends' understandable to all. When public policy is changed or re-invented, and when government initiatives are promoted, the language and meanings can be distorted, and the 'ends' of social work diverted, subverted and suborned. Upholding them, refusing to be knocked off course, challenging, resisting and combating, these are all leadership behaviours. Social work can enter new policy initiatives, confident if the ends remain the same. Its 'means' can be deployed, continuing to build and lead, in terms of the evidence and practice skill base. If business systems, like call centres or computer-generated practice structures, get in the way of the 'ends', waiting for a government review or government-funded academic research is too passive and too late.

Public policy and political initiatives can use language that alienates and distances social work from its ends – for example, 'high-cost high-harm families' (Newman et al, 2007). The evidence base for such initiatives is limited, and social work needs to be part of the challenge, critically constructive and bringing leadership in its engagement with formal, standardised or manualised programmes. They have a value, although they need to be used selectively, as part of a range of intervention skills and methods (Barth et al, 2012). They are attractive both to empiricists as standardised working methods, and to policy makers seeking quick-fixes. However, they can fail to recognise the complexity of the needs faced by the people social work serves, risking standardising problems and using cognitive methods rather than the psychosocial, recognising the person in their environment (Unrau et al, 2007), and the relationship base of social work. However, if social work turns its face against such approaches, rather than bringing critical engagement, it encourages the marginalisation of social work in public policy and the blanket imposition of alien working methods. Social work can be at the heart, rather than at the margins, of social policy, if it brings confident and authoritative knowledge, evidence and competent practice.

The *Adult social care outcomes framework* includes broad aims, which, while consistent with social work ends, has a problem of language and meaning for day-to-day practice; for example, when something like safeguarding is turned into a measurement, 'The proportion of people who use services who say those services have made them feel safe' (DH, 2014, p 37). This has no direct or arguably any indirect relevance to social work practice. The articulation of the social work 'end' would encompass the effectiveness and accessibility of any intervention to protect *all* potential victims of abuse or neglect, not just those already using services. The focus on the easily measurable ignores the actual work of social work.

The independent social work practices instigated in 2008 (Stanley et al, 2012) offer a model of self-governance and leadership of services commissioned and delegated from local authorities. While the number of independent practices is small, and some services have returned to the commissioning local authorities, this is an interesting development to watch if they increase in number and retain the original aspiration to be run and led by social workers. They are both the consequence of a commissioning, business-orientated culture and conversely, an opportunity for social work to take control and lead part of its core business and expertise. Social work, however, has a longer pedigree than both state provision of social care and of the welfare state, in addition to its well-developed value base of social justice, which is inevitably and appropriately at odds at times with state employer and statutory direction. The ends of social work in terms of protecting vulnerable people, promoting independence and choice in solutions to problems, as well as choice in the services used, are fundamental. The origins of social work in charitable or voluntary organisations, with families and children at home or cared for elsewhere, the ebb and flow of community development work and supporting older people and people with disabilities, are part of the narrative (Younghusband, 1978). In the field of medicine, too, the issue of state-mediated healthcare, through government-funded services, is also seen to have a significant effect on the relationship between doctors and their patients. Social work is not alone in inhabiting a world where external prescription is common and real dilemmas of what works exist. Evidence-based medicine with prescribed algorithms can be just as much at odds with 'patient-centeredness' (Armstrong, 2007) as the prescribed processes faced by social workers.

If the state determines and owns the *ends* of the service social work provides, it would be likely that the full ambitions of promoting social change, empowerment and liberation of people to enhance wellbeing (IFSW, 2014) will not be pursued. It can be argued that discretion in the *means* of the delivery of a service (Lipsky, 1980; Dworkin, 1997) may be negotiated. However, the detailed prescriptive processes in children's social care (Wastell et al, 2010), and the reality of implementing the tasks of care management in services for adults (Audit Commission, 2012), demonstrate even the *means* of delivering what has been seen as a social work service can be subjugated to process. The delivery of universal direct payments for adult social care and the opportunities for exercising discretion by an individual social worker (Ellis, 2007) are restricted by enduring and unresolved issues in the evolution of this part of the personalisation agenda, and in particular, the amount of funding available being determined by local eligibility criteria, rather than national entitlement. In addition, decisions on 'hard cases' are made by managers or commissioners. This study suggests that any discretion is used negatively by social workers, showing a tendency to resist its implementation using words such as 'let', 'allow' or 'give'.

Managerialism has its roots in 'the belief that there are common ways of organising and delivering any service, focussing on direction, efficiency, external accountability and externally defined standards. It is centred on developing the skills and focus of senior staff on this agenda, rather than the professional skills to lead and provide the service' (McKitterick, 2012a, pp 103-4). Some commentators have identified managerialism as part of the 'New Right' (Clarke and Newman, 1997), identifying particular features of management as a distinct, separate function with an emphasis on measurement and developing competitive markets: 'It gives priority to the managerial and economic concerns of service funders and providers, focussing on service costs and efficiencies' (Asquith et al, 2005, p 5). In addition, a change from inputs and processes to outputs and outcomes is promoted, although for much of the performance management culture in social work this is far from clear.

The growth of professional elites, in terms of specialised knowledge, education and competitive merit, has been a feature of the later 20th-century history (Perkin, 1996). This historical narrative analysis includes managers, particularly as an elite, alongside other specialist occupations, including bankers, with power derived from role authority, as well as expertise. It is arguably a modernist account of power, located beyond the more traditional power base of professions with reserved duties, self-governance and public deference. Perkin argues that the authority of this new professional class is secured in a range of specialist knowledge and skills, often acquired after a period of unrelated study, often in elite higher education. An earlier analysis by Burnham (1941), an American radical philosopher, had suggested that as capitalism declines, 'virtual control is passing into the hands of a new ruling class, the "managers", by whom he means the administrators of industry and government' (quoted in Woodcock and Avakumovic, 1950, p 449). Both analyses place specialist knowledge and skills as subservient to management and administration.

To return to the wider world beyond social work, there are other voices questioning the effectiveness of leadership and even the end of leadership. Kellerman (2012) describes a lack of evidence in the 'leadership industry', despite her working within it, the loss of a culture of deference and in particular, a failure to examine the positive attributes of followership. This is an argument that suggests power is progressively dispersed and shared as followers become stronger and titular leaders become weaker. This does not feel to be the case in social work. A vacuum is an opportunity to fill vacant space. I use the word 'vacuum' because it suggests that there is the opportunity for social work to fill that space, for it to regain its own destiny and for social workers to take responsibility for themselves, for effective work, to achieve positive change and to hold on to the agenda of the relationship-based practice and social justice, which may be outside the expectations or wishes of employers and managers.

The enduring trend identified by Kellerman is that the trajectory of history moves towards democratisation, a trend from leader power to the expansion of follower power. This is seen in models of collaborative leadership, with a focus on team effort, empowerment and flatter hierarchies. This language is expressed in the principles of leadership practice set out in The National Skills Academy for Social Care in England and DH (2013) as social purpose, co-production, innovation, improvement, integration, and risk and responsibility. However, this also demonstrates an enduring conflation and confusion of concepts of leadership and management. The personal qualities are general, and are arguably aspirations for and by everyone, developing self-awareness, managing oneself, continuing personal development and acting with integrity. Significantly, the Academy reserves creating the vision and delivering the strategy for senior staff only. This begs the question of where the skills and knowledge to provide a service comes from, and where responsibility for knowing or showing the way is located. The framework is spookily identical to that developed within the NHS without the additional work specific to clinical practice that is undertaken by the authoritative and collegiate, profession-led membership bodies in health services. When social work was included in the review of the clinical leadership competency framework (NHS Institute for Clinical Innovation and Improvement and the Academy of Medical Royal Colleges, 2011), the leadership of social work was identified as under-developed compared to professions across the health sector. I can see no response to this challenge from the institutions that claim to lead social work or social workers.

THREE

Sources of leadership in the profession

Introduction

The spectrum of traditional or conventional sources of leadership are located within institutions, membership subscription organisations, role or title, the law and regulation. The development of the use of self-leadership, through knowledge, competence, experience and peer respect, is less advanced. In this chapter I explore the ideas of self-leadership and distributed leadership that can enable, encourage and validate the contribution of *all* social workers, addressing the current vacuum and lack of efficacy of those organisations or interests that might claim to lead. Knowledge, evidence-informed practice and purposeful interventions are key elements of the way forward, built collectively from within the profession and embedded in rigorous continuing professional development.

Much leadership literature and policy is couched in terms of conditional delegation, and fundamentally, that the overall direction and strategy are already determined and are not negotiable. In this regard the concepts are akin to 'followership' (Kellerman, 2012). In addition, the theories of managing oneself are evolving through the concepts of emotional intelligence (Goleman, 1998), knowledge about oneself, and mindfulness (Dolman and Bond, 2011). These are the personal competencies, as opposed to professional ones, identified by Sydanmaanlakka (2002), of clear objectives in work, sufficient competence, feedback about performance and continuous development. Neck and Manz (2013) associate self-leadership with self-empowerment. It is often focused on learning personal skills and how this prepares people for formal leadership positions, and more importantly, for leadership to be exercised by everyone.

In social work, with increasing experience and expertise, working with colleagues, some with less access to professional training, belonging to other professions or less experienced peers, *showing the way* is an integral part of the job. With colleagues it includes explaining the inter-play of the social and personal or psychosocial influences and the interventions needed, sharing and demonstrating skills in direct practice, sharing evidence from research and examples from good practice and fostering an enquiring, curious and reflective culture in the workplace. Integral to relationship-based interventions is the sharing of information, insights and the development of skills in direct practice. This is not to lose sight of the 'non-judgemental' and empowerment traditions of social work. The insights of social workers, drawn from direct work with individuals and families, working with colleagues in a multi-disciplinary environment, all influence the practice of others and demonstrate the effectiveness of the servant leader relationship with individuals and with families (Cullen, 2012).

Self-leadership and distributed leadership

The NHS and some of the professions within it have given substantial attention to the exercise and location of leadership. The model of leadership frequently cited is 'distributed', both for social care (Hafford-Letchfield et al, 2008), and for health services (NHS Institute for Innovation and Improvement and Academy of Medical Royal Colleges, 2009). The recognition of both the complexity of the service being provided, and the range of expertise of individual team members, are the reasons given for avoiding leadership being located in one person or one position. The activity of leadership is shared and distributed among members of the team. A specific service example comes from mental health:

> Psychiatrists should complement and respect the vital roles played by clinicians from other professional backgrounds; delivery of mental healthcare is a team activity in which all members make important contributions to improving mental health and service provision. The ability to unite this diversity of talent and perspectives to meet

organisational aims is a hallmark of a successful medical leader. (Royal College of Psychiatrists, 2013, p 2)

Or:

Clinical teams perform best when their leaders value and support staff, enable them to work as a team, ensure that the main focus is on patient care, and create time to care. Team leaders are most effective when they work in a group that emphasises shared and collective leadership and when they establish well-structured teams. (The King's Fund, 2013, p 32)

Within education and schools there is a substantial interest in this model as a way of embedding leadership towards high aspirations and achievement for all pupils (Bennett et al, 2003). Notwithstanding this model of distributing power, discretion and authority may not be translated into a reality for all frontline workers of a sense of being responsible, accountable and trusted, or as seeing managers demonstrate this distribution and sharing of authority and power. There is a risk that distributed leadership is conditional and continues to be focused on direction from a managerialist agenda of national policy, performance indicator targets and local political expediency, rather than direction from evidence-informed practice, relationship-based work, the direct voice of people who use services and their carers, and social justice.

Self-leadership promotes and retains responsibility for practice, quality standards and continuing development within the individual and their collective consciousness, within the community of colleagues or peers who share responsibility for similar work. It can encourage and build on internalised, personally owned standards of practice. Within this personal and community world rest the opportunities for remembering the overarching aspirations of social work, the commitment to skilled intervention, at both the levels of the individual case and of social justice, and dedication to continuing professional development: 'Empowering managers will be concerned with motivating individuals and teams to achieve more towards organisational objectives by granting them greater independence from managerial control' (Hafford-Letchfield et al, 2008, p 28). The conditionality of this approach relies on the duality of the trust by managers to devolve authority, and for individuals and teams to have objectives that coincide or that are shared with the organisation. Where this is not the case, there can be strategies to achieve resolution, or at least tactics to accommodate the achievement of the different objectives around the ordinary organisational restraints. If the core expectations of job role are met, working in innovative and creative ways, undertaking developmental work in wider areas of the service can be negotiated or undertaken with peers away from the immediate work environment. Enthusiasm, energy and evidence of awareness of current knowledge and learning can never be unwelcome, even if it feels as if the work setting did not initiate it!

Organisations and institutions

The landscape of social work and the wider, more diffused world of social care is rich in (or crowded with) organisations that in their own objectives seek to improve services, almost exclusively funded from statutory sources. Consequently, their existence and future is dependent on national or local government financial support:

- The Social Care Institute for Excellence (SCIE) shares knowledge about what works.
- The National Skills Academy for Social Care helps employers increase staff skills, gives employees ways to improve their own skills and endorses training (in 2014 it merged with Skills for Care, see below).
- The National Children's Bureau works to improve the lives of children, promoting evidence-informed decision making and cost-effective sector-led improvement.
- Research in Practice supports evidence-informed practice with children and families.
- Research in Practice for Adults promotes the use of evidence-informed policy and practice in adult social care.
- The Centre for Excellence and Outcomes in Children and Young People's Services works to help those working in children's services improve the life chances of all children and young people, in particular those who are most vulnerable.
- Skills for Care and Development, one sector skills body for the UK, has the function of helping social workers, care workers and those

working in children's services to do the best job possible, supporting employers and to develop a world class workforce.

There are four linked bodies for each of the four UK countries – three combine the regulatory role with the development of skills and professional standards:

- The Scottish Social Services Council is responsible for ensuring staff are properly trained and qualified.
- The Care Council for Wales is responsible for promoting and securing high standards across the social services and social care workforce.
- The Northern Ireland Social Care Council is responsible for strengthening and supporting the professionalism of the social care workforce and improving the quality of social care through the development, promotion and regulation of education and training.
- In England, Skills for Care is responsible for supporting employers in creating a capable, confident and skilled adult social care workforce. It merged with the National Skills Academy in 2014.

There are two social work organisations in the UK:

- BASW
- in England, the College of Social Work.

If the funding of such a plethora of undifferentiated bodies had come from a range of sources, rather than from central government and local authorities, the situation could be more explicable. They appear to have avoided, or to have survived, the 'bonfire of the quangos', or the reduction of government-funded arm's-length bodies planned by different political administrations. Such a number, located and sheltered under the large social care and children's services umbrella, brings the hazards of the diffusion of focus, duplication and unclear accountability. Social work practice, its knowledge and skill base, its qualifying education and continuing professional development, are potentially helped or hindered by these organisations.

The multiplicity is arguably a sign of inchoate action by the public bodies funding them, or perhaps a sign of desperation to do something to improve services, through a myriad of initiatives to improve the development of the employers and staff providing them. The sector skills body model is one drawn from employer-led models of self-improvement. Employers, through a shared and collective common interest, seek to invest in the development and training of their own staff. However, with central government being the largest funder of both social care and children's services, albeit mostly through local authorities, and despite there being a large independent sector, for-profit and not-for-profit, national government finance sustains the sector skills bodies in adult and children's social care, including specific provision for social work.

The situation is markedly different in other skill sectors, where employers from a predominantly market economy have a greater commitment to collectively funding the development of skills and knowledge in the workforce. As social work is located within the remit of all these bodies, they cast a shadow, and the breadth of responsibility for adult social care and children's services dilutes the attention for the specific requirements of social work. It causes a generalisation or homogenisation of social work within social care, adding to the lack of clarity of purpose, knowledge and skills base, and most pernicious of all, the lack of a focused and ambitious attention to social work and social workers.

There are two bodies specific to social work and social workers in the UK: the College of Social Work in England was established in 2012, funded by government grant and contracts, member subscriptions and employer corporate membership, and BASW was formed in 1970 from the amalgamation of seven social worker member organisations that had been members of the Standing Conference of Organisations of Social Workers formed in 1962 (some of these organisations had been founded before the First World War). The eighth member of that organisation, the National Association of Probation Officers (NAPO), decided not to join. The requirement for a social work qualification for the probation service was abolished in 1997.

The Social Work Task Force (2009, p 45) recommended 'the establishment of an independent national college of social work. This will articulate and promote the interests of good social work. It will give the profession itself strong leadership; a clear voice in public debate, policy development and policy delivery; and strong ownership of the standards to be upheld.' This echoes a call from the Chief Social Services Officer in Northern Ireland: 'Social workers, individually and as a profession, need to be more confident, committed and enthusiastic, and to speak with one strong, unified voice. There needs to be a willingness to learn lessons and to change, to solve problems, not just to state them, and to have a higher profile by sharing good practice and celebrating success' (Martin, 2007, p 269).

Looking at the two statements, the latter places responsibility on individuals and the profession, rather than a structural solution. In 2009, senior civil servants in the Department for Children, Schools and Families (DCSF) and the Department of Health (DH) invited organisations responsible for social work

> ... to discuss the first steps in establishing the College of Social Work in England. The Social Work Task Force's Report to Government (2009) recommended the creation of an independent national college of social work, developed and led by social workers. The Government has accepted the recommendation as an essential step in enabling social workers to gain a strong voice and to work with Government, employers, social work educators, the public and media on a more equal footing. (Correspondence from the Department of Children, Schools and Families and Department of Health, 11 December 2009)

The two government departments invited SCIE to provide 'logistical support in the form of accommodation and corporate service functions' to support the establishment of the College (Correspondence from the Department of Children, Schools and Families and Department of Health, 11 December 2009). This was subsequently underpinned by a government grant of £5 million. The relationship between the College shadow body, SCIE, and BASW was fractious and litigious from the outset (Oral evidence to the House of Commons Education Committee, 2011; Graham Stuart MP, chair of the Education Committee, letter to Tim Loughton MP, Parliamentary Under-Secretary of State for Education, 9 November 2011). Discussions ebbed and flowed, culminating in a complete stand-off and cessation of any collaboration for the development of the profession or social work services in 2013. Although a large membership is seen by both organisations as important for credibility and for revenue, it is interesting that in countries such as the US, Australia and South Africa, the credibility and effective leadership of professional associations for social workers seem unaffected by the proportion of potential members where subscribing membership is far from universal. Are social workers not good joiners or weak in collective action? Other professions manage mass membership through a greater sense of commitment to continuing professional development, or have a greater ownership of their own professional identity (Reynolds, 2007), or perhaps feel able, or are made more welcome, to make a significant and direct contribution to their own profession's development and professional standards. This is embedded in the professions' own commitment and taking of direct responsibility for ensuring they receive their own professional supervision and continuing professional development. The current responsibility for this and the standards rest with the regulatory registering and inspection bodies, and in addition in England, with the national organisation for local authority employers (DfE, 2011a). Research showed two years later that only half of local authority employers were applying these standards (Holmes et al, 2013).

This is a striking indication of the lack of effect in relying on employers to lead, through their managers. The standards were fully supported and endorsed through the Social Work Reform Board, by social worker representatives, local government employers, and by the Association of Directors of Adult Social Services (ADASS) and the Association of Directors of Children's Services (ADCS). The standards were developed as the direct result of substantial government investment in the reform of social work and social work standards following the deaths of Victoria Climbié in 2000 and Peter Connelly in 2007. The standards are not high, contain no new ideas and are familiar in other professions; they should not be challenging. The responsibility for adhering to and delivering the standards rests with staff who are usually registered social workers. For employers to reach 50 per cent compliance after so much time and public expenditure is shameful. One could record this as an example of evidence of the failure of top-down, government and managerialist activity, as well as social work not owning and applying its own basic professional standards. To blame employers may be to miss the point. The issue is that an organisation formed of local authority employers is not the appropriate location. The standards rest within social work, and the failure to uphold them is that of social work. The means and the people to rectify the problems are not the employers.

Reflecting on the rise and fall of the social work organisations over the past 50 years (Bilton, 2010), five organisations were responsible for social work in the 1970s. These were:

- The Central Council for Education and Training in Social Work (CCETSW) formed in 1970, a statutory body responsible for promoting and approving social work education courses and qualifications.
- The National Institute for Social Work (NISW), established in 1961 following a recommendation in the Younghusband Report (1959) that there should be a staff college (it closed in 2003 after the establishment of SCIE).
- The Social Work Service of the Department of Health and Social Security (DHSS), which changed into the Social Services Inspectorate, whose responsibilities now lie with the Office for Standards in Education, Children's Services and Skills (Ofsted), and the Care Quality Commission (CQC).
- The Personal Social Services Council (PSCC), a non-statutory, non-executive advisory body funded by the DHSS and local authorities.
- BASW.

As Bilton (2010) points out, of these five organisations, only BASW continues in existence, and is the only organisation that has been totally reliant on the contributions of its members. All the others were dependant on central government funding.

I was in the thick of the early discussions for the planning and formation of the College of Social Work as member of the College Development Group at the outset of the work in 2009, and was an active member of groups within the College and BASW. Three features stand out from that experience. First, BASW was not seen by the Social Work Task Force, the Social Work Reform Board, ADASS and children's services or civil servants as a potential predecessor body for the envisaged college. The reasons expressed were the membership level across the profession, the perceived history of quasi-trade union activity, both in its professional representation service and challenge of government, and employers' policies and practice. There was also the broader aspirations from the Social Work Task Force for a body to agree and articulate high standards of social work practice, an area of work in which BASW had not been strong or particularly active. Clearly the perspectives in all the organisations involved in the early discussions clashed, and I observed this was a problem coming from all sides. There was quickly an entrenched refusal from all quarters to support any collaborative or constructive working together.

Second, for BASW, the formation of a college was a challenge to its way of working and the balance of work undertaken by staff and by members. Organisations and institutions can, like living organisms, display extraordinary levels of resistance to change or perceived threat to their existence. While its professional representation service for members with their employers, now potentially split off with the formation of the legally separate trade union arm, is arguably not part of a publicly credible collegiate professional body, the College of Social Work shadow board had carried out very detailed, secret, negotiations for a joint membership agreement with a single union, Unison. These negotiations were later abandoned following critical scrutiny by the House of Commons Education Select Committee in November 2011.

For other organisations and interest groups, the formation of an ambitious, truly social worker member-led, independent and properly *collegiate* body is a challenge and a threat, as opposed to a state-mediated body (Johnson, 1972; Cousins, 1987). It became clear that it would be a real irritant and challenge to employers and managers if social workers had their own professional standards and a base of confidence, beyond the authority of managers and the power of government regulation. The government sponsorship of the College of Social Work also came at the same time as the formation and development of other state-funded 'colleges', the National College for Teaching and Leadership in 2013 formed from earlier bodies, and the National College of Policing in 2012, both of which are distinctly different in funding and governance from the historic medical colleges.

What has been missed is the potential shared authority and public credibility, embedded in common standards and a shared body of evidence-informed practice expertise. Such a collegiate body would call into question the existence of the quangos in the field, and it would weaken the authority of employer-led bodies. A minor detail was the fact that BASW is a UK-wide body, albeit with separate named structures in each of the UK countries, and the College as proposed by the Social Work Task Force was for England alone. The discussions between the two organisations, when they were taking place, identified straightforward ways of resolving this issue. BASW could have taken the initiative and demonstrated how it was capable and competent to undertake most or all of the functions being identified for a college of social work even before the Social Work Task Force had completed its deliberations. The reasons why it did not are unclear. What I observed was a resistance to change, a strong, nearly overwhelming feeling of threat, and a refusal to rise to the challenge of moving to a collegiate way of working which used the expertise and energy of its members. On the other hand, there was an assumption by other organisations and interests that it did not have a legitimate role to be part of the college foundation. Could this be part of the historic resistance within the profession to take a lead to itself, albeit with proper provision for a strong and assertive user and carer voice at its centre? It was a time for energy, action, ambition and work to grasp the initiative. This did not happen, and that opportunity has now passed.

The word 'college' has a number of meanings. These include an educational institution, or a body whose members work together as peers, collaboratively, in a collegiate way. Education can be part of that collegiate body. Recently, a number of organisations called 'colleges' have been formed by government initiative and funding, for example, the College of Policing (2012), the Leadership College for Further Education and Skills (2012), the National College of Teaching and Leadership (2013), and the proposed formation of a Royal College of Teaching (Leslie, 2013). These are wholly government-funded bodies and 'membership' for individuals is free, management is distant and inextricably linked to current political will. It is as if the two meanings of college have been conflated with an educational focus and an inferred status claim to be akin to the royal colleges in medicine. The common feature of the new colleges is their dependence on state funding and a membership distanced from governance and from a direct or collective contribution to the work being undertaken. The formation of the colleges rests within government initiatives; the ultimate control is in reliance on government funding and the very weak direct voice, influence, or any meaningful authority in the day-to-day work or the governance of these very *un*-collegiate bodies for the people providing the public services concerned. Thus, they could be the ultimate manifestation of managerialism and the ascendancy of a managerial elite, secure in power and its relationship with the civil service and government, as opposed to a demonstration of direct experience, skill and knowledge in practice coupled with an independent motivation for social justice. There is a paradox in the neoliberal reduction of the state as a social care provider, the state seizing direction of the means of control of a key component of social care and other public services.

A subtle distinction may be becoming evident in central government creations – the separation of the work being undertaken by state-funded staff from the people undertaking the work, policing, teaching, further education and social work being the focus of these new institutions, split off from police officers, teachers, lecturers and social workers. This arguably continues the potential for ownership of knowledge, practice evidence, skills and standards being split off from the people directly providing the service. There is a bitter irony for social work and social workers who sought statutory regulation and registration of the profession, separate from the interests of the members of the profession, now finding that all the institutions responsible for their work are beyond their direct influence, split off through funding and institutional interests.

There could be a post hoc justification of the stand-off between the College of Social Work and BASW being legitimised by a separation of the interests of social work and social workers. However, this argument is undermined by the College's earlier negotiations with a single trade union, Unison. By 2013 the stand-off had reached the stage of no open lines of communication, and even with a significant shared membership, it had proved impossible for members of both organisations to successfully initiate any rapprochement or joint work. The result has been direct competition, two different codes of ethics, two sets of member benefits – a situation as incomprehensible to those on the outside as it is unnecessary. The combined effect has been to weaken social work in England.

BASW and the College offer strikingly similar benefits for their members, knowledge information systems, professional indemnity, mentoring and member news or a magazine. Each has developed similar ways of working, members being invited to meetings or to consultations, but decisions on any issues of import being made elsewhere and by staff, including commissioned external work. Is this an adoption of quango working methods? Is this what civil servants had wished to deliver to government all along? Is it the result of social workers being seen or experienced as unwilling or unable to work collaboratively on policy and practice development? Is it a perception that no one would listen to or heed the collective outcomes of social workers working together? The most chilling aspect is that both organisations seem to have internalised the managerialist culture, and regard ordinary members as inappropriate and incompetent pilots of their own destiny and even their practice, their contribution neutered in arcane governance structures that are far from any activity being undertaken. Other smaller social work organisations are more informal and not reliant on significant state funding. Their work comes from the personal energy and commitment of individual members. Two such organisations currently operating in the UK are the Social Work Action Network (SWAN), a member network with an active annual conference, and Making Research Count, a collaboration across 11 universities promoting national research discussions. These two coalitions are located in both the social justice-radical and the 'techno-rational' traditions of social work (Parton, 2000).

Combining social justice and the personal, with evidence-informed practice

The two aspects of social work – social justice and the personal – are not divisions; while the personal will be to the fore in much social policy, it is the policies themselves that require the active engagement and contribution of social work and social workers. SWAN has a strong commitment to preventative services (2004), and much formal evaluative research, particularly in children's services has been on prevention programmes (Maquire et al, 2012). The re-focusing on the importance of relationship-based practice and consolidating the evidence base demonstrates how the 'techno-rational' can be accommodated in practice, how the personal, the therapeutic, is not separate from wider issues for intervention and change.

The bridge that joins these two perspectives, practice wisdom (Sheppard, 1995) and evidence-based or informed practice (Newman et al, 2005), needs constant maintenance and strengthening. While the ambiguous politics of social work, of the two powerful, dual commitments to society and to the individual (Pearson, 1975), can too easily be articulated as being in opposition, in the 'artificial bifurcation of practice validity and theoretical validity' (Sheppard, 1998, p 763), the direction of social work lies in living and working with these uncertainties, drawing on the full range of sources of knowledge and skill, as an internalised and collective awareness across practitioners, educators and researchers, as opposed to directed methods of operation.

Knowledge, evidence-informed practice and purposeful interventions

In making the argument for more open use of knowledge, research, explicit practice skills and mutual reflective professional supervision, there needs to be a sense of purpose and direction, beyond the simple administration of public services, be they directly provided or purchased. For the most empowering models of self-leadership, professional development and personal ownership of practice expertise, knowledge and research are central. In the universities there are two further self-organised organisations that have substantial influence and positional authority – the Association of Professors of Social Work and the Joint University Council Social Work Education Committee, which represents universities providing social work education across the four UK nations. Could it be that this is the location of the most confident or assertive corpus within the profession? Is this where there is sufficient time and energy available to invest in the articulation of purpose and effective methods of working? There are real challenges for university teachers and researchers to maintain direct practice skills and knowledge of the current demands and needs in services. These challenges are similar to those social workers who are senior managers, who risk being driven by national policy initiatives and performance management.

Universities are dependent on student numbers – it is calculated that the Social Work Degree and postgraduate course student numbers increased by 126 per cent between 2003 and 2011 (Holmes et al, 2013). In 2003 the national requirement for all university social work education to be delivered in formal partnerships with employers was removed, despite strong objections from directors of social services, in the changes in qualifying education, only to be reinstated following the deliberations of the Social Work Reform Board in 2012! It is another example of the world of social work sliding back, or being pushed back by government edict, and then having to re-learn.

The employability of NQSWs and their calibre is questioned again with the instigation of two separate government reviews of social work education by government ministers in 2013, one from the Department for Education (DfE) (Narey, 2014), and the other from the DH (Croisdale-Appleby, 2014). There are initiatives in 'fast track' social work qualifying education for graduates that existed in residential social work with children in the 1960s, in the Home Office Emergency Social Work Courses in the 1970s, and in Scotland in 2003–07. The two current schemes are Step Up to Social Work, initiated in 2010 and Frontline in 2013. Both programmes focus on learning while in employment, with a lower level of university-based learning, and aiming to be completed in less than the two-year postgraduate norm. Again, one can see the tension between the drive from central government and employers to direct and control the profession and the universities. Consensual leadership may be achieved by authoritative professionalism, with a greater degree of autonomy being granted, or taken, through competence and expertise. Poor training and education, with a weak knowledge and skill base, leads to no authority and no autonomy. Is it in the interests of the powerful to keep the workers competent in a narrow technical range of prescribed skills? Leadership is harder to exercise with more competent, better educated followers (Kellerman, 2012).

The education and research capacity of the universities engaged in social work is substantial – social workers are trained at over half of the universities in the UK. Their potential for leadership is huge, both in terms of the training provided, and the intellectual capital garnered from practice and policy research. It is significant that the core of the two self-organised groups, SWAN and Making Research Count, are based in universities. One would expect the universities to provide the thinking and reflective space to both promote clarity of purpose and to identify, through rigorous research, how social work practice and related social policy can be effective. The impediments have been the ebb and flow of national policies on the relationship expected between employers and universities referred to above. Social work research is largely commissioned by central government rather than organisations that provide social work services or by professional associations. The ambiguities of social work can become more fascinating and pre-occupying to academics than to busy practitioners and their supervisors.

Part of this is a phenomenon shared way beyond social work. Debates about the links between theory and practice are universal.

Tenkasi and Hay (2004) identified the role of the 'scholar-practitioner' who acts as a bridge between the world of academe and the workplace, by a process of framing, influencing, making sense of and demonstrating the linkages. This is a role well established within medicine, with joint appointments between university medical schools and the NHS, the role being a combination of direct medical practice, research and teaching. Social work has a very limited tradition in this sharing of roles, although practitioners and their supervisors undertaking university-based post-qualifying awards fulfil a role with valuable similarities. If knowledge is seen as objective, independently verified and external to the practitioner, who is simply expected to use that knowledge in their practice, then it would not be surprising if knowledge producers – researchers, thinkers and teachers – are perceived as separate from knowledge users – practitioners and the organisations where they are located. This is akin to the separation of the knowledge base used to develop formal social work assessment systems embedded in computer programs from the context, practice and judgement of social workers. 'Increasing audit and challenges to professional discretion are exemplified in child welfare practice. We can detect such constraints within electronic assessment. Put crudely, we "fill in" the screen with information, the characteristics of which are pre-determined by the IT programme' (Pithouse et al, 2009, p 604). The use of formal systems for prescribing and managing and recording social work processes, based on knowledge, albeit research-based, which is unknown or unfamiliar to the practitioner, distances them from their task, mechanises the process and prevents the use of discretion. The assumption has been made that social workers cannot understand or remember the research and knowledge base, that social workers cannot internalise and own this as a core part of their working, to be used creatively, with judgement:

> There is always going to be an insoluble paradox between the drive for consistent and evidence based standards of care and unique predicament, contexts, priorities and choices of the individual. (Rawson, 2002, p 120)

However, to prescribe process based on research evidence which is unknown or not owned by the operative denies creativity, discretion, judgement and responsiveness to individual or complex situations.

The 'scholar-practitioner' or 'scholar-facilitator' (Morrison, 2010) can mediate the separation of knowledge, whether drawn from formal research evidence or practice wisdom, but it is not always easy. The pressures on academic researchers in universities to deliver highly ranked academic research are so great that some in social work and social policy are not available to teach or personally tutor social work students. Equally, apart from their research fieldwork, they may have few opportunities to spend time with social workers in practice and with the individuals and families they serve. The loss of learning is two-way. In addition, some research in the field of social work and related social policy is undertaken by universities that are not engaged in social work education. Their work inevitably becomes a commodity for policy makers and managers, rather than part of a growing body of practice wisdom and evidence-informed practice. This is not 'the uncritical assumption that evidence based practice provides the answers to all, or at least most service users' difficulties' (Ferguson and Woodward, 2009, p 62). It is recognition that it is an important and influential component alongside the current direct experience of practitioners, and in particular, their learning from people who use their service and their carers. Social work recognises that people have complex needs, beyond the sole solutions of pre-ordained treatment or intervention programmes.

An important and often missing component in current research in practice is the role social workers can and should play in practising above the level of the individual case. This can be both in influence and challenge within the team or employing organisation and outside the workplace in collective action and campaigning (Ferguson, 2008). An example of this was the campaign by social workers in 1973-74 against the reception into care of children whose parents were homeless. Social workers, with the backing of their professional association, refused to do this, and collectively and successfully campaigned with others to alter the law. National social work campaigns like this have been rare in the UK. Leadership from learning, continuing professional development and research in social work practice has a critical part to play. To accomplish the full potential this has to be located close to services and with strong social worker direction. In exercising self-leadership practitioners, their social worker supervisors and social worker managers of the service each have the personal responsibility to be constantly abreast of new knowledge and learning, rather than being reliant on policy edicts, government guidance or legislation. Without accepting and undertaking this accountability and obligation, as an internalised norm and discipline, social work has no cause to complain if others prescribe and control. The provision of post-qualifying training programmes, beyond in-house learning provided by employers, has a long pedigree as a means for delivering continuing professional development, informed by current practice research, which is to a consistent standard, validated by both employers and partner universities. This remains the most tested and secure way forward.

The sources of leadership in social work from organisations and managerial hierarchies have proved conditional and often primarily concerned about organisational interests or second-guessing what government funders may expect. Positional social work leaders, with recent examples initiated in England in 2013 – the chief social workers for adults and for children and families and the dedicated role of principal social worker (now in most local authorities) – can provide a focus for promoting best practice, the use of research knowledge and the reinstatement of externally validated, progressive continuing professional development. However, they cannot be a substitute for confident, competent self-leadership. The slow growth and slow acceptance of evidence-informed and evidence-based practice has arguably hindered the development and acceptance of practitioners as authoritative self-leaders with a sense of personal autonomy and responsibility. The shift required is for all social workers to work as practitioners, as professionals and as social scientists (Croisdale-Appleby, 2014, p 15). There is nowhere else to go for the leadership of social work in *showing the way*, except from within social workers themselves, from within each and every one of them. Social workers should not sit back and wait for others to tell them what to do.

FOUR

Clarity of purpose in social work practice

Social work seeks to help individuals, families and communities who have difficulties in their relationships resulting in conflicts and deprivations. A social worker moves between the inner and the outer worlds of the person(s) they are seeking to help; that is, they may focus on the feelings, attitudes etc of the person(s) or on the adverse social circumstances in which such person(s) exist, or, most likely, both. They are not either psychotherapists or social reformers (except indirectly) but employ some of the attributes (but not the depth of expertise) of both. (Stevenson, 2013, p 75)

Introduction

Social work literature and policy documents can demonstrate extraordinary claims to usefulness and woeful lack of clarity on working practices. They can appear to glory in complexity and unrealistic ambitions. The contradiction is that in the over-ambition for the use of social work, its effectiveness or specific contribution can be easily denied. In this chapter greater focus is sought, combined with a confidence in its role, specific knowledge and skills. In particular, the challenges of personalisation and personal budgets and child protection are addressed.

Complexity or confusion

In all social work practice there is a range of roles and responsibilities, often in tension, competing, if not in outright contradiction. Part of the challenge to the cognitive and emotional abilities of social workers is the way in which this complexity is internally processed, and how it is explained and demonstrated coherently in direct practice, in work with colleagues and with the people who are served and their carers. In the first instance, the internal language is developed to explain and to be able to articulate, drawing on knowledge and insights from the diverse academic disciplines that collectively form the basis of the academic social work curriculum, the evidence of what can be shown to constitute effective practice, and the progressive gathering of practice wisdom. This is then embedded into day-to-day thinking, systematic analysis, reflection, synthesis, evidence-informed practice (Hodson and Cooke, 2007), and expressed, shared and explained with both colleagues and people who receive social work services.

In both national and international definitions of social work and the role of social workers there are consistent themes that encompass the personal, social and structural territory of the tasks and responsibilities, and the knowledge and skill base:

> Social work is a practice-based profession and academic discipline that promotes social change and development, social cohesion and the empowerment and liberation of people. Principles of social justice, human rights, collective responsibility and respect for diversities are central to social work. Underpinned by theories of social work, social sciences, humanities and indigenous knowledge, social work engages people and structures to address life challenges and enhance wellbeing. (IFSW, 2014)

It is interesting that 'problem solving in human relationships', which had been in the 2000 definition, is now not included.

The language is dense, arguably the result of multiple translations and the necessary generation of an internationally shared articulation of a universal, shared understanding and broad consensus. It is interesting to reflect that it uses the term 'theories' rather than 'knowledge'. Is this another sign of social work's uncertainty about a knowledge base, or a reluctance to acknowledge one? This definition has proved robust, enduring and capable of application across many countries and cultures. Narey (2014), in his review of the education of social workers in England, commissioned by the Secretary of State, regarded the definition as 'thoroughly inadequate' in describing the work of a social worker with children. He drew back from calling it 'appalling'. The challenge in international and generic definitions is to be both specific and inclusive enough. The hazard for social work, and in particular, the people served, is that definitions for particular areas of work and responsibilities excise its social justice and relationship-based nature.

In this chapter, definitions of social work are examined alongside the narrative of the development of social work's location, roles and responsibilities. While some writers have relished the uncertainties and the contested nature of social work, there are enduring themes, continuity, in the knowledge base and relationship-based skills:

> Social work's disciplinary territory is the poor, troubled, abused or discriminated against, neglected, frail and elderly, mentally ill, learning disabled, addicted, delinquent, or otherwise socially marginalised up-against-it citizen in his or her social circumstances. (Sheldon and Macdonald, 2009, p 3)

> Social work is, and should remain an eclectic discipline. Its field of operation – the troubled and/or disadvantaged and/or discriminated against individual in society – ensures that it will depend for theoretical sustenance on concepts and findings from a wide variety of sources. (Sheldon and Macdonald, 2009, p 46)

Davies (1994) formulated a description of the function of social work in terms of maintaining a stable society and rights and opportunities for people who, in an unplanned, uncontrolled community, would not survive. This expresses how social work is simultaneously located in social control and in social justice, in the memorable terminology of Case Con of the 1970s, the 'soft cop'. In the renewed radical tradition of Jones et al (2004), 'More than any other welfare state provision, social work seeks to understand the links between "public issues" and "private troubles" and seeks to address both.'

Brand et al (2005, p 55) identified the key characteristics of social work as:

- the focus on the whole of the person's life, their social context, and environment
- the capacity, in circumstances that are often difficult:
  - to engage quickly with people to establish trust,
  - to persist in efforts to engage even when this has proved difficult and others have given up
- consciously to move into situations that would be avoided by most people because they are complex and high risk
- the relationship established between the social worker and the service users involved is integral to achieving quality
- the capacity to manage situations where risks are very finely balanced so that 'you are damned if you do and damned if you don't.'

Focusing on the relational perspective in social work, Folgheraiter (2012, p 103), after an exhaustive analysis of the international definition, concludes:

The social work professional area – the set of the various 'social professions' carried out within or without national welfare systems – promotes and accompanies the desired social changes which emerge, as a reaction, from shared perceptions of severe hardship, actual or potential, in social life. It promotes problem solving, whatever the origin of the problems, by exploiting the energy present in human relations. In accordance with the spirit of empowerment, it promotes the liberation of people by showing trust in their real powers of initiative, so that they feel that they are able to contribute towards the building of a common well-being, and even help the 'helping professionals' themselves in the exercise of their statutory tasks. Based on all the social sciences, with special reference to the phenomenological and humanistic oriented ones, social work operates at the points where people interact among themselves, joining together to more effectively cope with shared difficulties within their environments. The principles of self-determination and reciprocity, as well as the defence of human rights and the redress of concrete social injustices, are fundamental to social work.

He also articulates a very short one, 'Social work is every professional activity whose ultimate purpose is to transfer people's concerns about their lives into human energy to change them for the better' (Folgheraiter, 2012, p 105).

There is a broad and international consensus on the combination of working for social justice, seeking positive change for individuals and groups by a variety of interventions, based on understanding people in the psychosocial matrix, with a value base which is shared with other professionals working in human services. However, this international definition is under review by some because of the strong commitment to social justice and its links to the contested nature of social work in some countries: 'Unless we reflect on our history (even the grimmest chapters of it) and acknowledge the clear political nature of social work activity, we are unable to develop a global social work distinctly and unconditionally committed to social justice' (Ioakimidis, 2013, p 188). The College of Social Work at the University of Mumbai (2013, p 1) includes a definition in its vision and mission: 'building a new social order based on human dignity and social justice, work for a preferential option for the vulnerable and exploited and a value base of compassion, personal integrity, moderation, tolerance and self-respect.' Social work practice encompasses social change, the interpersonal or therapeutic, and social order. The balance of perceived importance of each of these three and their contemporary definition change over time, but the centrality of the themes at the core of the social work role and purpose endure. Equally, the emphasis on one or more of these themes may be more to the fore in particular roles and work settings. Croisdale-Appleby (2014, p 14) sees the duality of social work to both enable and to protect.

Another prism through which to view the complexities of social work is the dual historic traditions of social casework or therapy and the administration of welfare, what came later to be termed 'social care services' (Burnham, 2011, 2012). The excessive focus on the process of case management in the tasks allocated to social workers in adult social care arguably turned into the administration of eligibility criteria and the allocation of providing direct services by others. The relationship-based, counselling skills of social work can be squeezed out by the scale of numbers of referrals, the undifferentiated allocation of work, the focus on performance measures on throughput, rather than positive outcomes for individuals and families. The enduring nature of social work is affected but not altered by changes in demographic need, new social problems and public policy. Nevertheless, social work can be profoundly affected by these changes and at times unbalanced by shifts in public policy, such as the introduction of personalisation and personal budgets as a government initiative across all four UK nations in adult social care.

There is a continuing contrast between social work with adults and with children and families, with a clearer focus on knowledge and skills in the latter. For example, the DfE (2014b) published a consultation document on what a child and family social worker should know and be able to do. This is positive evidence of the new role of chief social worker (children and families) in the English civil service. It includes refreshingly clear statements, such as: 'apply a wide range of knowledge and skills to help build family relationships, resource and resilience so that the welfare of the child is paramount', 'build purposeful, effective relationships with children and families, which are both authoritative and compassionate; demonstrate a high level of skill in evidence based, effective social work approaches to helping children and families which support change' (p 1). This work must always be tempered with humanity (Featherstone et al, 2014), and a greater focus on the structural and economic disadvantages that many families face. The aspirations for knowledge and practice skills are high, not only to include in the initial qualifying education academic and practice curriculum, but also in structured and validated continuing professional development. It is also imperative not to forget other social workers who have not had the benefit of good training, and critically to bring social worker managers up to these standards and to meet these expectations. The national structure for university and employer partnership post-qualifying awards in validated learning and assessment of practice has been lost following the Social Work Reform Board, coupled with the failure to build on the positive experience of using these awards in the NQSW pilots (Cambridge Education and Children's Workforce Development Council, 2009; Carpenter et al,

2011) and in the implementation of ASYE. Nevertheless, there has been some determined local retention of the discipline of these systems.

Social work, personalisation and personal budgets in adult social care

There has been a degree of scepticism and caution among social workers about the steady development of personalisation. While its focus on placing the individual at the centre of the design and delivery of the services they use shares the values and principles of social work practice (BASW, 2012), it has been a government-led initiative. As such, it is also linked with other evolving government strands of policy, shared across political parties. The introduction of personalisation across the UK and the accelerated pace for individual social care budgets in England and Scotland emphasise a strong user voice for individual choice and control and more recently, an emphasis on preventing the need for continuing social care through re-ablement (Leadbeater and Lownsbrough, 2005; DH, 2008; DHSSPS, 2011; Welsh Assembly, 2011). Personalisation is consistent with the core values of human rights, personal dignity, self-determination and person-centred practice of social work identified by Carr (2008, p 25), but whether it is legitimate to claim it has directly grown from them may be a claim too far. Social work might wish to claim the credit for showing the way, but the evidence trail is weak.

Despite the commonality with social work practice values of choice and self-direction,

> ... the testimony of both professionals, care staff and clients is that the social work system often fails to deliver on these goals. In practice social workers seem to be risk managers and resource allocators, gate-keepers and controllers, often working with clients in crisis when the task is to save them from harming themselves and others. (Leadbeater and Lownsbrough, 2005, p 19)

Arguably this has much to do with how local employers have deployed social workers as care managers following the community care changes (Davies and Challis, 1986) which identified and prescribed in government statutory guidance the functions of assessment of the circumstances of the individual who might need social care, including the needs of their carers, negotiating and arranging the provision of social care services within available resources, and arranging and then reviewing that care (DH, 1990). While this was combined with an organisational separation of the arranging and purchasing of care from the provision of direct social care services, it failed to articulate the complexity of personal relationships and circumstances, together with informal community resources that are the territory of social work. Lymbery (2013) identifies how radical social work can combine the transfer of choice and control to each person using services while at the same time engage and agitate for a more just financial settlement of resources for social care.

The personalisation changes were quiet on what is now termed 're-ablement', actively working with individuals, their carers and within communities, to regain or extend independence. It is interesting to reflect that initiatives in this area seem to originate from developments in social policy, linked to the public recognition that state funding for social care, whatever the state of public finances, cannot keep pace with the long-term increase in the number of older people and people with long-term disabling conditions, rather than any contribution from social work.

The emergence of the term 'social care' from the 1980s, often used as a catch-all to include social work among other services, even in the English context of so-called integrated children's services, could be seen to describe a more passive activity than social work. The focus has been on the quality of services and the care provided, including vital issues of respect, personal choice and individual attention. Social work, as distinct from social care, arguably has a greater and historic sense of a narrative of change and challenge. This was recognised by Croisdale-Appleby (2014, p 14): 'capability to transform rather than merely deliver a service is the overriding motivator'. However, re-ablement for older people is being evaluated by social policy researchers, rather than social work researchers (Glendinning et al, 2010). This may reflect the lack of attention to skills and knowledge in the field of services for adults as well as a limited supply of social workers in this field with a background in rigorous practice and policy research (Milne et al, 2014).

There are issues within the delivery of universal individual payments for people to arrange and purchase their social care. There are administrative challenges and a need to make proportionate checks on the use of the payments in circumstances of uncertain mental capacity of the individual recipient. There is a concurrent reduction in public funds available for the steadily increasing demand for social care that has yet to be adequately confronted (Wanless, 2006; Dilnot, 2011; Lloyd, 2012; Commission on the Future Funding of Health and Social Care in England, 2014). Social workers have been reticent or even reluctant to identify personalisation as a logical consequence of social work methods and values. Personalisation can be focused on prevention and re-ablement, emphasising the role of individuals with complex needs as active participants in shaping, choosing and delivering their own solutions. The results of an acceleration of the delivery of individual social care budgets in England have been encouraging – over 70 per cent of budget holders reporting a positive impact on being independent, getting the support they need and want, and over 60 per cent reporting a positive impact on physical health, mental wellbeing and control over their support (Hatton et al, 2013). The caution or reticence within social work appears to be linked to concerns about its association with service budget reductions and encouraging greater provision of direct services by the independent sector and individuals. Personal or individual budgets have the potential to mark a shift in the relationship between the state and the individual (Glasby, 2014). While this has the potential to increase the authority and power of the individual needing a service, through choice and control in their own life and the form their care takes, it could be used as a means for the state to move back from ensuring universal provision of services. While this is arguably a reality during reducing public finances and increasing need, it is not a reason for resisting the positive aspects.

There have been major organisational and technical challenges in implementing a major change in how social care budgets are deployed that have a direct impact on the work of all staff. This may have contributed to a lack of clarity on the roles and responsibilities of social workers in supporting the planning and use of the individual budget in both government guidance or from the profession. Nevertheless, the heart of the distinctive role and skills of social work is moving at the pace of the individual, starting where the client is, supporting through crisis, engaging with individual biographies, and promoting strengths and resilience (Kerr et al, 2005). This is consistent with the central thrust of the personalisation agenda, promoting direct payments for social care and re-ablement.

Child protection and safeguarding

The social work task has excessively focused on screening, assessment and attempting to manage risk, at the expense of directly working with families, children and young people to protect them from neglect or abuse (Ayre and Preston-Shoot, 2010). While there is a rich history and credible practice evidence on effective social work interventions to enable families to care safely for their children (Macdonald, 2001), and equally to identify those families where removal to a temporary or permanent family is necessary (Farmer and Wijedasa, 2012), the scale of what child protection guidance (DfE, 2013a) calls referring 'into social care' can overwhelm the capacity to undertake this in any depth. In particular, the relationship-based nature of effective work with children and families is inevitably compromised. The Munro review (2010, p 27), and subsequent government data (DfE, 2014a), highlight the scale of referrals coming 'into social care' within local authority children's services in England, 600,000 in 2013/14. This was an increase from the previous year of 10.8 per cent, with an attendant increase of children subject to a child protection plan of 12 per cent to 48,000. The scale of this activity is vast, despite the aspirations of *Every child matters* (DCSF, 2003), which had a focus on universal and 'upstream' preventative services. This included the bringing together of all local authority services for children and young people, universal, targeted and specialist, into a single structure and a single management. However, 'social care' remains identified as a specific entity, and a convenient repository for separated accountability for child protection. The inference is that social care is isolated, open to separate blame when things go wrong, and a disposal point for children and families who are difficult or challenging for universal services. The statutory guidance relating to the implementation of the Children Act 1989 consistently repeats the requirement to make referrals 'into social care services' of children who may be 'in need' or for whom there are child protection 'concerns'. It flies in the face of the aspiration for an integrated service, where the responsibilities for children and families who need direct help and protection are shared, and all services are available to be deployed. How much authority have social care services to mobilise or call on the services of the wider local authority, the NHS and other key agencies? How much authority, influence or direct call on in-house or purchased services do social workers have to support them in helping children, young people and families? The responsibility of the Local Safeguarding Children's Board to achieve coherent and joined-up services can feel very remote to the social worker and their local managers, pre-occupied with screening and assessing scores of referrals into their service, and facing off the 'thresholds' for agreeing to undertake an assessment, before the potential provision of a social work or social care service. The reaction of government, including local government, to tragedies in child protection has been increased prescription of practice and process, particularly in assessment systems, the suppression of professional judgement and the deletion of a national policy on professional post-qualifying training with employer and university partnership-validated awards.

An interesting study by the UK government Cabinet Office Behavioural Insights Team (Kirkman and Melrose, 2014) indicates an understanding in at least one part of government that the decision making in social work with children and families at the 'front door' requires improvement. It was found that time and workload pressures increase the reliance of social workers on intuition; rather than the focus of other professions on overt, evidence-based and skilled intuition, there was a tendency to judge cases on their relative rather than objective merits, and the complexity and scale of social workers' decision making engendered 'depletion' or 'decision fatigue'. Kirkman and Melrose (2014, p 5) conclude that 'there is an over-arching issue that complicates all of these behavioural factors: there is an almost total lack of robust evidence available or given to social workers on what works in particular contexts. This weakness in analytics compromises both current diagnostic practice and the development of better approaches.' While the study was small-scale, many of us will recognise this critique for many local services. It is a castigation of the civil servants responsible for social work services, an indictment of the enormous public funds expended on the reform of social work education in 2003, and the Social Work Task Force and Reform Board from 2009 to 2012. Equally, social workers, including social worker managers, social worker educators and researchers, are culpable. Rather than waiting for yet another ministerial initiative, via a special adviser or quango, each social worker has a responsibility to address these shortfalls individually and collectively.

The Munro review (2011) was welcomed by both the profession and by government; nonetheless, while the avowed aspiration was to give greater value to professional expertise, the resulting revised and shortened *Working together to safeguard children* (DfE, 2013a) continues to stress the referring 'into social care' services, the setting of thresholds for assessments and all social work decisions directly overseen by a manager. The large-scale assessment processes remain, gathering information about children and families, an analysis of needs, the risk and level of harm, determining the category of a 'child in need' or with 'child protection concerns', and concluding with the potential to provide 'support' to address these needs in order to improve the child's outcomes and to make them safe. The reality for most children, young people and their families is a return to pre-existing universal services, however effective or successful they may be. The finite resources of social workers are swallowed up by the sheer numbers of referrals and assessments. The focus of practice remains on process and risk aversion. While there is a recognition of the need for analytical skills and constructive challenge in reflective supervision and shared consideration of judgements and intervention plans, the screening and assessment processes squeeze and compress the opportunities for relationship-based interventions.

The managerialist agenda and limited trust in the skills and judgements of social workers remain evident in the child protection guidance. Social workers and their managers are cited together a total of 14 times (in DfE, 2013a). No other organisation or profession has a prescription of managerial oversight in the document. The guidance does not address whether this manager is expected to be a social worker or how capable, knowledgeable or research-aware they should be. It is entirely appropriate that important decisions about risk, need and the complexity of the situations are shared, in the context of thoughtfulness, analysis and reflection. However, to locate and describe this as a managerial activity rather than one of skill, competence or peer review demonstrates lack of confidence in social work practice and a reluctance or refusal to acknowledge the capability of social work practice or the presence of knowledge or research awareness.

Claiming and offering to do too much

The breadth of ambition of social work can lead to extraordinary claims to usefulness. This not only overwhelms services with the demand for help, but also lays it open to questioning of its claims for effectiveness and benefit. It suggests an overweening ambition and arrogance. The initial report of the Social Work Task Force in England (2009) gave the following description for the public. It is quoted in full to demonstrate the breathtaking scale of the territory claimed.

> Social work helps adults and children to be safe so they can cope and take control of their lives again.
>
> Social workers make life better for people in crisis who are struggling to cope, feel alone and cannot sort out their problems unaided.
>
> How social workers do this depends on the circumstances. Usually they work in *partnership* with the people they are supporting – *check out what they need, find what will help them, build their confidence, and open doors to other services.*
>
> Sometimes, in extreme situations such as where people are at risk of harm or in danger of hurting others, social workers have to *take stronger action* – and they have the legal powers and duties to do this.
>
> You may think you already do this for your friends and family but social workers have specialist training in fully analysing problems and unmet needs, in how people develop and relate to each other, in understanding the challenging circumstances some people face, and in how best to *help them cope and make progress.*
>
> They are qualified to tell when people are in danger of being harmed or harming others and know when and how to use their legal powers and responsibilities in these situations.
>
> You may think that you'll never need a social worker but there is a wide range of situations where you or your family might need one, such as
> - caring for family members
> - having problems with family relationships and conflict
> - struggling with challenges of growing old
> - suffering serious personal troubles and mental distress
> - having drug and alcohol problems
> - facing difficulties as a result of disability

- being isolated within the community
- having practical problems with money or housing.

(DH and DfE, 2009)

While this is purposely written in straightforward language and to be as generic as possible, it is very quiet on knowledge, evidence base, skills and methods. The focus is on assessment and arranging care, 'check out what they need, find what will help them, build their confidence, and open doors to other services'. The direct intervention beyond this is 'help them cope and make progress'. This is hardly a description of purposeful activity, focused on change, drawing on a body of practice knowledge, research and skills. The *Statement on the roles and tasks of social workers* from the General Social Care Council (GSCC) (2008) was similarly over-inclusive, with most of its claims for social work applicable to most workers in services for the public.

Another strikingly similar over-inclusive inventory comes from Australia:

How we can help you

Social workers can help if you are experiencing a crisis, are in need of support or are unsure how to access the right assistance.

People of all ages can talk to social workers about:

- family and domestic violence
- homelessness
- relationship breakdown
- loss and bereavement
- mental health and
- addictions

Social work help can include:

- short term counselling and support for difficult personal or family issues
- exploring options
- information about, or referrals to, government and community support services
- discussing difficulties you are having in meeting your activity test or participation requirements

Who we help

Priority is given to people with complex needs who don't have support from family or other services in the community, particularly:

- those thinking about suicide
- those with untreated or unstable mental illness
- young people
- those experiencing distress as a result of family and domestic violence, homelessness or hardship
- those caring for an adult or child with a disability or serious illness

[This information is correct as of January 2015 and was sourced from the Australian Government Department of Human Services website: humanservices.gov.au]

In Scotland, Brand et al (2005, p 4) proposed criteria that indicate the need for social work intervention:

The child's, adult's, family's or social situation is unusually complex with a number of interacting factors affecting assessment and decision-making.

The child or adult is at risk of serious harm from others or themselves and requires skilled risk assessment and safeguards.

The child or adult is likely to put others at risk of harm, distress or loss and a response needs to take account of the individual's interests and others' welfare.

The child's or adult's circumstances, including their health, finances, living conditions or social situation, are likely to cause them or others serious harm, social exclusion, reduction of life-chances or well-being.

The situation requires assessment of, and intervention in, unpredictable emotional, psychological, intra-family or social factors and responses.

Relationships, rapport and trust need to be established and maintained with a child, adult or family who find trusting relationships difficult.

There is a high level of uncertainty about the best form of intervention and/or its likely outcome.

The circumstances are such that there are significant risks in both intervening and not intervening, and a fine judgement is required.

The person is facing obstacles, challenges, choices and/ or life-changes which they do not have the resources (personal, intellectual, emotional, psychological) to manage without skilled support.

Prescribed or standard service responses are inadequate, and sensitive, creative and skilled work is needed to find and monitor personalised solutions.

The child's or adult's situation is getting worse, either chronically or unpredictably, and is likely to need additions or changes to interventions.

While these are more contained and restrained criteria for the deployment of social work skills and active interventions, Brand et al's discussion paper is largely silent on the nature of the contribution of social work practice skills, knowledge, research, methods of working or the outcomes they are expected to deliver. It is also silent on social justice and empowerment. All these descriptions are too broad and generic to give clarity of purpose. They stand in the way of maintaining a knowledge and evidence base for practice, and can prevent any consensus on expertise and specific skills. The contradiction in the over-ambition for the use of social work, or its role, is that its effectiveness or specific contribution can be easily denied.

Model of 'reserved duties'

An alternative approach to role definition is the 'reserved duties' that may be defined in statute, government guidance or prescription by a professional body. It cannot be expected that these will necessarily embrace or emphasise the social change, challenge or justice aspects of social work. In England the duties reserved by statute and government guidance for registered social workers include child protection investigations, children in need assessments, the lead professional in child protection plans, foster and adoptive parent applications and professional responsibility for each child or young person in public care. There are no such reserved duties in services for adults since the AMHP replaced the approved social worker role in 2007. It is noteworthy that this was the only reserved duty for social workers that required assessment of knowledge and skills at a post-qualifying level, initially in a national examination, and subsequently as a university and employer partnership award. These reserved roles can help clarify the particular sets of knowledge and skills in social work practice that enable these responsibilities to be successfully discharged.

The College of Social Work in England (2013a) identifies 18 situations where a social worker 'should always be both responsible for dealing with directly with people and overseeing cases'. While some are clearly reserved duties in legislation for children's services and others relate to protecting children and adults at risk of abuse or neglect, the focus on the complexity of needs and social circumstances is limited to assessment and review, rather than identifying the specific, purposeful intervention or help of a social worker to achieve positive change. For 17 other tasks it is advised that a social worker 'should *usually* be responsible for dealing directly with people or overseeing cases'. The list is hugely ambitious, including providing or arranging advocacy for people who do not have a voice, and helping them to be more in control of their own lives, taking a lead in community development and re-ablement services, and helping parents develop the skills and understanding to be more effective in meeting their children's needs for care, development and control. It is silent on how hard-pressed social workers, who are managing their own workload or the workloads of social work colleagues, should prioritise and deploy their finite capacity to meet this long list of human need.

The size of the pool of situations described that give the potential for needing a social worker is presumptuous and over-reaching, so vast as to be ultimately overwhelming. There are echoes of the over-ambition for which Brewer and Lait (1980) castigated the profession. This is different from the earlier acidic questioning of the legitimacy of social casework methods by Wootton (1959) in her challenge to social workers seeking psychological explanations of poverty and disadvantage, rather than focusing on practical help and guidance, coupled with campaigning for social justice. Doubts about the efficacy of counselling, or at least its applicability to problems that share both personal and social causations, did have an effect in challenging a focus on direct work with individuals and family groups, with critiques of 'the faith of the counsellors' and 'secular priests' (Halmos, 1965; North, 1972).

In one of the minority reports appended to the Barclay report (1982), Pinker argued for a less ambitious mandate for social work than the central thrust of the report for community social work focused on neighbourhood development, social work as a selective, rather than a universalist, service, with a reactive rather than preventative approach, focused on social casework methods, what might now be more usually named as therapeutic, relational and counselling methods. In the end the Barclay report had little impact on how social workers were deployed. There was growing emphasis on more effective child protection services, improved outcomes for children and young people in public care, and the massive wave of the community care reforms from the Griffiths report (1988). Interestingly, the College of Social Work (2012) has returned to the same term, 'community social work', with a focus on cultivating social capital, building resilience among individuals and families, and reducing reliance on state services.

The challenge is how social work articulates for itself, and shares with others, the full breadth of the psychosocial knowledge and insights brought to the work and exercised in interventions or modes of therapy, in advocacy, and as agents of change. This is not complicated, but it is complex. By ordering knowledge and understanding roles, appropriately marshalling and deploying practice skills based on the evidence base of what is effective, the way can be shown, leading both in work with colleagues and with the people who are served. Social work contains, not uniquely, challenging and potentially confusing variables in both its practice and in the description of its practice and purpose.

Affliction of uncertainty

The complexity of the work environment and the causes of the problems that are sought to be alleviated can encourage ambiguity and lack of resolution, as opposed to an inspired, tireless seeking after greater certainty. Is this a quality inherent in those who are drawn to social work, both as educators or practitioners? Is it a feature of the social sciences? The variety of roles and the historical narrative of the development of social work over the last century seem to encourage an unnecessary lack of clarity and consensus on the core knowledge, skills and methods of intervention. The first university-based social work training started in London in 1903, in Manchester in 1904, in Birmingham in 1908, and soon after in Bristol, Edinburgh, Glasgow, Leeds and Liverpool (Younghusband, 1978). Clearly the nature of some social problems changes over time. For example, as the state has taken greater responsibility for income benefits, judgement about the need for charitable funds has gone from social work. It is intended that personal budgets for older people and people with disabilities to purchase their own social care will be 'rights'-based. It remains to be seen, since the funding available will be finite, whether social workers could be drawn in again to assessing eligibility through judgements of merit. Some areas of advocacy have receded – for example, the right to housing families as a whole unit through homelessness legislation has radically reduced the admission of children to care solely due to lack of a family home. Other areas have moved to the fore such as the greater awareness of abuse of older people and people with disabilities. Another, on the horizon, is for social work to demonstrate its own effective interventions that enable older people to regain or retain a greater level of independence and social interaction.

> Social work has to be seen as a collection of competing and contradicting discourses that come together at a particular moment in time to frame the task of social work. (Cree, 2003, p 4)

The knowledge base, the core of relevant knowledge and insights from the social sciences, from life-long human growth and development and social policy, including legal frameworks, endure. The 'competing and contradicting discourses' while in flux and of changing intensity, remain remarkably resilient, enabling people who are older, who have a disability or who have a mental illness to enjoy safety, maximum independence and a full quality of life, supporting families to provide a safe and secure childhood. What alters over time are the ideas on what is effective in achieving positive change and the relative allocation of resources.

> A central problem for social workers is how to maintain helpful illusions about their work while facing up to the reality of what they are being asked to do. Are they merely functionaries in the government's cost-cutting

agenda? Are they nothing more than the human face of a surveillance state? Furthermore, is the traditional caring role gradually being destroyed by the business culture? Perhaps 'professionalism' is an illusion if the traditional social work identity, the relationship skills and expertise in decision-making are all being eroded. (Searing, 2006)

Social work has an authoritative part to play in these discourses at a practice level, in the methods and interventions used, and at a more strategic level, in advocacy, building and sharing practice knowledge and wisdom and social action/campaigning. When social work abdicates from that role, or allows policy makers or managers to prevent or close down that discourse, it is reduced to an administrative or purely technical activity.

FIVE

The social worker manager as leader, colleague and champion

Introduction

The opportunities and responsibilities for using leadership rest with all within the work or team setting. The social worker who is a manager cannot abrogate their practice and educational leadership roles by restricting or curbing their activities to administrative management. In this chapter I seek to make the case for social workers who are in management positions to reclaim and reinvigorate their own professional identity. They remain practitioners, responsible for case decisions, the use of current research evidence and fundamentally, the quality of practice through supervision and delivering continuing professional development. But they are failing as social workers if they deny the social workers they manage the educative, reflective and analytical opportunities needed to enable them to provide a continuously improving service. Supervision is a source of professional development, shared reflective analysis and mutual learning. Administrative and management support is important, but not to the exclusion of these professional responsibilities. Supervision is the location of the exchange and synthesis of complex information that enables the social worker manager to make the case and resource decisions they procedurally are unable to delegate to practitioners. Also, by remaining skilled and knowledgeable practitioners and educators, they are in a better position to trust, delegate and grant greater autonomy and individual judgement to the social workers they manage. There is a paradox for social worker managers, however; if they allow their practice knowledge, skill and research awareness to fade away, they become less able to delegate, and of less value in supervision and ensuring the professional development of their team. They progressively move into a general management and administrative mode of working, and fail to promote the professional capabilities and individual judgements of social workers.

Supervision practice and standards

Despite the longstanding professional traditions and standards in reflective supervision (Mattinson, 1975; Kadushin, 1976), and the understanding of the role of the supervisor, as enabler and helper, backing up and showing trust (Young, 1965), an enduring proportion of social workers in surveys and studies report not receiving it in adequate quantity or quality. In a survey of social workers in direct practice, 63 per cent reported receiving supervision at least once a month, 16 per cent every two months, 7 per cent every three months and 10 per cent rarely or never. It was rated 'excellent' or 'good' by 40 per cent, 'fair' by 35 per cent and 'poor' by 25 per cent, and 62 per cent reported that it did not adequately cover personal development and training (Godden, 2011). A NQSW survey in 2012, undertaken by Helen Donnellan (Plymouth University) and Professor Gordon Jack (Northumbria University), found that 41 per cent reported not receiving regular supervision and 42 per cent considered continuing professional development was neglected in supervision. Carpenter et al (2012) found that out of NQSWs in the English pilot programmes, 52 per cent received supervision to the expected standard in the first year, rising to 77 per cent in the third year. Another survey of social workers, including students, experienced practitioners and frontline managers (McGregor, 2013), found that only 45 per cent received it monthly, and 54 per cent reported that none of their supervision was reflective. Less than 70 per cent of local authority employers reported implementing the Social Worker Employer Standards, which include supervision and continuing professional development (Wiseman and Davies, 2013). A focus in supervision on direct practice with individuals and the interventions used has a positive impact on improving practice skills and on the outcomes for individuals (Harkness and Hensley, 1991). In inspections of social work in child protection the quality of reflective supervision is found to be vital to good and confident practice (Ofsted, 2012).

Looking across to the medical profession, the General Medical Council (GMC) has stringent expectations for doctors: 'You must recognise and work within the limits of your competence and you must make sure, to the best of your ability, that you are appropriately supervised for any task you perform.' For doctors with extra responsibilities,

> You must make sure that the people you manage have appropriate supervision, whether through close personal supervision (for junior doctors, for example) or through a managed system with clear reporting structures.... You must support any colleagues you supervise or manage to develop their roles and responsibilities by appropriately delegating tasks and responsibilities. You must be satisfied that the staff you supervise have the necessary knowledge, skills and training to carry out their roles. (GMC, 2012, p 25)

The registering body for social workers in England, the Health and Care Professions Council (HCPC) (2012a, p 12) requires:

> You must effectively supervise tasks you have asked other people to carry out. People who receive care or services from you are entitled to assume that you have the appropriate knowledge and skills to provide them safely and effectively. Whenever you give tasks to another person to carry out on your behalf, you must be sure that they have the knowledge, skills and experience to carry out the tasks safely and effectively. You must not ask them to do work which is outside their scope of practice. You must always continue to give appropriate supervision to whoever you ask to carry out a task.

The enduring problem in social work of the lack of regular, reflective, analytical supervision, linked to progressive, validated continuing professional development, will not be solved by more managerial action, government edict or critical inspections. The solutions lie with each individual social worker ensuring they receive it themselves, and each supervisor social worker providing it, through an internalised sense of responsibility and a personal commitment to provide and assure a safe and effective service. It essentially needs to be a feature of self-respect, respect for colleagues and respect for one's profession.

There can be benefits in devolving a proportion of reflective supervision to others (Carpenter et al, 2011), and this will be enforced where the manager is not a social worker. To fail to give or secure adequate reflective supervision prevents the social worker manager's real engagement in the casework where they are responsible for case decisions. The oversight, managerial and administrative functions, the growth and the inappropriate use of managerialism all have the potential to diminish, dilute or neutralise the leadership of professional practice and the provision of an effective social work service. Conversely resistance, passivity, resentment and avoidance of supervision can accentuate the manager role, to the detriment of professional development and reflection. It can institutionalise the managerialist agenda, creating a spiral of dissent, lack of trust and intrusive oversight, just as much as neglect and stagnation.

There is the risk that professional reflective, developmental supervision becomes reduced to over-seeing, controlling and prescribing, with the potential to reduce or prevent autonomy, creativity and the development of critical analysis and judgement (see Figure 5.1).

Figure 5.1: The circularity of the semi-professional

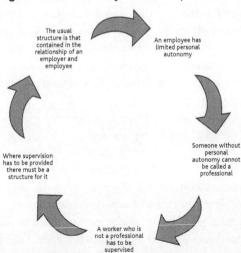

The usual structure is that contained in the relationship of an employer and employee

An employee has limited personal autonomy

Someone without personal autonomy cannot be called a professional

Where supervision has to be provided there must be a structure for it

A worker who is not a professional has to be supervised

Source: Hugman (1991, p 79) and Glastonbury et al (1982, p 120), reproduced with the permission of Palgrave Macmillan

This rather depressing portrayal of supervision and lack of recognition of the competence and capability of social work will be familiar. The lack of trust and respect is shown in the child protection guidance (DfE, 2013a), and there is limited employer commitment to continuing professional development (Wiseman and Davies, 2013) despite employers being allocated responsibility for assessing the responsibility for progression in capabilities. Experience shows that changing this sorry situation will not be achieved by task forces, government reform, reviews and pilots. The change has to come from within each social worker, in their demonstration of their knowledge and skills, and from within each social worker manager in their own knowledge, skills and energetic commitment to continuing professional development, rather than simply focusing on the administrative management of their roles (see Figure 5.2).

Figure 5.2: The circularity of a confident and assertive social worker

Social worker earns greater autonomy and respect and contributes to practice learning for students and less experienced colleagues

Social worker demonstrates knowledge and skills informed by research evidence

Manager provides professional supervision, with shared reflection on complex work, joint decision making and a focus on continuing professional development

The social worker manager

The management of social work entails providing professional reflective supervision for each social worker, or ensuring they receive it from another experienced social worker. In addition, the manager is commonly responsible for case decisions, defined in national policy guidance, for example, in child protection (DfE, 2013a), and in much resource allocation. If these are regarded as management decisions, then the social work task is arguably suppressed to a technical, administrative role of gathering information in order for another to make decisions. If, in the context of a discussion between two professionals, in shared critical analysis, two colleagues, albeit one with more experience and positional authority, come together, these decisions can be seen as part of professional leadership. The culture of risk avoidance (Kemshall et al, 1997; Barry, 2007) and adherence to procedures militate against creativity, flexibility, risking an impersonal service, far from the relationship-based work origins of social work. Within a team or service, Honey (2001) identifies distinct team roles, all of importance and all contributing to the whole. The manager as leader in this analysis has the first built into their role, but just as they need to be ready to fulfil *all* the team roles as necessary, as part of their repertoire, most successfully they fulfil their responsibilities by sharing and devolving the leader role:

> The *leader* who ensures that the team has clear objectives and makes sure everyone is involved and connected.
>
> The *challenger* who questions effectiveness and presses for improvement and results.
>
> The *doer* who urges the team to get on with the job in hand and does practical tasks.
>
> The *thinker* who produces carefully considered ideas and weighs up and improves ideas from others.
>
> The *supporter* who eases tension and maintains team harmony. (Honey, 2001, p 38)

The central thesis of this book is that each and every social worker has the responsibility to be a leader – how and by what means is dependent on the circumstances; social workers are never without a leadership role or without leadership responsibilities. The alternative is to succumb to a technical, administrative, passive and ultimately victim role.

How a manager models good practice in social work

- Publily refers to themselves as a social worker.
- Introduces, promotes and debates the current and past evidence from research and evaluations, in service meetings and in individual case discussions.
- Shares references and copies of their current reading.
- Provides regular high-quality professional reflective supervision, distinct from task and performance management.
- Shares their own positive use of their own supervision and demonstrates how they prepare for it.
- Personally invests in progressive continuing professional development that is externally validated.
- Retains professional registration and progression on the *Professional capabilities framework* or equivalent.
- Provides practice learning for student social workers and positively supports colleagues who are also doing this.
- Shares difficult dilemmas about resources and other issues that risk compromising their own professional standards in service meetings and individual case discussions.
- 'Rewards' good practice and energetic professional development with greater discretion and autonomy.

Special role of team manager

A team manager is a:

- leader by example
- deputy and co-worker practitioner
- coach
- fellow professional colleague
- role model
- guide
- facilitator of continuing professional development
- conduit for professional concerns and issues to the wider organisation and senior managers, including whistle blowing
- skilled administrator who supports and who solves problems.

A team manager is not a personal therapist or counsellor.

Inspections of child protection social work practice have found

> The most important form of support was provided informally and formally by line managers through their detailed understanding of work, reflective supervision, and their direct involvement with parents. Social workers considered that scrutiny and knowledgeable challenge were integral to their feeling supported and empowered to exercise their professional judgement. (Ofsted, 2012)

Part of the process that managers are undertaking in their leadership of social workers or the social work service they directly manage is the nurturing of the internalisation of the values, skills and personal vocation of these colleagues. Internalisation can be described as a 'metaphor' (Scott, 1971), the process of understanding values and behaviours, and incorporating them into day-to-day ways of working and a sense of what is good practice. While the manager will have pre-occupations with processes, procedures and resources, they risk providing a role model of a deft administrator or adept operator within the organisation, rather than a thoughtful, personally committed fellow professional, who shares the vocation, who demonstrates their continuing quest for constantly improving practice, based on analysis and research.

The overwhelming management agenda

How do managers prevent themselves being overwhelmed and wholly preoccupied by the administrative agenda? How can we resist, or at least temper or mediate, the managerialist culture? Ruch (2012, p 1318) identifies, 'By adopting more managerialist approaches, the potentially anxiety-provoking aspects of practice are avoided. Such approaches configure practice as simple and straightforward and involve predominantly surface-level structural responses to practice shortcomings.' All of this can be internalised at the expense of, and to the exclusion of, what was already within social workers. This can be characterised by "I used to be a social worker", "I have not maintained my professional registration or continuing professional development as I do not really practise any more". By demonstrating 'social worker-ness', social workers not only provide a model of valuing skilled practice, an active and enduring quest for the latest thinking and research, a personal commitment to continuing professional development, but they also demonstrate the highest qualities of leadership. This demonstrates how they value and respect the status of social work.

The bombardment of demands on services, even when there is no austerity in public spending, has the potential to blunt the emotions inherent in a human response to need. The response to this is both individual at a personal level and procedural, with social workers using organisational systems to protect themselves, as well as to contain the need. Their defence can be to distance themselves, to objectify the demands as workflow, and to forget their original vocation or ambitions on entering the service. Processes, protocols, reviews and audits can divert attention to paperwork and data, away from the direct service, inadvertently encouraging a passing or abdication of personal responsibility and accountability. The organisational response is technocratic, impersonal and procedural; referrals go through processes of call handling, computer-driven screening and assessment systems (Hall et al, 2010), the social worker becomes just an assessor and a navigator, rather than a service in their own right. The person referring, even fellow professionals who may be seeking advice, consultation and guidance, can find themselves having to go through a call handler and receive a response based on whether thresholds for an assessment or a service have been met. Referrals about abuse are recorded as 'concerns', a conscious dulling of the emotional edge, worse still, a denial of human suffering. The defensiveness and denial of both the individual and the organisation, often backed by national legally binding government guidance, can coalesce, congealing into process and systems, which deny or deflect personal responsibility and accountability. This is the territory where managers have to hold on to their social worker-ness, retain their values, knowledge and practice wisdom of what does and does not provide effective help.

The social worker manager, like the social worker expert practitioner, promotes and participates in the deliberations within their service about how these opposing forces can be examined and addressed. Ultimately, while the conflict may not be fully resolved, in their day-to-day exercise of leadership they can try at all times to ensure that the complexities and uncertainties inherent in most social work practice, as in other fields of human services (White, 2002), are not resolved by formulaic, procedurally driven responses. Inspiration, rather than discouragement, can be drawn from the glacial progress from the Munro review of child protection (2011); process may still rule, but it is increasingly recognised that social workers need to be better prepared and better equipped to exercise judgement in the context of relationship-based practice.

Managers can and do exercise their practice skills and knowledge in the form of case supervision and oversight. A positive and proactive approach to the detail of the children in care by senior managers can minimise drift and help ensure that children move on to stable and secure placements (Chamberlain and Ward, 2013). While these issues are captured in the performance and financial data of indicators and budget pressures, it is the close attention to each child, and the support each social worker needs, which lift the work of senior managers back to social work practice. The quality and active engagement with practitioners and about practice, by most senior managers, have a direct impact on the service provided and the quality of relationships with the people served (Ofsted, 2012). This can transcend the managerialist culture if coupled with expertise in practice and a respect for social work and investment in validated professional development.

Autonomy and discretion

Perceptions of the degree of autonomy enjoyed, or exercised, vary enormously. They range from the enormous power that many parents who may be at risk of losing their children feel is held by social workers, through the experience of them being part of an inchoate multi-purpose local authority, and the circumscribed activities of care management and mass assessments. The work of Lipsky (1980) explored both the freedoms and constraints in public services in how they are implemented and provided as a flexible and creative service by 'street-level' workers. Evans and Harris (2004), in the context of social work, argue against a simple view of 'all or nothing' independence in the exercise of judgement by an individual or freedom to act. Dependent on circumstances, including the level of experience and expertise of the worker, discretion, individual or independent judgement and action will vary. In the context of social work provided within public services and within the tradition of empowerment, the use of the word 'autonomy' may have its limitations. Freedom and discretion to form judgements and to act, to determine how best to provide a service, are dependent on the circumstances. The limitations or prescriptions of policies and accountabilities are not necessarily constraints on discretion; they can often be enabling, circumscribing discretion, rather than preventing it (Dworkin, 1997). Earning progressive autonomy requires taking responsibility for learning, while at the same time demonstrating accountability for competent and effective practice through continuing professional development of professional research-informed knowledge and skill development (McKitterick, 2012a, pp 88-9).

An extensive collaborative programme of work across a group of local authorities in West London, addressing substantial problems in recruiting social workers, found a lack of autonomy of frontline staff, with systems that gave little latitude for action or for decision making that did not require prior approval by managers. The term used to describe this was 'role slumping' (Searle and Patent, 2013). Tasks and decision making are escalated to higher levels, resulting in a lack of clarity in roles and responsibilities. This has a pernicious effect on the confidence and competence of practitioners, who identified this as a coercive impact from three key areas: exaggerated risk and fear from poor practice; limited workforce capability; and low organisational trust that coalesce to create an endemic drift for many tasks away from their correct level of responsibility, escalated inappropriately to higher levels, 'externally derived concerns are promoting a climate conducive to micro-management and task checking, which effectively duplicates effort.... This process can impact by eroding the confidence and competence of social workers whose roles are being performed by those more senior' (Searle and Patent, 2013, p 1111).

Experimental independent social work practice, where social work services are commissioned by a local authority, with their flatter management and arguably more inclusive structures, indicate how practitioners can have greater devolution of responsibility, including some finances (Stanley et al, 2012). In addition, shared responsibility for decision making made for speedier decisions, and carers of children in care considered that social workers in the practice pilots were more likely to be able to take key decisions (Holmes et al, 2013).

Lack of trust in the quality and effectiveness of university social work education can be used as a reason by employers and managers for not trusting the abilities of social workers with more delegated responsibility and autonomy. However, the practice learning element of social work education is largely the responsibility of employers. Through their managers they are responsible for working collaboratively with local universities and for providing practice learning placements. They are responsible for the quality, as well as the number, of good social work graduates they recruit. Arguably, the solutions to problems in these areas rest with social workers in titular leadership as well as in managerial positions, through their active contribution of substantive, high-quality practice learning for students, and joining university colleagues in ensuring qualifying and post-qualifying awards reflect the knowledge, skills and aptitudes required for the work. The solutions rest at a local level, through shared and energetic leadership across university education, practitioners and organisational management. On the other hand, in not actively contributing to local social work education, employers may be demonstrating a wish not to recruit or deploy social workers in roles where they will have significant responsibility. Perversely, the managerial aspiration may be for a technical, biddable, rather than professional, capable, challenging social worker workforce.

The escalation of tasks and responsibilities upwards, or the failure to delegate responsibilities to the person with direct contact with the person who needs a service and their carers, is familiar to managers in the context of allocating resources. Frontline practitioners rarely have the authority to directly call on services for the people with whom they are working, or the authority to make some key case decisions. Despite the substantial power social workers are perceived to hold by people who use services and their carers, in the context of direct practice social workers can feel untrusted, to have fettered discretion and little autonomy. The term 'autonomy' is included in the English College of Social Work's detailed documentation on the *Professional capabilities framework* (College of Social Work, 2013b), moving from effectiveness in interventions soon after qualifying, to greater independence, being responsible for offering expert opinion as they become more experienced, with 'advanced' responsibilities.

> To improve the situation, a culture which allows for mistakes and facilitates sharing and learning from experience needs to be fostered. Crucially, social workers with sufficient skills and knowledge should be supported by their employers in flexible decision making, enabling them to effect real change on the lives of service users. Sequencing here is the key; more autonomy for social

workers who lack necessary skills and experienced and are not supported by collaborative working practice and management, would not be desirable. In this respect, reforming training skills and practice is a necessary precondition of changes in organisational structure. (Holmes et al, 2013, p 52)

The manager as educator

Social work education operates in a complex world of competing forces. Universities are expected to rival one another in terms of student numbers and national and international ranking tables. All but a few are required to undertake research; some in particular are only permitted by their own governing bodies to continue teaching social work if the external research ratings and research income are good enough. The attendant sets of 'performance indicators' and income from student numbers can become more important than the views of potential employers of graduates, or the experience of graduating students on their quality and preparedness for practice. The practice education element of social work can become separated both from university academic teaching *and* current social work practice and patterns of service provision. Equally, the practice learning opportunities will, from time to time, be found to be so poor, or overall practice so unsafe, that universities place students out of necessity, with regret and trepidation. The elements of the valuable, academic rigour of universities in teaching, discovery of new knowledge, testing received knowledge and applying knowledge to good effect, the provision of education in practice and the provision of social work services can become disjointed with their respective languages, separate staff teams and different perspectives. The elements can seem to become separate worlds, impermeable and impervious to one another.

The reluctance of some employers to recruit social workers who are newly qualified because they lack experience (Holmes et al, 2013) or cannot 'hit the ground running' (Donnellan and Jack, 2010) indicates a chilling naivety on their part. This is not expected of other occupations where experience and wisdom is needed to provide a sophisticated and complex service. The responsibility for the paucity of appropriate practice learning placements rests with the same employers, exacerbated by a badly planned and executed doubling of enrolment of student social workers between 2003 and 2006, without attention being given to ensuring that the requirements for practice learning in the revised social work education standards were adhered to (DH, 2002). For example, the requirement for at least one practice learning placement to be in statutory services has been widely ignored, leaving many qualified social workers without the experience that local authority employers expect and require, and yet these employers are still not providing a sufficient supply (Holmes et al, 2013).

The *Professional capabilities framework* in England (College of Social Work, 2013b), implementing the initiative of the Social Work Reform Board (2010), separates out the roles of educator, advanced practitioner and manager at the advanced social worker level. While much of the specific capabilities are retained as common or shared, the description of the separated roles and responsibilities diminishes the professional leadership of the social worker who is a manager of social work services and social workers. The exclusion of the facilitation of the learning and development, and the interface with education and training, contributing to the development of knowledge, promotion of excellence in their field or using evidence-informed practice for managers, encourages the disfunctional separations identified above. Their vital role in practice, in terms of joint direct work, deputising for social workers in their team and the supporting, guiding and modelling leadership of analytical and reflective practice, are lost in the lack of expectations in constructive challenge to enhance practice, procedures and policies, to promote innovation, to introduce new ways of working from recognised sites of excellence, and to contribute to the development of knowledge and promotion of excellence in their field using evidence-informed practice. While part of this may be due to the drafting of large documentation for a new presentation, and perhaps an enthusiasm to promote the particular responsibilities in practice education and advanced practice, it is unhelpful to play down the educational leadership that managers can and should be expected to fulfil. To locate some of them solely with specialists splits the manager from their own social work responsibilities. The risks in this are to embed general management behaviours, to emphasise their administrative responsibilities, rather than to enhance their social work capabilities, particularly in the professional leadership, knowledge and intervention and skills domains. In the circumstances of the 'role slump' discussed above (Searle and Patent, 2013), the widespread phenomenon of a lack of delegation in much case decision by managers, it is important for those managers to demonstrate and develop these capabilities. Without the practice knowledge, wisdom and skills, and without being research-aware, the managers will not be equipped to competently make the case and practice decisions reserved to them. Equally, their capacity to judge when or whether to allow greater autonomy in judgements, conclusions in assessments and choice in intervention methods will be impeded. The playing down of the expectations of practice knowledge and skills for managers reduces their usefulness to the social workers they supervise and manage. Perhaps even more insidiously it enables them to maintain low levels of delegation, autonomy and trust.

There is a mismatch in the expertise and capability that is expected in managers held responsible for so many safeguarding case decisions set out in the revised government procedures (DfE, 2013a). It risks reinforcing and further embedding the separation of social worker managers from the knowledge development, training and education worlds. The tone and content is about management and administrative systems rather than leadership in practice or of social work. It may represent a reflection of the denigration of professional social work in seniority and authority in large public organisations, under the guise of reform, similarly diluted in the same framework for the 'strategic' level.

For the medical profession, the GMC's *Tomorrow's doctors* (2009, p 7) fulfils a slightly different but closely related purpose in the language of outcomes:

> The doctor as a scholar and a scientist,
> The doctor as a practitioner,
> The doctor as a professional.

The content and demands are more universally ambitious, encapsulating the breadth of knowledge sources drawn on, the complexities of roles and responsibilities, and the dimension of ethics and values. It is notable how comprehensively these are captured, with no reticence on the range of sources of the knowledge base, and a greater integration of legal and values issues within the whole. These can be issues that social work plays up or separates out at the expense of presenting a confident whole. Croisdale-Appleby (2014, p 15) has promoted these terms for social work with adults, the social worker as a practitioner, as a professional and as a social scientist. While it remains to be seen if this aspiration is accepted by government and quangos, it is for university students to expect this in their professional education, and for all social workers to demonstrate and to embed in their continuing professional development.

Changing from the language of competence to capability is new territory for social work in England; the former is still the language in the requirements of the registration regulators across the UK. There remains the inevitable challenge of finding good enough words to capture generic expectations across diverse social work services. In shifting from competencies to capabilities, the focus is on moving beyond an assessment of being able to practise at a specific level for specific tasks, to the greater ambition of assessing capabilities in skills and knowledge in a prospective way that can show the ability to meet new needs, develop new skills and adapt to changing circumstances. This ambition and the potential complexity, especially needing to 'populate' nine domains at nine levels, that is, 81 categories and descriptors, is fearsome. Quite reasonably the employer's line manager or supervisor is best placed to measure the impact of continuing professional development on practice and service delivery (Skills for Care and Development, 2013). The widespread aspiration to provide a framework that encourages career-long progression in practice capability is welcome, although the intricacies have the capacity to be self-defeating. Taylor and Bogo (2013) identify serious 'fault lines' with the regulator, the HCPC, retaining the model of competencies, and the Social Work Reform Board adopting the North American model of capabilities to describe what is to be developed, promoted and ultimately objectively assessed.

The potential risks are two-fold – it has heralded tortuous challenges in another overhaul of university education programmes and assessment systems, and in the development of a new language and assessment systems, which have the potential to be impenetrable and obscure to all but the fully initiated and immersed. This threatens turning off or losing even the most committed practitioners, supervisors and managers who ardently wish to remain part of the development of social work education, the development of the members of their team, and the pursuit of their own professional progression. Although the responsibility to uphold and pursue standards in continuing professional development has been allocated to employers (LGA, 2014), the drivers for quality assurance are weak or do not exist. The requirements of the registering body (HCPC, 2012b) are soft and require no concrete evidence of new learning or improving practice for revalidation for continued registration. While flexibility and avoidance of simplistic inputs, like courses, with encouragement to use a range of different learning activities is to be welcomed, the responsibility for quality assurance remains, in reality, with the determination and enthusiasm of the individual social worker, if possible, supported by their manager or supervisor.

The *Professional capabilities framework* (Social Work Reform Board, 2010; College of Social Work, 2013b) gives both the individual social worker and their professional supervisor the facility to progress their development together. The challenges are that, first, employers may only wish to support progress to the level of responsibilities in the current post, and second, their own quality assurance standards may not be robust, objective or ambitious enough to give credible 'portability' for future roles, responsibilities or new employers. There is encouragement for employers from a sector skills council body to include the measurement of impact of continuing professional development on practice and service delivery, measured by the line manager or supervisor (Skills for Care and Development, 2013), and collaboration in partnership across a group of employers and universities. The most 'portable' and enduring kinds of objective validation of continuing professional development, albeit achieved at a particular point in time, are university-validated post-qualifying awards, developed and run in partnership with employers. Where these are available in a modular form, the opportunity is given for bespoke learning and to spread the assessment of improving practice and knowledge over a period of years. The first post-qualifying awards in social work were well established by the 1960s at the Universities of Bristol and Newcastle, and the Tavistock Institute of Human Relations (Younghusband, 1978). From 1970 to 2001, CCETSW validated post-qualifying awards. This responsibility was taken on by the GSCC until 2012, but now has no location, beyond the scattered, thriving and committed partnerships between some universities and employers. It represents, alongside the failure to achieve the aspiration of the profession, and the Social Work Reform Board's requirement for a staged registration of social workers following structured professional development in the first year after qualifying with a formal assessment, another discarded opportunity in the improvement journey of social work practice. It is a serious backward step, indicative of limited ambition in the managerialist climate and culture, and a sign of the power of government-funded bodies that would be challenged by a growing, confident, and academically confident body of social workers.

The slow progress in the development of the NQSW programme from 2008, which evolved into the ASYE, has been a slow burn success for many, with continuing poor delivery in some areas (Carpenter et al, 2011). The programme is still organised as an initiative, rather than an evolution that becomes embedded in the ordinary expectations of social workers, recognised as both their entitlement and their personal responsibility. This is partly due to reliance on time-limited national funding streams, and consequently needing to be packaged as something new again and again, rather than the consolidation of well-established good practice. It is also in the interests of organisations that rely on their income for new initiatives to take their time and to keep reinventing the wheel. By the end of the first year, in 2009, two thirds of the employers were actively involved with their partner universities in linking their programmes with modular post-qualifying awards (Cambridge Education and Children's Workforce Development Council, 2009). Without a strong enough ownership across social work services, and without extrinsic, stronger expectations from regulators and the responsible government departments, the responsibility belongs to each social worker, in the internalisation of the ownership of basic standards of good professional development.

The limit on the rigour of externally determined standards for the profession, while sadly demonstrating low external expectations and internal lack of ambition, gives the profession, in each individual practitioner, and particularly in each social worker as manager and leader, the opportunity, as well as the responsibility, to:

- be a positive role model,
- generously give learning opportunities,
- build learning into the way they work,
- make learning and the validation of learning an integral part of how the service works, and
- champion the benefits of making continuous learning a priority (adapted from Honey and Mumford, 2000).

The direct line social worker manager or supervisor, familiar with the use of the *Professional capabilities framework*, will use it to guide and inform their own continuing professional development. It requires energy and tenacity to maintain the focus on its utility in developing and improving the provision of a good service for individuals and their carers, avoiding multifarious detail, and having the confidence to resist experts and specialists who could have an interest in building complexity and a tower of Babel. If its application and use is allowed to become a remote special realm of knowledge, or it is turned into another bureaucratic or management task, it will have failed, and in a few years' time another mechanism will be sent down the line. The framework has to be owned, used and led by the profession, in the form of practitioners and their supervisors, close to where the service is. Its evolution and refinement belong within each and every social worker, as part of their self-leadership, their own maturation and navigation of their professional progress. If it becomes an unquestionable, esoteric, centrally imposed regime, impermeable to the realities of service and the voice and wisdom of those providing social work, it will fail, becoming yet another centrally driven initiative to be changed after another scandal or policy shift. It should be the means, hopefully refined into a shorter, less cumbersome and user-friendly form, by which social work can continue to grow, progress, building on experience and knowledge, rather than be the subject of constant attempts at redefinition.

SIX

Leadership within direct practice

Introduction

Leadership in social work practice has two components. First, it is deployed in direct work with individuals, families and carers, and second, in working alongside colleagues within the team or organisation where the service is provided, and with colleagues in other agencies and professions. In this chapter the starting point is leadership as 'showing the way', focusing on the values and approaches of distributive and citizen models of leadership that emphasise participation, engagement and inspiration. Within direct practice the development of insight and understanding is the critical first step in empowerment and working towards positive change.

The social worker, by openly developing and sharing insights on the personal, drawing on psychological and social perspectives and knowledge, and working with individuals and families, jointly identifies the best ways forward. Explaining these complex interactions to colleagues gives understanding of the problems and challenges faced by individuals and groups in distress or in need of direct help. It helps colleagues gain a broader and more comprehensive appreciation of the complexity of individual circumstances, and the potential causes or origins of the challenges they and those around them face. It can build empathy and understanding in colleagues who may be irritated, impatient or simply perplexed by seemingly intractable problems, and demonstrate how interventions need to focus across a range of issues. Equally, colleagues gain from the demonstration of effective social work interventions.

The application of the qualities and skills of participative leadership and self-leadership are central to the practice skills in direct work with people who use social work services and their carers. The values and approaches of participative, engaging and inspiring leadership schools of thought accord with the social work methods of empowerment, sharing authority and knowledge, person-centred counselling, building shared goals and developing insight. This use of leadership is part of the narrative within the enduring traditions and values of social work, listening, heeding, sharing power, modelling, coaching and being grounded in where the individual and their carers are, starting from their direct experiences and the solutions *they* identify.

Moving beyond insight and understanding requires knowledge of what is likely to make a difference for the future, what interventions or changes in personal circumstances will resolve current problems and prevent or reduce the likelihood of their recurrence. This brings the knowledge and experience of 'what works', whether it be in local, available services, both specialist and universal, or in the specific interventions that the social worker can use in their direct practice. Alternatively, and in addition, they can enable, encourage or support colleagues to use vital components of their 'toolkit' or portfolio of skills and knowledge. These are the components for the leadership that all social workers have both the capacity and responsibility to exercise.

Using leadership in direct social work practice

The traditions and values of social work include a strong focus on self-determination, linked to the social justice praxis, and the consequent identification and development of strengths (Biesteck, 1957; IFSW, 2014). The relationship-based nature of practice has a long pedigree (Philp, 1963), yet is often squeezed out by the scale of case bombardment, an historic scepticism about the therapeutic nature of social work, and the varying levels of skills in communication, building relationships and in family work (Ferguson, 2014). Relationship-based practice (Trevithick, 2003; Ruch et al, 2010) provides the location for joint work in the exploration and development of a shared understanding of the origins and solutions for problems. However, as identified by Platt (2008) and Harris (2012), relationship-based practice can be lost in the increased focus on practice determined by procedure and a focus on assessment.

There are strong links to the heritage of family therapy and work with family groups within mainstream social work practice (Jordan, 1972; Nuttall, 1985; Goodman and Trowler, 2012). The social worker, in gathering information, checking and re-checking their understandings and insights, identifying potential solutions and achieving positive change, is exercising a shared leadership role with the person using their service, their family and their carers. If solutions were easy, if the problems were not complex, then the straightforward provision of technical or practical social care services would suffice. In this regard, the reductionist procedures of assessment and consequent care management processes over-simplify the essential co-production approach required for effective practice. This can be seen as the ceding of power and authority by a state-employed professional, notwithstanding the inherent power and social control explicit in work with children and families (Okitikpi, 2011). It is recognition that the person experiencing the problem has the rights and capacity to identify and determine the solutions, albeit with the support and access to the expertise and knowledge of the professional.

Co-production has been a concept that has reached an ascendancy in the public policy and practice discussions about the provision of adult social care (Needham and Carr, 2009). It is also used in a widening promotion in public sector service reform:

> Co-production refers to the joint production of services by the producer/expert and the consumer/user....The benefits of co-production are: the people who need to be involved are involved; people become more assertive; the range and quality of services is improved; and a constituency of support is created for that service. (Walker, 2002, p 8)

Again, reflecting on the discussions earlier in the book, it is easy to see how the values and traditions of social work practice can be gathered up or re-remembered to form part of a public debate on the nature of the relationship between the individual, their family, communities and the state (Horne and Shirley, 2009). The language or rhetoric used around co-production has resonance with the 'Big Society' big idea of the Conservative election manifesto in 2010 (Conservative Party, p 37), and like personalisation can be used or abused to justify or deliver lower levels of state-provided or state-funded services. For social work practice, these are potential distractions from the central tenet of working with people to identify and to put in place their preferred solutions, ones that they have identified as most likely to be effective and to give them the outcomes they seek for themselves. The issues of the level of public finance available for services, and the sharing of responsibility for these most disadvantaged in society, are critical in terms of social justice. The advocacy and campaigning on these issues remain central to the responsibility of each social worker, 'as advocacy and mediation for people experiencing discrimination or difficulties in accessing services and resources' and 'as practice that can bear witness and report on "social ills" as they impact on the lives of service users' (Trevithick, 2003, p 167). While personalisation and the 'Big Society' may be used as masks for reducing public funds, it is counterproductive to allow this to negate the longstanding practice wisdom of the effectiveness of co-production as an integral part of self-determination, and working to identify and develop the inherent strengths of individuals, families and communities. Within team working, as well as in direct practice, promoting and facilitating the hearing of the voice of the person using or seeking access to services as a citizen, with rights and expertise, is putting citizen leadership into day-to-day practice.

Working with children and families

The relationship-based and partnership model of practice and 'client self-determination' (Biesteck, 1957) do not outrank or 'trump' the responsibilities of social workers to all members of a family, including each child and young person and to the wider community. This is notable in the field of child protection, where the prime responsibility is the protection of children and young people from abuse and neglect, alongside the direct work with parents and other adults in the family to enable them, if possible, to provide good, safe care and positive outcomes for the children and young people. Brandon et al (2008) identified that in some families, where social workers had been working with families and children had died or received serious injury, the 'apparent and disguised cooperation from parents often prevented or delayed understanding of the severity of harm to the child and cases drifted' (p 90). They observed that children had become unseen and unheard.

In addition, the threats and intimidation experienced by social workers, both in investigating and endeavouring to work constructively with aggressive adults, can divert their attention and distract them from their responsibility to protect children. The threats and intimidation can lead directly to avoidance by the social worker (see Littlechild, 2008). The impact of the exposure to aggression and threats of serious violence on social workers inevitably affects their capacity to do the job. It is not unusual for them to visit family homes where the police would not visit alone. In court, they may be the only person who is giving evidence who has visited the home and experienced this level of threat and sustained intimidation.

High-quality, reflective and stringently analytic supervision and periodic joint visits with a senior social work colleague (Ofsted, 2012) can support the required respectful uncertainty and healthy scepticism identified by Lord Laming (2003), and militate against the risks of optimism in the constant pressure of new safeguarding referrals that lead to a need to show through-put and case closure. Fauth et al (2010) identify some key issues relating to the authority, power and potential effectiveness in working with 'highly resistant families'. Drawing on the albeit limited field of research evidence in this area, they highlight the child protection system as a powerful tool, whose power can be used in a positive and non-coercive manner, with honesty and transparency. However, they also note in their review of the research that social work practitioners 'may display a confrontational style' (p 16), which is not the respectful uncertainty promoted by Lord Laming.

The focus needs to be retained on the longstanding social work behaviours and practice skills, demonstrating empathy, establishing relationships, balanced by a 'healthy dose of scepticism' (McKitterick, 2008, pp 2-3). To achieve 'humane social work' (Featherstone et al, 2014) in child protection requires not only a recognition that most children and young people who have been abused or neglected remain with their families, but also that the adults in those families need direct help themselves, and are often best placed to help identify the successful ways of ensuring their children are cared for well.

So where does this leave social workers in this critical and exposed area of work as leaders? For families, the social worker is seen as both powerful, with enormous authority over them and their role as parents, and also open to distraction and diversion. For the social worker in child protection and safeguarding, they are, or feel themselves to be, a junior frontline member of staff in a large organisation that has numerous systems of control, in reviews, performance management and panel meetings. Brandon and Jordan (1979, p 1) characterised the institutional or positional pressures:

> Powerful forces push social workers into restricted roles. There is a strong public perception that they should be nicely and inoffensively helpful, never angry and disturbing. Some clients paralyse social workers' imagination and creativity with threatening and disruptive demands, but most see them as low-ranking officials of whom little is to be expected.

Plus ca change!

There are few, if any, resources that social workers have to call on directly beyond their own time and skills (Searle and Patent, 2012). Their judgements are potentially trumped by other more established and protected professions, expert witnesses, senior managers who are increasingly less likely to be social workers, and lawyers. In court they can bear the brunt of the challenge by other parties to legal proceedings, and there is strong anecdotal evidence that they may be expected to suppress their own professional judgements on the best decision to be sought from the court in favour of a decision by a manager or resource allocation panel. The use of their explicit role to ensure children are safe, including leading core group meetings in child protection work from the outset of their career, are roles that require great leadership skills, as well as self-assurance and confidence. The multi-agency structures to support their work need to recognise this, and support the development of the necessary skills, alongside a respect of the importance of what they are doing. The legal procedures available to their employer, if they work in a local authority, can underpin their individual expertise alongside the evidence-informed practice skills that provide the core of their work with families. This core of evidence is still being developed (Thoburn et al, 2009), and there is a range of promising approaches in working with complex families where there is evidence of abuse or neglect. In developing and enhancing their range of intervention skills, social workers not only need to access high-quality reflective supervision, research literature and rigorous continuing professional development, but must also have the space and time to provide the relationship base for the direct work they are undertaking.

Social pedagogy

In exploring how services for families and children and young people are delivered across Europe, some learning can be drawn from how professional responsibilities are allocated, and in particular, how social work practice and professional development might be enhanced in the UK. There has developed an enduring interest in social pedagogy in other European countries. While the word 'pedagogy' has had an essentially educational meaning in English, the origins are in Greek, meaning the guiding of a boy or young person. The application of the term has a range of meanings across countries in northern Europe, and is sometimes interchangeable with social work (Petrie et al, 2005; Boddy and Statham, 2009).

In the context of leadership within practice, the educational origins in the broadest sense (Lorenz, 2008) are centred on direct work with children and young people, usually with a focus on working as an 'emancipator' rather than a deficit or problem-orientated approach, which Boddy and Statham (2009) contrast with the focus on child protection and very high levels of need in the deployment of most social workers in services for children and families in the UK. Nonetheless, the overall approach builds a useful conceptual bridge in social work and related practice between the participatory, emancipatory and capacity-building mode of social work and the interventionist focus on problems and risk, which can so easily dominate practice.

Empowerment

Empowerment has been one expression of the social justice tradition of social work, alongside the personal and more individual therapeutic or casework traditions of self-determination and promoting choice; while social workers have no legitimacy to give power or claim to devolve power, social justice determines that individuals have rights. These are non-negotiable and non-transferrable. A related term is 'consciousness-raising'. Women, people from black and other minority ethnic communities, people with disabilities and other oppressed groups can be negatively valued and be denied the skills and resources:

> Social workers of the empowerment tradition do not encourage clients to place their faith in the judgement of experts. Instead they prompt clients to develop trust in their own capacity to discern, through dialogue and reflection, the respective merits and pitfalls of any recommendation, whether that of a professional, a government official, a supervisor at work, a friend, a support group, or family members.(Simon, 1994, p 187)

She identifies the self-conceptions of social workers as 'nurturers, facilitators, mobilisers and social and organisational reformers' (p 177) and 'developing leadership among those who are disenfranchised' (p 6). In an evaluation of the common elements in successful social work interventions to achieve behaviour change or a reduction in problem behaviours McNeil et al (2005, p 22) identified the importance of the establishment of a working alliance in a therapeutic relationship that is collaborative, taking the client's perspective and concepts of the problems, with a mutual understanding or agreement about the nature and purpose of the intervention.

A mother of vulnerable children, who are subject to a child protection plan as a consequence of her close relationship with one or more men who pose a real risk to their safety, and who incidentally abuse her, can address with her social worker where her choices and ultimate interests lie. The social worker, in jointly developing insights, raising self-confidence, ultimately enables the mother to assert and take back her own power. How do we prevent our claims to practising and upholding empowerment as being little more than the offering of 'titbits of autonomy', as continues to be a risk within services for people with learning difficulties (Flynn, 1992)? Empowering people is contained as a key component in the BASW *Code of ethics* (2012, p 13); however, it can risk being relegated to one of a number of professional values, as opposed to a specific way of working. It can come to be seen as a focus for positive policies rather than an integral part of practice with individuals and families, as well as in advocacy, working with groups and communities, and in campaigning. Payne (2006) critically analyses power and empowerment in the context of the positional location of social work with attendant authority, including from duties enshrined in statute, and their role in allocating scarce resources. Recognising this does not negate the empowerment and consciousness-raising techniques of social work practice:

> Social workers should recognise that they feel vulnerable when they give up control of a situation, and find strategies for gained support and approval for risky strategies in their work. They should also take responsibility for identifying where differences between them and clients may lead to inappropriate use of power and responding appropriately. (Payne, 2006, p 136)

Guiding and navigating

In the large-scale screening and assessment of people coming to adult and children's services *and* in their work in complex cases, social workers have the role and responsibility for identifying and, if necessary, mobilising other services or particular interventions that will either meet particular needs or complement their own. This is more challenging than straightforward advice and diversion to more appropriate services. The complexities of needs and promoting choice for preferred solutions require an appreciation of the effectiveness or evidence base of the service or intervention. For a family faced with the near failure of an older person to maintain their independence at home, aggravated by increasing dementia and depression, a simple referral on to a rehabilitation or 're-ablement' service risks failure. The social worker needs to be fully aware of how the range of local rehabilitation and dementia services work, for whom it is known to be successful, who it suits less well, and how to ensure that the issues of dementia and depression are factored in to the overall service provided. In sharing hard information on the evidence from the service on 'what works' and what does not, alongside the complementary interventions required to achieve success, the social worker is guiding, leading and sharing their expertise and knowledge. Their skills in communicating and considering options with the older person, and in working with family and community carers, are fundamental to the contribution they can make for enhancing the quality of life, emotional wellbeing and maximising independence. They are actively working with the older person to achieve positive outcomes, not simply seeking navigation away from a social work service.

Parents facing almost insuperable behaviour problems in their child may be enormously helped by the range of parenting programmes available. Social workers' awareness of the evidence base for these programmes, the expectations on family members, and how they may need to be complemented or supported are all critical parts of the knowledge and expertise that they need to share with families and to directly use in their practice. The same applies across a wide range of specialist services, for example, community mental health and drug misuse services. The reductionist model of care management, alongside the remote commissioning of specialist services, in both services for adults, as well as for children and families, should not absolve the social worker from the responsibility to be research and evaluation-aware and to know how they may be able to enhance the effectiveness or success of services provided by others. These services and specialist skills are also sources to be used to add to and complement the social worker's own portfolio of interventions they can use in direct work, not a one-way referral away from themselves.

Public education and information are powerful resources, used at varying levels across social work specialisms. In adoption and fostering there is a substantial literature available for carers, which recognise and respect their expertise and responsibilities. The NSPCC booklet *What can I do? Protecting your child from sexual abuse* (2012) is another example of focused advice and information that is of direct benefit to families. The authoritative and respectful style of such educative material is effective in complementing direct practice, as well as being important in wider public education. Practitioners, growing in confidence, will identify the material relevant to their area of work, and contribute their own writings as authoritative experts, leading and sharing information and education. With the return of responsibility for public health to local government in 2013 in England, there is great scope and resource to develop this further, through the expertise and experience of social work practitioners.

Leadership with colleagues and across other services

In much of social care, social workers have had the benefit of a more substantial level and time in education and training than almost all their colleagues. Much social care is provided by colleagues, many with invaluable experience, who have not had access to the benefits of formal qualifications. Other professional colleagues in partner agencies will benefit from the psychosocial insights and evidence base of social work in the collaborative working that is at the core of most social work. The leadership role is explaining and sharing these insights, and modelling effective practice. Recently qualified social workers are likely to be more up to date with current research evidence and innovative in new ways of working from their time at university. New graduates will have 'a systematic understanding of key aspects of their field of study, including acquisition of coherent and detailed knowledge, at least some of which is at, or informed by, the forefront of defined aspects of the discipline [of social work]' (QAA for Higher Education, 2008, p 18). Those who have qualified at Master's level will have 'a systematic understanding of knowledge, and a critical awareness of current problems and/or new insights, much of which is at, or informed by, the forefront of their academic discipline, field of study or area of professional practice' (QAA for Higher Education, 2008, p 20). In this regard they are experts, and to be valued, and a 'fresh pair of eyes' (Galpin et al, 2012). This is particularly pertinent with the variable level of participation in formal university and employer partnership-validated post-qualifying awards. The absence of these programmes for many experienced and social work staff cuts them off from current and new knowledge and emerging research.

While an NQSW may feel a 'rookie', they are often the best placed to introduce a critical awareness of current and new thinking in practice and public policy research. In England, the College of Social Work's *Professional capabilities framework* (2013b) identifies the leadership responsibilities of social workers in their first year after qualifying: 'Show the capacity for leading practice through the manner in which you conduct your professional role, your contribution to supervision and to team meetings' and 'take steps to enable the learning and development of others' (College of Social Work 2013b, under 'Professional leadership-AYSE'). By the next stage, these expectations are extended to 'Contribute to and promote development of practice, taking the initiative to test new approaches' and 'Contribute to the learning of others' (College of Social Work 2013b, under 'Professional leadership-professional leadership-social worker'). These are quite tentative, and show no sign of a wish to use their recent university education. The reasons for this limited ambition may reflect the work location of most social workers in local authority employment with an overwhelming managerialist culture. It may reflect employer perceptions of how well prepared for practice many social workers have been by their university training and education, with limited access to an appropriate range of practice learning settings. The absence of reference to the important role of leadership in working with colleagues and with other agencies is a critical omission (see Chapter Seven). Progressing through the levels in the *Professional capabilities framework*, the extending leadership expectations for experienced, advanced and strategic-level social workers focus on progressive responsibility for leading service and practice development, a progressive focus on promoting a culture of professional curiosity, responsibilities for reflective supervision, professional development, including ensuring employer standards for supervision and continuing professional development are met. There are strong arguments for drawing aspects of these to the expectations at the starting point of the social work career.

In the field of medicine, the responsibility of doctors to be leaders in their practice and in their teams at the beginning of their career is recognised, expected from the outset, including as trainees.

> Psychiatrists should recognise their responsibilities to wider systems of care and not just to individual patients, and work collaboratively with managers, united by a shared desire to learn from experience, improve services and enhance patient safety. (Royal College of Psychiatrists, 2013, p 2)

> All doctors must contribute to discussions and decisions about improving the quality of services and outcomes … contribute to teaching and training doctors and other healthcare professionals, ideally acting as a positive role model. (GMC, 2012, p 7)

This, in part, is recognition of the importance of team and partnership working within clinical teams. In health services terms, social workers within local authorities and in co-located health and social care services are 'clinicians'. A current mantra from the health service is 'Management and leadership needs to be shared between managers and clinicians and both equally valued' (The King's Fund, 2011). Can we be confident that this behaviour is common in social work, social services and social care?

These are affairs of organisational culture, public policy and ultimately, for internalised praxis. While external and prescribed, the risks are that they are subject to organisational, or public policy, changes in wind direction, rather than hard-wired into a sense of self and self-worth. BASW places part of this self-leadership within its *Code of ethics* (BASW, 2012, p 16), in particular shared responsibility for professional development, evaluation and research:

> Social workers should contribute to the education and training of colleagues and students by sharing knowledge and practice wisdom. They should identify, develop, use and disseminate knowledge, theory and practice ... should use professional knowledge and experience to engage in research and to contribute to the development of ethically based policy and programmes. They should analyse and evaluate the quality and outcomes of their practice with people who use social work services.

This expectation from BASW can be contrasted with the more lowly ambitions for social workers in England from the College of Social Work, particularly in the early stages of their career. The risk is the loss of the resource of social workers to promote a professional culture, continuous service improvement and being a central part of distributed and shared leadership. These are too important to be left in the hands of social workers in strategic positions or general managers. My advice to social workers, reviewing their progress through the levels of the College of Social Work's *Professional capabilities framework* (2013b) with their professional supervisor and manager, is to address their contributions and development at the higher levels from the outset, with particular regard to the domains of leadership, knowledge and intervention and skills. Even if this opportunity is denied to them, they can still record this in their own record of supervision, their personal record of their continuing professional development, and information recorded for professional registration. This would be a powerful illustration, an exemplar, of self-leadership, modelling assertive ownership of continuing professional development among colleagues.

Professional leadership at advanced level includes 'Promote a culture of professional curiosity embracing research within your area of responsibility, encouraging the exploration of different cultures and ideas' and 'Take responsibility for ensuring individuals and workplace practice is informed by and informs research and current professional knowledge.' For experienced social workers the equivalents are, 'Play a leading role in practice development in the team and help sustain a learning culture' and 'Contribute to organisational developments.' In the intervention and skills domain at the strategic level the expectations include

> Maintain a well developed understanding of knowledge relevant to your area of practice, and a confident self-awareness of knowledge limits. Be able to access and make critical use of relevant knowledge from a variety of sources, and apply this knowledge in practice. Develop expertise, informed by knowledge, in both established and emergent areas relevant to their field of practice.

At the advanced level the linked capabilities are

> Be able to gather, analyse and review complex and/or contradictory information quickly and effectively, using it to reach informed professional decisions. Engage and facilitate research and evaluation of practice. Promote use of evidence and theory to support practice in complex and changing circumstances; for experienced social workers. Maintain and expand a range of frameworks for assessment and intervention.

To allocate these expectations later in a social work career, rather than as an integral expectation of professionals who have qualified at graduate level, and for a substantial proportion at post-graduate level, indicates a lack of ambition, a lack of trust and a lack of willingness to acknowledge and use their capacity or capability. Arguably, the reservation of higher professional expectations to those who are more experienced and those in designated senior roles denies both the opportunity for these attributes, skills and routine ways of working to be used in the first flush of professional development after university, and to become embedded in the internalised, personally owned expectations of professional behaviour and performance. It assumes these capabilities can be learned at a later stage of career development. It denies these attributes are of value in the part of the social work workforce that provides the large of majority of the social work service to the public. It limits the capacity and potential power and authority of the core of the social work workforce both to challenge and, more critically, to directly contribute to service development, including the promotion of new knowledge and skills. Finally, it indicates a lack of a culture of participative or shared leadership within the formal organisations, including employers, central government and quangos, around social work.

All social workers work alongside colleagues who have not had access to formal professional training who are helping provide the total range of services for which they are responsible as the key worker, care manager or lead professional, including leading regular core group meetings and reviews. This includes staff who may work within the same organisation or team, who may or may not share the same manager. It is unlikely they are the line manager; nevertheless, they have a leading position, which may be explicit or implicit. Working together requires shared objectives and clarity on the respective responsibilities of each worker. In these situations the social worker has clear leadership responsibilities and a partly supervisory role that needs to be acknowledged and owned. The social worker will almost certainly have responsibility for the care plan, in particular, the social care components of it, and the lead professional accountability, while they may not directly supervise these staff in a managerial sense. They have the responsibility to oversee the work, to ensure all are working in harmony, to a common purpose, and are part of the formal case-reviewing processes. This is a substantial, but unavoidable, responsibility that comes early, from the outset of the social worker's career. This is at the same time as they are learning to take responsibility for their own practice, and are gaining confidence in their own skills. There will be a difference in life experience and in experience in the service area; nevertheless, the social worker has greater responsibilities and personal accountability that can only be exercised by a combination of mutual respect and an explicit acceptance and demonstration of leadership.

It cannot be assumed that co-working, informal discussions or waiting for case reviews will ensure a cohesive and effective service will be provided. Shared planning for providing a service may include continuing assessment, managing risks, seeking changes in behaviour, increasing independence and substantial emotional and practical support. It needs to be focused, skilful and provided in a seamless way. In order for this to be successful, clarity is required on the arrangements for delegation, supervision, professional support and case accountability. Systematic care planning and review is required, assessing disagreements, recording and sharing of records, alongside the provision of specific training or development opportunities for the support worker (Chartered Society of Physiotherapy et al, 2006; McKitterick, 2012a, p 92). This can be regarded as routine management and supervisory business, although it is often missed or assumed to be in place without acknowledgment. The leadership skills come in quietly, ensuring all of this is explicit, having the confidence to speak out, record and show the way, using all the skills and attributes of respect, openness and clarity of purpose.

SEVEN

Leadership within a multi-disciplinary environment

Introduction

There are two aspects to multi-disciplinary and inter-disciplinary working: first, the social worker, within their organisation or team, professionally qualified, working with unqualified, but experienced and knowledgeable colleagues who often have shared responsibilities for work with individuals and families. In this context they are the leader of practice and de facto supervisor of these colleagues. While this may not be explicitly recognised or respected in organisational or hierarchical terms, their leadership skills are critical in the provision of effective, good quality, consistent services. And second, social workers have the scope and responsibility to lead within teams that include other professional disciplines, contributing their particular knowledge and evidence base, insights and values. This is not a managerial or team leadership role, but one of an active and influential contributor. There is therefore valuable learning from other professions working in this way.

Integrated, multi-disciplinary and inter-disciplinary working

The social worker's own confidence in their professional base is critical, in terms of knowledge, practice skills, evidence and capability to articulate and persuade, what could be called the 'rhetoric' of social work. Social workers demonstrate and practise their particular and specialist skills, grounded in evidence, and use these to complement and supplement the contributions of other professional groups. In joint service settings such as health and education, they bring a fresh pair of eyes, half in, half out, working together in a team or joint service, but at the same time, distinct. They are the proponents of the psychosocial, 'Drawing attention to the whole dimension of family and community ... highlighting the strengths of individuals and families' (Cullen, 2013, p 1357). They bring the perspectives of social justice and empowerment, for example,

> Social work nurtures hopes and aspirations and promotes citizenship, inclusion and human rights. As society grows more complex, the values, knowledge and skills of social work should become ever more vital. Social work has also taken a lead amongst welfare professions in involving and taking its priorities from people who use services and their carers and families themselves. (SCSN for Mental Health, 2010, p 10)

Social work has a distinct but complementary role to that of health colleagues in relation to building community and family resilience, working in partnership and within a rights-based approach. The social justice value base also requires a challenge to low expectations of recovery and difficulties in accessing universal services, tough advocacy, a sharp-elbowed proxy parent, partner or friend. In addition, if they have developed groupwork skills within their training and in subsequent practice, the insights and methods of working are invaluable in facilitating teamworking, particularly as many social workers are located within integrated services, and rarely operate as sole workers (Pullen-Sansfaçon and Ward, 2012). McAuliffe (2009, p 140) explores the role and responsibilities of social workers within inter-disciplinary teams working with people who have learning difficulties and their families, citing Donzelot (1997), who describes social work as 'a profession that seeks to liaise, to mediate, and to negotiate between professions and between the professions and the service users and families'.

It is worth exploring what is meant by 'multi-disciplinary working'. Social workers provide their services from many different kinds of settings, working alongside and collaboratively with colleagues from other professions and occupational groups. Examples include integrated health and social care and youth justice, as well as postings of social workers in schools and early years services. They also work in settings where their professional training is seen as valuable, but not necessarily essential, for example, wider social care services, work with asylum seekers and refugees and in community development. The complexities and challenges can be ignored, because multi-disciplinary working is considered so common that it becomes conceived as a self-evident 'good thing'. However, a systematic review undertaken for SCIE (Cameron et al, 2012, p 1) found: 'The evidence base underpinning joint and integrated working remains less than compelling. It largely consists of small-scale evaluations of local initiatives which are often of poor quality and poorly reported.' Bowyer (2008), in a review of the social work literature and research, found little evidence of improved outcomes for people who use services from multi-professional working.

Notwithstanding the caution in such a systematic reviews, it is notable how in the case of child protection, multi-agency working and multi-disciplinary working on a case-by-case basis is regarded as an imperative. It is enshrined in longstanding professional literature (Hallett and Stevenson, 1980) and government guidance (DfE, 2013a). Furthermore, when a child dies or is seriously injured, failures in multi-agency working are enduringly cited as a contributing cause (Brandon et al, 2012). While serious case reviews are less developed in safeguarding adults, having a more recent history (Manthorpe and Martineau, 2011), similar issues of multi-agency communication and joint work arise, although, as with safeguarding children, social care receives much of the attention. There is a steadily growing evidence base on the factors that aid effective joint working: explicit shared aims and objectives, clarity on respective roles and responsibilities, coupled with some flexibility in work roles, a local past history of joint working, good communication and information sharing. In addition, adequate funding was found to be an important factor. Much of this is dependent on the personal qualities and competence of each team member, where each can have a positive impact, and can enhance these factors in the way they work to good effect. Reflecting on the dynamics and personal experience of joint work within teams, or around a specific case in supervision, can be a prime opportunity to enhance effectiveness, as part of continuing professional development.

Wilson and Pirrie (2000, p 7), in a review of multi-disciplinary team working, found the key issues to be:

- bringing more than two groups together;
- a focus on complementary procedures and perspectives;
- providing opportunities to learn about each other;
- a motivation, a desire to focus on clients' needs;
- developing professionals' understanding of their separate but interrelated roles as members of a multi-disciplinary team;
- the need for 'clearly negotiated team roles'.

Cameron et al (2014, p 9 et seq), in a later review of research evidence, identified a wider set of issues:

- shared aims and objectives at both strategic and operational levels;
- appreciation of respective roles and responsibilities;
- flexibility;
- good sharing of information;
- co-location;
- strong management *and* professional support;
- positive local history of joint working;
- adequate resources;

with caution on issues of enduring organisational differences and a lack of appreciation of the contribution of different professions. Overall, their conclusion from their review is that while 'it demonstrates that joint working can lead to improvements in health and well-being, reduce inappropriate admissions to acute care or residential care and that intermediate care can save costs it remains difficult to draw firm conclusions about the effectiveness of UK-based integrated health and social care services' (p 4).

Because integrated working and working in the context of teams drawn from different disciplines are considered the norm and expected, it does not mean that it is easy, straightforward, or that it does not require the development of skills. Although the terms 'interdisciplinary' and 'multi-disciplinary' are sometimes used to mean the same thing, some researchers distinguish very clearly between the two:

> A multidisciplinary approach is one that involves a limited exchange of information between the collaborators, with each providing one's own expertise to the problem through

a division of labor. In this approach, collaborators learn little about the other disciplines involved in the project.

An interdisciplinary collaborative approach ... [involves] persons from different disciplines working together in an 'integrated' way in which the collaborators work closely together and combine their knowledge to create a solution to a problem. In this approach, collaborators learn something from each other outside of their areas of expertise. (Borrego and Newswander, 2008, p 7))

In considering what is really expected of collaborators in each model of working together, there will be a range of experiences and aspirations. Within teams of health professionals there is a substantial shared knowledge of physical conditions and potential medical treatments – each profession has particular specialist expertise and responsibilities, underpinned by a shared organisation and shared accountabilities as part of the NHS. Social workers have a distinct and separate knowledge and practice base and, except where they are directly employed and managed within the health service, have different managerial accountabilities. The NHS has a foundation in empirical research and scientifically validated treatment methods, and while these are subject to complexity and uncertainty, there is a confidence and conviction in how their professional staff operate, which can be a challenge in the social work tradition of agnosticism about empiricism (Newman et al, 2005). The confidence and assuredness the social worker brings is founded on their own distinct knowledge and skills in the psychosocial insights and methods of intervention. Working across disciplines includes a willingness to share skills and expertise, and to share work. It includes acknowledging and debating differences: 'This means that social work practitioners must develop skills in advocacy, negotiation and presentation of evidence in order to contribute to the resolution of dilemmas and disagreements' (Ray and Phillips, 2012, p 121). They also bring the potential of a fresh pair of eyes, both in terms of values, and often a far greater knowledge of what life is like within the person's home and within their family and social milieu. The hazards and devaluation of the leadership of social work within the team come when this is not asserted, or when there is such a joining and confluence of approach and working methods that the distinct contribution of social work is lost.

Arguably, the inter-disciplinary approach of collaborative working, where knowledge and skills are fully integrated, can militate against this distinctiveness and descend into homogeneity and the lowest common denominator of approach. In this scenario, the lower evidence base for social work interventions and the strong managerialist structures around professional development push social work out of a leadership role and function. The challenge for managers of social work services, for educators and researchers, is to provide the distinct clarity of knowledge, effective practice skills and role expectations to arm the social worker to enter the complex and challenging arena as an active, assured, articulate, confident, assertive, full participating member of the collaborative team, whether it is multi- or inter-disciplinary.

Social worker as lead professional

In both child protection and for children and young people in public care, a social worker is required to take the lead. Their work is comprehensively overseen by review meetings, case conferences, resource panels and independent reviewing officers, and when courts are involved, by lawyers, expert witnesses, family court advisers, magistrates and judges. Nevertheless, the designated social worker has lead responsibility. On the one hand, the social worker can regard this array of overseers as disempowering, slide into passive working, awaiting the next meeting or court hearing to direct what is to happen next, the behaviour that Farmer and Lutman (2012) term 'passive', as opposed to 'proactive case management'. On the other hand, recognising and relishing their responsibilities, this same array of colleagues is used as a set of resources, to help them achieve the best outcomes for children, young people and their families. This 'proactive case management' is based on their clarity of purpose and their clear exposition of the evidence that informs their practice and their interventions. They tenaciously pursue the interests of the children and young people by a combination of advocacy and direct therapeutic, relationship-based work, with them individually, with their families, and with other carers. In this way they are champions, leading, battling when necessary, to achieve the best outcomes for each child and young person who is their responsibility. For a child and young person in care, they are the sharp-elbowed parent, with the authority, if not always the power, to demand the best.

The extensive oversight of all these systems and bodies evolved as sets of checks and balances on the quality, competence and integrity of social work practice. They are resources to help and assist, as much as sources of constraint and obstruction. The oversight may be used to fetter and constrain. To escape the restrictive, and at times oppressive, nature of their contributions, an energetic and assertive demonstration of practice and competence founded on research and practice wisdom is required. This should be combined with assured contributions in reports, case discussions and meetings to counter any unhelpfulness. To support and encourage this, managers need to be providing the respect, the means, the tools and skill development for the social worker. Rigour in reflective supervision, with a focus on learning and development, rather than control, and rehearsing skills in discourse and explanation, can be liberating oversight. The recognition and empowerment through continuing professional development, addressed as mutual and shared learning, enables social workers to demonstrate their practice that merits respect and trust, and which can demand this.

Child and adolescent mental health services will typically include social workers, who, despite the challenge of being labelled as child and adolescent mental health workers, a generic job title that also encompasses nurses, psychologists, youth workers and others, potentially have a powerful and authoritative role within the team, drawn from the profession's lead responsibility for children and young people in public care, as well as specific expertise in child protection – children and young people in care are a group that is well recognised as having very substantial and specific needs for services addressing their mental health, both in terms of defined psychiatric morbidity and the severity and complexity of their emotional health needs (Milburn et al, 2008; Rao et al, 2010). Children in care are specifically identified as benefiting from dedicated specialist services (Tarren-Sweeney, 2010). The link across from a social worker having lead responsibility for a particular case does not always automatically translate into the application of skilled and effective interventions, and their role becomes perforce one of both determined advocate *and* therapist. Simply slipping into the adult social work role of care manager, identifying an external service to provide help and reviewing that service at intervals, does not fulfil or discharge the responsibilities of the lead professional. Notwithstanding this, the adoption of generic job titles in both adult services and in child and adolescent mental health services has lessened the confidence and clarity in the specific contribution of social work practice (Ray et al, 2008).

Promoting independence, empowerment and re-ablement

The importance of grasping and promoting these specific roles is illustrated by a study of integrated teams for care for older people and people with mental health problems. Social workers expressed the least satisfaction of all occupational groups with their current team job and the understanding of their role. They considered they had less autonomy than all the other professional groups in their team (Huby et al, 2010). The reasons for this were not part of the study, but this could be a manifestation of lack of confidence in intervention skills specific to social work, and perhaps part of the heritage of a role solely determined by care management expectations. In the field of adult social care there are no duties reserved to social workers, no activities or responsibilities deemed by statute or government guidance to require the specific skills and knowledge of a professional social worker. Equally, the profession has not yet consistently or systematically identified the particular practice wisdom or practice research evidence base that can and should be brought to the highly pressured and complex world of social care and its interface with the health service: 'The coverage of research studies evaluating social work contributions to mental health practice is patchy and many areas of practice remain under-researched' (McCrae et al, 2005). Pritchard (2006) is more positive, perhaps with a wider acceptance of what constitutes evidence than might be acceptable in the rigour of health service-funded evaluations. In the area of re-ablement for older people, seeking to extend and enhance independence and quality of life, the research and evaluation literature is largely silent on the contribution of social work, although Wilde and Glendinning (2012), and SCIE (2013) identify a growing recognition of social and psychological needs. Perhaps this recognition would have already been present if social work had been present.

Much of the evaluation of integrated re-ablement services for older people has focused on recovering physical ability and building confidence. Parker (2014) examined the 'fuzziness' of definitions of re-ablement, and sought to differentiate the key characteristics that distinguish intermediate care, re-ablement and other health and social care services. The first two share the objectives of avoiding acute hospital admission, short- and long-term re-admission reduction in the use of home care, and avoidance of admission to long-term care, and are only short-term services. In addition, re-ablement aims to be restorative, enabling people to regain self-care skills. In this regard it shares the active focus of social work as opposed to the arguably more passive approach of social care and care management.

Meeting social needs and psychological support to build confidence are often neglected: 'There is good evidence that re-ablement improves service outcomes, prolongs people's ability to live at home, and removes or reduces the need for standard home care' (SCIE, 2013, p 32). The evidence for improving morale is moderately good, which may indicate the limited focus on psychological and social needs (SCIE, 2013). This evidence suggests that social work needs to join re-ablement services for older people, having a positive contribution to make. The empty husk of care management, the process of assessment, arrangement of a 'care package' and review (Davies and Challis, 1986) is a way of describing a process, a generic way of working, not a set of skills and knowledge. It is interesting to note that one of the evaluation studies that led to the embedding of care management as the primary role for social workers in much of adult social care identified budgets for care decentralised to social workers as a key part of the early successes (Hudson, 1993). Few social workers in adult social care have direct access to care budgets or a direct call on specific services. They enter a process of matching need (or levels of disability) against eligibility criteria, and then negotiate with the budget-holding manager or the provider of a specific service. They have no authority, no discretion.

'Autocratic or directive leadership' can prescribe the pace of the process, the speed of hospital discharge, the paperwork to be completed, and will decide if services are to be provided. In circumstances where a vulnerable adult needs to be protected, actions by the social worker can be prescribed by procedure and legal advice, decisions not made the social worker, but at meetings and case conferences. The 'pace-setting leader' will do the same, *and* would also allow a degree of devolution on spending decisions and discretion to enable the social worker to take prompt and effective steps to provide direct protection of a vulnerable person. The 'transactional leader' would welcome some determined advocacy on behalf of the person needing a service and their carers. They would receive with open arms the social worker providing direct help in the form of addressing complex and competing needs, giving skilled advice, counselling and family work to address emotions, feelings and ambiguities, and moving forward with concrete action. Creative and unusual resolutions would be encouraged and welcomed. Processes and procedures are to be used flexibly as ways of facilitating a good service, not for controlling or constraining. The same issue of the location of resource decisions is identified in the evaluations of the implementation of personal budgets, where social workers undertake an assessment of need, choice, how any risks could be managed and to identify costs, but all case decisions are taken by a budget-holding manager. It is not easy here to see the place for practice skills, the scope to achieve positive change, or even the potential of assertive advocacy. This was addressed, together with the potential interplay of the reluctance of some social workers to embrace and enthusiastically implement personalisation and individual budgets, earlier, in Chapter Four.

The historic lack of clarity in professional and government policies on the role of social workers in adult services, and the strictures of management through performance indicators, makes it both timely and vital for a more assertive professionalism, built on both the experience and the voices of the people served, and the experience and knowledge of what works in social work practice. Failure to rise to this challenge would be a passive yielding to the forces of managerialism, technocratic prescription and the drowning of the voice of experience: 'The lords of earth are only great, while others clothe and feed them!' (Cole, 1846). Social work failing to exercise its own leadership through every social worker, to show the way and to make best use of practice wisdom hands power to other professions, to employing organisations, and ultimately takes power from those social work seeks to serve. Shifting to the mode of 'citizen and servant leader', the roles of the social worker are explicitly advocate, navigator of potential and available services, creative problem solver and champion of maximising independence and full participation in an ordinary and valued life (Thomas and Wolfensberger, 1999). The 'package of care' arranged under a process of care management can take into account the full range of activities and social interactions that promote, regain and maintain independence and wellbeing. The very rich maintain their independence because they have servants, they do not need social care. The organisation providing social care and a social work service supports and enables the social worker as 'citizen' and 'servant' leader to promote independence and to ensure the best care possible. This is not to deny that resources are finite – of course they are rationed – but the trick is to provide the best possible, the most effective, and the most skilled, firmly founded on the best research evidence of what works. At the same time, social work has a wider social justice responsibility to highlight resource service deficits through collective campaigning, beyond the individual case, and beyond the constraints of employment.

Social work with older people is embedded in social care as distinct from healthcare services for older people. A study by Windle et al (2009) indicates savings to the NHS in pilot joint health and social care early intervention services. Another study (Steventon et al, 2011) found that there was no overall reduction in emergency hospital admissions or in time in hospital. One explanation suggested is that the 'case finding' of older people may have brought to light previously unidentified needs for hospital treatment. A study of a mixed team of professionals working with older people found that the impact of social work seemed to have an impact on the healthcare of older people (Emilsson, 2013). This study focused on the form of the team as 'trans-professional', where the different professions were working together in a way that integrated working processes and where disciplinary boundaries were partially dissolved. This is a form of 'inter-disciplinary' working (Borrego and Newswander, 2008), where colleagues working closely together can share and model working methods, adapting and adding to their skills, thus avoiding the need for constant changes in worker for different specialist tasks. Another study explored the successful substitution of social work or social care by nurse-led care case management (Manthorpe et al, 2012). The educative leadership role of social work can be deployed in extending the professional perspectives and interventions of professional colleagues, often through deliberations about some individuals and their circumstances. It does not need to be present physically around every individual, but available to be called on, and contributing to wider discussions within the service.

Some of the evaluations of the effectiveness of integrated working, including early interventions, are disappointing evidence for policy makers. It had been hoped that substantial, collaborative preventative work with older people living in the community could reduce the use of expensive hospital care. If it is considered as an aspect of the help older people require to retain their health and consequent quality of life, then it gives the opportunity for a more evidence-based public policy. There has been much attention on older people as perceived 'bed-blockers' or given a diagnosis of 'acopia', meaning 'not able to cope' (Oliver, 2008). In an analysis of the care provided for older people in hospital, Tadd et al (2012), with a particular focus on care behaviours and the dignity accorded to them, clearly exposed the competing interests within hospitals, which include infection control, maximising the use of beds and risk avoidance. Each of these was found, at times, to be pursued at the expense of the older person and their ultimate recovery and their regaining of independence. Infection control caused some people to be isolated in side rooms and encouraged to use incontinence pads. Maximising bed use caused people to be moved between wards, using an enormous amount of ward nurse time. Risk avoidance was seen in the unnecessary use of wheel chairs and bedrails. All of these 'safe' practices and efficient use of resources lead to unintended consequences of confusion, isolation, reduced mobility and increased dependency. Older people, through these practices, risk leaving hospital more confused, less mobile and more incontinent. While it is not for social workers to manage hospital colleagues, their fresh pair of eyes should be mindful of these features of hospital care, and seek to support change. The national mantra may be on reducing 'bed-blocking' by older people, but as Tadd et al point out, not only do these people need expert treatment in hospital, since older people are the greatest users of hospital inpatient services, the hospital regimes need to be better adapted to their needs, and in particular, to maximise their independence at discharge. The social worker leading in the multi-disciplinary work in hospital is well placed, although perhaps not necessarily welcome, to promote recovery, regaining independence and the capacity for a good quality of life, to help reduce the gap between life expectancy and the number of 'healthy years' that can be subsequently enjoyed. Simply to clear the bed is not necessarily to increase independence or to help achieve more 'healthy years': 'Effective leadership, time to reflect on practice and confidence to question inappropriate practices that have become accepted norms require urgent attention if dignified care is to become a reality for acutely ill older people' (Tadd et al, 2012, p 42).

Wood and Salter (2012) report that, while re-ablement moderately reduces care costs over the longer term, it does not always reduce health costs, as hospital re-admissions are higher than they should be. Their research identified a narrow application of re-ablement to focus just on 'within the home' tasks, rather than enabling older people to re-engage with their community networks, a cliff-edge of support ceasing after a finite period, without adequate steps taken to ensure that a 're-ablement ethos follows to maintain the good work achieved during the intervention ...' (p 12). In addition, when people are subsequently funding their own social care, the studies usually do not have access to follow-up data to identify outcomes, since there is no cost to state funds.

Promoting the psychosocial

A small-scale, but revealing, study of professional interactions in a health setting (Atwal and Caldwell, 2005) in consultant doctor-led multi-disciplinary team meetings found in an analysis of the interaction of social workers, therapists and nurses that they were reluctant to voice their opinions or contribute information or judgements that could give direction to the planning of outcomes of care and treatments. They suggest that this demonstrated conformity to a dominant culture, and that these professionals are not 'respecting their own autonomy or being an effective advocate for their client' (p 272). It does suggest that the contribution of different professional judgements, perspectives and skill contribution requires a greater and more assertive contribution in multi-disciplinary settings, where a single professional voice may dominate. Rintal et al (1986) found that in health rehabilitation settings physical issues were emphasised (65 per cent) while psychosocial issues were under-emphasised (14 per cent). The perspectives that social workers bring to the personal and social circumstances of an individual using healthcare and treatments are of greater significance than the straightforward sharing of information and arranging social care services of the passive care management role. Without this leadership in multi-professional deliberations, the voices of the individual and their family will not be heard, nor an appreciation of the resources available in the wider community and social settings. While there is likely to be a tacit understanding among all the different professions that these issues are of importance, unless the social worker is active, assertive and effective in their communication, their contribution in facilitating recovery, maximising independence, reducing the need for future health treatments, with all the concomitant enhancement of quality of life, will be absent.

The presence of social workers in multi-disciplinary services that straddle health and social care, for example, community mental health teams, is not universal. There is a common practice of using generic job titles such as 'child and adolescent mental health worker', 'care coordinator', 'youth offending officer' and 'mental health worker', open to recruitment of people with a wide range of professional qualifications, social work, youth work, nursing, psychology, counselling and a range of therapies. This approach to workforce planning may be the result of shortages in the supply of certain disciplines, or may be an indication of homogeneity of approach and lack of acknowledgment of the range of specific needs for specific interventions that people require from the service. Anecdotally, it is telling that such 'workers' report that they are frequently asked what profession they belong to. It certainly makes it difficult for each professional to retain their identity and particular contribution, and potentially leaves their continuing professional development at the basic level required for registration. Huxley et al (2012a), in a review of the literature and survey of the composition of multi-disciplinary mental health teams, found that while there is little evidence that the overall team composition is justified, there is some evidence that greater professional diversity, in the inclusion of social workers, is linked to greater effectiveness. This could assist with issues of clarity of purpose (see Chapter Four).

Mental health had been the only 'reserved duty' for social work in social services for adults until the creation of the approved mental health professional (AMHP) in 2007, open to a number of different professions, which replaced the approved social worker created by Mental Health Act 1983, with the requirement for specialist post-qualifying training and assessment. Perhaps the change from approved social worker to AMHP is a cautionary tale of how reserved duties do not necessarily protect skills and responsibilities. It may have distorted the skill base, narrowing and diminishing the longstanding, earlier psychiatric social worker role, skill and knowledge base. The social worker is the champion of psychosocial factors in mental health recovery as well as the cause of psychosocial vulnerability. The complex interplay of physical causations, including potential hereditary vulnerabilities, the role of medication, psychological treatments alongside the necessity for positive social support systems, including family and wider social capital (Webber et al, 2011), are widely known across the range of health professionals. Their very familiarity may have altered the professional authority that social workers traditionally brought to multi-disciplinary working in mental health, but this awareness does not necessarily translate into the direct practice of these other professions. It is for the social worker to bring the psychosocial into the assessment, care planning and delivery of recovery.

The insights and understandings of the Brown and Harris research (1978) demonstrate the links and associations between factors of vulnerability and provoking agents for depression. Their research found these to be early maternal loss, lack of a confiding relationship, several young children, and unemployment. The seminal earlier social work study by Goldberg (1967), and later work by Leff (1976), demonstrate the importance of family and home circumstances, and how relationship-based interventions have a positive impact on enduring recovery. These kinds of evidence enable the social worker not just to bring understanding to their professional colleagues from other disciplines, but more importantly, to work collaboratively with the individual, their family and wider social network to build or rebuild a more robust social support and secure emotional attachments (Webber et al, 2011). The wider context of quality of life (Oliver et al, 1996) transcends the simpler suppression or alleviation of psychiatrically defined symptoms, and links recovery to social inclusion and positive personal relationships. While there may be risks in formalising the measurement of social inclusion (Huxley et al, 2012b) which could objectify, excluding the personal experience of the people whose lives are being measured, this needs to be integrated with the empathy of the workers who are tasked to provide a relationship-based service.

Herod and Lymbury (2002), in a small-scale study, demonstrated the clarity that some health service professionals have regarding the role and distinct features of social work, their critique and challenge within the multi-disciplinary team, the holistic perspective they bring, and the quality of the relationships forged with individuals and families to form the basis of effective interventions. In order to assert these authoritative roles and responsibilities, the social worker needs not only to know the family and social circumstances well, but also to be able to insert and articulate this knowledge and these insights coherently into the multi-disciplinary deliberations. These consequently inform and guide the care and treatment plans, which draw on the skills and evidence base of the whole of the multi-disciplinary team, from the full range and heritage of the academic, research and endowments of colleagues from other professions. Social workers in these teams need an acute awareness of their own value and the impact of their own contribution, and to be able to articulate this in an assertive and acceptable way to influence, inform and ultimately help shape the overall plan of care and intervention. This needs to be grounded in critical awareness of current practice research.

At Winterbourne View Hospital for people with learning disabilities (Flynn, 2012) there were social workers who had been heavily involved and who had been providing a social work service for the individuals who lived in this private facility, funded by public monies, but who were arguably not personally and individually responsible for the placement. Nevertheless, they had an enduring role in the reviews of care and treatments of each of the people living there. An emphasis on commissioning and resource management is insufficient to secure expertise and personal responsibility. 'Commissioning is the key to this agenda. The right commissioning by expert commissioners, based on the right data, is the way to ensure the right capacity' (DH, 2013, p 9). This approach on its own is de-personalising, de-professionalising, it articulates the provision of services as a commissioning system. It lifts the responsibility for services for an individual, their quality, appropriateness and effectiveness of care to procedures. It potentially places all of this beyond the personal accountability of an individual who knows the person placed in care, knows their families, and who owns a personal responsibility.

Conclusions

Looking across services for both children and adults, the health service can be more alert and tuned in to the wider needs of children, accepting shared responsibilities beyond the definition of medical presentation of need as simply medically treatable. The risks of abuse, neglect and poor attention to complex health conditions causes wider psychosocial issues to be to the fore. This is augmented by the potential of legal testing of diagnoses in care proceedings. It is part of the social position of children as citizens who potentially need the protection from outside their own family. In the multi-disciplinary settings in child health the social worker's leadership in both the questioning and positive contribution in the formulation of judgements on abuse, including neglect, is critical. Where the social work service, and in particular the child protection services, are organisationally disconnected from paediatric services, where experienced social workers and paediatricians are not routinely engaged in the shared deliberations about diagnosis and child protection planning, the risks of unjust medical diagnoses and missed abuse are high. In an ethnographic study within child health services, White (2002, p 431) observed the sharing of uncertainties over a series of conversations about individual children and families, 'using knowledge and "know-how"', they are clearly making knowledge'. The similarity of paediatric and geriatric services in patients being categorised in professional talk as medical or social is seen in the study, and yet, a 'psychosocial' classification does not remove children from a perceived entitlement to health services. The reasons behind this may be rooted in the social value of children as potentially in need of protection. More sinister is the potential explanation of a lower social value placed on older, dependent people. The higher level of social work skills deployed in services for children and their families is arguably a reflection of these values. The challenge for social work is to lead a way out of this, both in multi-disciplinary discourse and practice. The community capacity building envisaged within a resurgence of 'community social work' (Barclay, 1982; College of Social Work, 2012) is a partial contribution to the exploration of a more clearly defined role for social workers working with adults. Rigorous and prompt evaluation of the potential success of a renewed community social work is required if it is not to be another short-term fashion.

Social work, with a distance, often organisationally, and in its knowledge base, brings to multi-disciplinary working a wider perspective to bear, and a willingness and potential expertise to widen the range and scope of interventions or treatments. For example, in a user-led research study of the CPA in English mental health services, the essence and meaning of recovery, as defined by service providers and psychiatric professionals, was found to be very different to the understandings and definitions of people receiving the service (Zucchelli, 2013). When the discernment of the outcome – recovery, the avowed purpose of services – is not shared, or is at least the subject of different expectations, recovery is inevitably jeopardised. Social work's confidence in multi-disciplinary settings needs to draw on its longstanding experience and knowledge of what had been referred to as 'social treatments' (London County Council, 1947), and avoid the bedevilling uncertainties about role, status and evidence base. The social worker in the multi-disciplinary team is best placed to initiate and lead these conversations, both in terms of direct work and conversations among the different disciplines, to lead by good practice, by the application of good practice in listening, respecting and ultimately heeding and being guided by the wisdom and aspirations of people receiving joint or integrated services.

Services are integrated or organised in a multi-disciplinary way for a range of reasons. When the expertise of a number of professions is sought within a particular specialist service to meet complex needs, a multi-disciplinary team, either around a particular individual or family, or as a standing shared service, social work's contribution is needed in an assured and authoritative confidence. While attempts to homogenise team membership in titles such as 'children's services worker' (Purcell et al, 2012, p 87), 'youth justice officer', 'child and adolescent mental health worker' and 'care coordinator' can suppress expectations of specific expertise, within the health service in particular, where professional identities can be stronger and continuing professional development more prominent, there are opportunities to emulate these features of professional behaviour. This includes, where line management may be shared across different professional groups, ensuring regular reflective supervision from a registered social worker is received, including structured, externally validated, progressive post-qualifying training and education.

To conclude this chapter, the issues of funding for services need to be understood as part of the context and an explanation of inevitable tensions and challenges. The adequacy and source of funding is particularly pertinent in times of economic stringency. Policy makers may see more integrated working as a more cost-effective way of delivering services or masking the enduring uncertainties about the boundaries of responsibilities for health and social care, between the NHS, local authorities and means testing the individual. Some studies have suggested that targeted investment in social care can decrease healthcare costs (Windle et al, 2009), but, in public policy terms, this can muddy the waters in the respective funding streams of health, funded directly by central government, and social care, funded by local government, local charging regimes and direct payments by the individual (McKitterick, 2012c). For social workers deployed in settings where these complex and often unfathomable issues of resources are played out, they can become the proxy for the confusions and a diversion, rather than focusing on direct practice skills, expertise and knowledge. When faced with these, the only solution is to push unresolved national and local public policy issues back upstairs to the senior managers in their organisation, and to consider how these can be brought to public attention. It is not the role of social workers to act as a buffer or a sponge to enable them to be avoided or denied.

EIGHT

Optimism, filling the vacuum and taking the lead

Introduction

There are three central and enduring themes of leadership for social work. First, much that is written about leadership in the public sector, and specifically in relation to social care, continues to conflate management and leadership as a single activity, with fixed positions of the leader manager and the follower operative, confusing much administrative support for practice with top-down management. Second, leadership is presented as a separate activity from knowledge and expertise in the service or the activity being led. Third, social work practice, and the oversight and development of practice, are fundamental leadership activities that can be subverted and submerged in the general management and procedurally driven culture in which most social work services are located. Leadership is an integral component of all social work practice and social work roles. While there are opportunities and responsibilities for all to advance successful leadership across the profession, there are no organisations that do this, and nor can it be expected that they will, in the foreseeable future, reform sufficiently to give or support the leadership that both social workers and the people they serve need and deserve.

Promoting the authority of the practitioner and renewing the focus on relationship-based, therapeutic and evidence-informed practice provide the foundation for optimism for social work services. A key component of this requires a review of the separation of the roles and capabilities, skills and knowledge of supervisor, social worker manager, educator and senior practitioner. In England, the Secretary of State for

Education (DfE 2014c) has announced a government intention to assess and accredit social workers in children's services at three levels after qualifying: as practitioners, practice supervision and practice leadership. Another government rather than profession initiative. There remains a fundamental need for clarity of purpose, core skills, knowledge and a research evidence base for social work practice, in whatever role or position. Supervisors, managers, review, case conference and panel chairs, educators and resource and case decision makers all need to reclaim and assert their identity and authority as social workers, as practitioners, and to respect and promote the authority of *all* practitioners. The context of constant emergence and re-emergence of new structures, architecture and roles will endure, with national and local service delivery organisations continuing to be the subject of repeated reorganisations and restructuring. The language, the jargon of management change can be vacuous, devoid of meaning and a distraction from the real world of providing an effective and valued social work service: 'Management speak is a matter of cramming the maximum number of feel-good words into the smallest amount of meaning' (Beckett, 2010, p 172). There will continue to be initiatives which government-financed organisations will recycle and present as new, as fresh discoveries, in order to justify their continuing funding and existence. But more alarming is the forgetting or ignoring of the learning and experience of the profession. The enduring wisdom and knowledge of social work has yet to find a home, or to be internalised within the assertive identity and practice of each social worker.

The benefits of self-management and earned autonomy in self-leadership encompass the capability and capacity to remind and assert these as the products of collective longstanding practice wisdom and knowledge, rather than new, to be re-sold to government and senior managers alike, as fresh discoveries to be imposed on social work. These conclusions are focused on optimism for the opportunities to deploy the skills of social workers as leaders, to counter managerialism, and to successfully compete against contesting power bases in providing services for the most vulnerable and marginalised people and groups. At a time of reducing public finances, there should be no place for a hollow recycling of ideas. There should be no place for organisations that are more concerned for their own survival and power. There is no place for marginalising the practice wisdom of social work, no place for suppressing the optimism for social justice, the effectiveness of relationship-based practice or the therapeutic imperative to achieve change.

Before reviewing how an optimistic future for social work, and for the work of social workers, can be led from within, a re-statement of what managerialism is can help to guide our strategies and behaviours. Descriptions of its characteristics include proceduralism, where centrally determined task-specific instructions, which de-professionalise practice, take the place of judgements, and creativity (see Ayre and Calder, 2010), and deny the need for sophisticated training and education. It seeks a narrow definition of efficiency, rooted in numerical measures or indicators, which enables managers and organisations to be less involved in practice skills, evidence and judgements. At a political level a definition is offered. It is

> An ideology which tries to eliminate political debate about the rival merits of competing ideals. In its stead, managerialism relies on a central elite which believes that it, and it alone, has the skill and know-how to devise policies to cope with the inexorable forces of economic change. (Dillow, 2007, p 11)

This approach reverberates in the closed, impermeable world of social work policy making within government and its funded bodies. It is then transferred down the hierarchical lines of management as practice 'guidance'. The absence of open and public discourse and the 'tyranny of transformation' and constant restructuring (Clarke and Newman, 1997) belie any claims of servant leadership, or even organisational citizenship (Parker, 2002). The organisational hackneyed terms of 'co-production' and 'communities of interest' become as banal and meaningless as the earlier words, 'consultation' and 'engagement'. It is not accompanied by evidence of listening, remembering, heeding and change. It denies and even rejects a shared history and accumulated practice wisdom. The promotion of evidence-based practice can combine both the discipline of rigorous research and the authority of the experience of people using social services, 'Refocusing on the training and integration of evidence supported elements and factors with a practice framework that builds on social work values and client preferences will best advance our effectiveness' (Barth et al, 2012, p 116).

Competition and the development of 'markets', with the attendant commissioning culture and structures, have separated the skilled worker from the organisations responsible for providing the service, and those with the skills and knowledge base in the service. The separation of management, administrative and organisational processes from social work practice, while being part of these pervasive and powerful forces, is also a force or method of organisational behaviour that social work has been weak or passive in successfully challenging or successfully combating. The Munro review (2011) of child protection, commissioned by a government minister, not by the service or by the profession, identified this from the outset as an impediment to effective practice, and yet there is no significant evidence of a reduction in centrally defined processes and procedures (DfE, 2013a). The issues are not new. The Association of Social Workers (ASW), at a study conference in Oxford in 1965, were deliberating on the relationship between professional work and administration, the term 'administration' encapsulating then what would now be called 'general management', as well as 'administrative support' (ASW, 1966). What is striking from that time is a willingness, optimism, to envisage a degree of integration and the maintenance of a commonality of interest. With greater confidence social workers can assert their leadership in what they know best, to question and challenge the slavish or even dangerous focus on performance indicators or the latest government policy initiative. At the same time, it is necessary to articulate and campaign for the appropriate management and administrative systems to support them to do their job. This requires a greater engagement in the building of the evidence base of what works, a greater investment in professional input into policy development, both as individuals and working collegiately within professional organisations. These organisations need to learn or re-learn how to welcome and encourage the full participation and contribution of their memberships, rather than operate as impermeable mini-quangos. This is a challenge – it requires these organisations to reform, with the development and respect in the mobilisation and use of the experience and expertise of all their members.

The preoccupations of managers, local government and national government can be seen as remote or unstoppable, but they can include positive resources for service improvement if engaged with and occupied as part of positive work (Taylor and Campbell, 2011). Leadership lies at the heart of all effective social work practice, in both the terms of 'servant leadership' (Greenleaf, 2002), and in the most straightforward meaning of the word, 'showing the way'. The authority to hold responsibility for this, rather than awaiting the guidance or direction of government, or government-funded bodies, rests with the accumulated practice wisdom of each individual and the collective memory. This has been, and will continue to be, garnered through research, critical analysis and above all, with the people who receive the service. Making clear what social work is doing, owning the complexity and explaining when things go wrong, or when they seem to have gone wrong, is the responsibility of all. When local authority spokespeople refuse to speak to the media about a perceived scandal or the inexplicable, the understandable media and public reaction is to assume something is being hidden, and to move on to blame social work and social workers. This may suit local authorities and central government – hiding behind dubious claims of confidentiality enables them to stand by and watch social work, rather than their own services being blamed, pilloried and damned. In my experience, the media 'social work bashing' is down to this failure to explain, to be open, and the failure to show how social work can put its own house in order.

There is a dynamic inherent in social work that attracts suspicion, and is arguably a reflection of the value wider society accords to excluded and downtrodden people (Sheldon and Macdonald, 2009). Does social work relish public opprobrium or low status? 'The fault dear Brutus is not in our stars, but in ourselves, that we are underlings' (W. Shakespeare, 'Julius Caesar', Act 1, Scene 2,1, line 134). Rein and White (1981) postulated that social workers are reluctant in the use of power, and tend not to wield professional authority based on status and position. The evaluation of the national programme for NQSWs (Carpenter et al, 2012), which evolved into the employer-led ASYE, examined 'self-efficacy' (Holden et al, 2002), their confidence in their ability to successfully undertake specific tasks and roles, and 'role clarity'. This provides the basis for some further examination of issues of authority, confidence and consequent influence.

The 'reluctance of the social work profession to absorb the concept of leadership' (Brilliant, 1986, p 327) may be the consequence of experiencing power as negative, but it does not wholly explain or excuse passivity or the suppression of ambitious standards. McDonald and Chenoweth (2009, p 4) suggest that social work has actually 'recoiled from the idea of leadership, harbouring an historical view that leadership is somehow contradictory to its social values and its underlying philosophy'. Credible practice, influence and impact in achieving positive change all require a confidence and explicit knowledge and skill base. Locating practice leadership, or the leadership of practice, in roles, in organisations or in government initiatives, without an attendant and far stronger leadership exercised by each social worker, leaves social work weak, both in its practice and its future development. The distinction between active and passive case management, identified by Farmer and Lutman (2012), which can be exercised by both social workers who are managers, as well as practitioners, is shown in the active contribution in the case-by-case work analysed by Chamberlain and Ward (2013). This is concrete evidence of both leadership *of*, as well as leadership *within*, practice.

One of the strengths of the *Professional capabilities framework* created by the Social Work Reform Board (2010) and built up by the College of Social Work (2013b) is including the domain of leadership at all levels. While the dilution of professional knowledge and expertise for the higher levels, with a diversion into general management activities, is a serious weakness, practitioners, their supervisors and educators could turn this to advantage. They will become much more expert, knowledgeable and research-aware than their managers. Their leadership will be stronger. This requires a personal commitment, with investment in continuing and continuous learning, reading and study, and working beyond the 'case load', both within and outside the workplace. It also requires a far more assertive and challenging approach in the workplace, a confidence and assuredness that will not always be welcome in a culture where practice has historically been driven by national policies and administrative edict.

A danger would be that those 'strategic managers' could strive to restrict the ambitions, authority and expertise of social work through their own lack of knowledge, awareness or interest in practice evidence or skills. Two indicators of this are the interest in employer-based social work training and the loss of momentum, and the absence of a national, professional consensus on a policy for formal post-qualifying awards. More positively, if the 'distributive' leadership model commended by Purcell et al (2012, p 89) for directors of children's services in England is adopted, there will be 'a more subtle and less linear form of leadership [in which] the leadership function is shared or distributed amongst those with the ability and experience necessary to ensure the function is carried out to the benefit of the wider organisation' (Wilkinson, 2007, p 1). While this model of leadership is still conditional and assumes the managing organisation shares the objectives of social work, it gives the opportunity to negotiate self-leadership through 'ability and experience'.

The elements of the description of a leadership programme for social care leaders (The National Skills Academy for Social Care and DH, 2013) can be triangulated with concepts of management and those of managerialism. The content includes substantial elements more aligned to these rather than to leadership, for example, improving productivity and effectiveness, developing commercial and political awareness, developing a performance culture. While it also includes collaboration, raising confidence and the ability to aspire for excellence in social care, it is silent on the skills and knowledge of how to provide this, or how to show the way in the delivery of good services. This is a government-funded organisation, closely allied to other quangos which I observe share a common interest in social work and social worker practitioners not having a direct voice in sharing their experience or taking a place at the table of government or funder public policy making. Because of this, such bodies lack credibility, locus or authority in the provision of good social work services.

Organisations that employ social workers and that are responsible for social work services will have a range of priorities that will not necessarily accord with those of social work. Inspection regimes and national performance indicators can become more important, or at best only a proxy, for providing an effective, humane and high-quality service. Timescales for child protection work can be measured by performance indicators, manipulated at times to appear positive for inspections. Minimising delays in the discharge of older people from hospital and reducing the number of people who receive publically funded social care are priorities for managers. The individual social worker and their professional supervisor, assuming effective medical treatment is being provided, are more interested in 're-ablement', maximising independence, social inclusion and overall quality of life. In order to be competent in achieving these outcomes, managers need to know what social work skills make children safe and what enable older people to lead a 'good life'. These cannot, with any good effect, be delegated to others if they themselves do not have direct experience or evidence of the efficacy of these services.

Renewed focus on relationship-based and therapeutic practice

There has been a growing recognition or re-discovery of the centrality of the therapeutic responsibilities of social work, sometimes now referred to as 'relationship-based' practice (Trevithick, 2003; Hamer, 2006), and one of the valued qualities recognised by the user-led movement Shaping Our Lives, National User Network (2013). Stevenson (2013, p 88) highlights the old potential over-reach of the therapeutic nature of social work practice towards the psychotherapeutic traditions and working methods that have a greater focus on the unconscious. While the doubts about the effectiveness of talking therapies, including counselling, are longstanding, they came to the fore when the generic imperatives of the Seebohm Report (1968) widened the scope and expectations of social work practice, and in particular the breadth of knowledge to be covered in generic social work training. This was also linked to a renewed focus on social justice and the efficient and humane administration of a wide range of social care and welfare services. The biting critique of the therapeutic ambitions of social workers by Barbara Wootton (1959) were picked up by Halmos (1965), although he later sought to build a more effective bridge across the personal and the political, for active social work practice and action (Halmos, 1978). The near ridicule of later writers such as North (1972) and Brewer and Lait (1980) kept the therapeutic traditions of social work in the shadows, counselling devolved to others, and even direct work with children who had been neglected or may have been harmed was missed (Laming, 2003). Paradoxically the political, social change and action components of social work values and traditions had not risen to the fore as an alternative.

My first social work tutor, Robert Morley, whose career included probation, social work, marital and individual therapy, stressed both the primacy of the relationship as the base of work and also the centrality and imperative to recognise the active and defining role of the person being helped, be they client, user or analysand: 'Whatever the particular theoretical stance of the psychotherapist, it is common ground that the process differs from medical practice in that the patient is not simply the object of the "treatment" flowing from the diagnosis, but an active participant in it' (Morley, 2007, p 128). The challenge for social workers is in settings where time available for individual attention is limited, where the sheer scale in numbers of referrals prevents enough direct contact to form more than the most basic, fleeting relationship or interaction. If the communication is focused on gathering information for screening or assessment, it is even more important that personal respect, warmth, empathy and competence are displayed up front, from the first moment of contact (Trevithick, 2012).

Whether the term 'therapeutic' or 'relationship-based' is used, the direct personal relationship between a social worker and the people they are seeking to help, and the quality of that relationship, are critical to the effectiveness of the service provided. It may be based on empowerment and working with people to make their own choices on how they access social care and increase or maintain their independence (Beresford et al, 2011). It may be quite intense explorations of feelings, personal circumstances and relationships that aim to achieve insights, resolve conflicts, increase confidence and rehearse new skills. The qualities of reliability, empathy, warmth and a perception of genuine concern remain at the heart of relationship-based social work just as much as they were the core of the 'casework relationship' of Biesteck (1957), each individual treated as such, with work focusing on the purposeful expression of feeling and use of emotions, accepting and not judging, and fundamentally enabling the individual to make their own choices. Another American text by a contemporary (Keith-Lucas, 1957) covered very similar ground, adding, significantly, 'the idea of movement', focusing on the need to achieve some momentum for positive change. Another way of expressing this is the 'therapeutic imperative', the purposeful, positive and change-focused work of social work, as distinct from social care. The undue emphasis on assessment across social care service, without the follow-through of direct help by the social worker, can dominate how social workers are often deployed – it can lead to a failure to develop or maintain relationship-based and change orientated practice. Confident, change-focused social workers do more than screen, categorise and ration: 'Organisational life must be reconfigured to enable social workers to have the time, knowledge, skills and confidence to work creatively and freely with children and parents' (Stevenson, 2013, p 80). The same applies across all specialisms.

Followership

Followership can be seen as a necessary corollary of leadership, the leaders and the led. However, this dyad can ignore the context, and more importantly, can deny the authority, power and capability of the people leaders claim to lead. Kelley (1988, p 8) described qualities of 'effective followers' as:

> The ability to self manage
> Commitment to the goals of the organisation
> Competence, including the pursuit of knowledge and improving their own skills
> Courage, in upholding standards
> Challenging incompetent or dishonest leaders.

This is a potential clarion call for social work, exercising caution in ensuring 'the goals of the organisation' accurately accord with the function and objectives of social work, albeit over 25 years old!

The risk to social work lies in the potential differences between the goals of an employing organisation, focused on performance measures, and the goals of social work, with the inherent challenges for change, social justice and empowerment. Local government has been an uncomfortable location for social work, both in terms of respect for its objectives and recognition of the investment needed in skill and knowledge development. Looking at the dimensions of whether the follower is a critical thinker or not, and whether they are active or passive, five follower types are described by Kelley (1998, p 11):

- The Sheep, who are passive, who require external motivation and constant supervision from their leader.
- The Yes People, who are conformist, unquestioning and committed to the cause.
- The Pragmatists, who work in the background, not trail blazers, committed but not independent thinkers.
- The Alienated, who are negative and critical of both the leaders and the group.
- The Star Followers, who are active, positive, not blind followers, and who succeed without the presence of a leader.

Kellerman (2012) challenges the lack of a significant interest in what makes or defines a follower, and what she calls the leadership 'industry' which, despite her being very much a part of it, she sees of unproven value. She defines followers within the web-like relationship of leaders, context and followers, as subordinates who have less power, authority and influence than leaders. This 'web' is distinct from the 'dyad' of the leader and the led. Looking at the engagement of followers with their work and with their leaders, she distinguishes five levels:

> Isolates, who do not respond to or care about their leaders.
>
> Bystanders, who have some limited commitment but stand aside and do not engage with their leaders or team.
>
> Participants, who are involved, either positively or in opposition to their leaders.
>
> Activists, who have strong positive, or negative, feelings about their leaders and act upon these and are actively engaged with both colleagues and process.
>
> Diehards, who are prepared to either die for their leader or aspire to displace them. (Kellerman, 2012)

These descriptions of engagement show how leaders can be ignored or marginalised, how followers may be subordinate, but have a degree of power, the opportunity for some authority and the potential for influence. The title of Kellerman's book, *The end of leadership*, shares words from *The end of history and the last man* (Fukuyama, 1992) which predicted that history is ending with the steady growth of liberal democracies leading to an eventual end of historic conflicts. This thesis of the coming of a post-historical age has also been considered in the context of the cooling of conflict in Ireland (Jackson, 1999). These optimistic analyses of recent history, with the arguable lessening of historic conflicts, can ignore new influences and new sources of contest and struggles. Equally they can underestimate the capacity of old enmities and struggles to re-emerge and endure. Nevertheless, there remains the opportunity to remember history as such, to build on wisdom learned, and to move forward.

The end of leadership has not come for social work. The external drivers remain powerful, performance management through indicators rather than practice standards, government-designed and binding practice guidance and a government Social Work Reform Board (2010, 2012) in England with government-commissioned reviews of social work education (Croisdale-Appleby, 2014; Narey, 2014). Partnerships between employers and universities are not universal, and professional organisations are not included. The limited literature on followership is illuminating in demonstrating the similarities with positive leadership. The expectations are high, for example, courageous followers 'do not expect the leader or the organisation to provide for their security and growth, or to give them permission to act' (Chaleff, 2009, p 6). The focus on leadership in public services, and in particular in social services, education and health, can be centred on the leader, to the exclusion of leadership by the subordinates who actually provide the service through their own practice, through competence and skill, knowledge and critical appraisal, energy and ownership of their own development.

Rising above the bombardment of 'the case'

The scale of referrals to social care, and social work in particular, can not only blunt the sensitivity of the individual worker, but can also invite systems of workload management which are antithetical to effective practice. While the technologies and working methods of call centres can be helpful for straightforward inquiries, requests for information and signposting, they can be blunt instruments for sifting out those whose circumstances require social work intervention. Equally, they can facilitate the emotional distancing caused by overwhelming demand and formulaic expectations of practice. Camila Batmanghelidjh, who leads a charity for children in London, Kids Company, has enormous empathy for the local authority social workers she sees missing what her young people need from them (Batmanghelidjh, 2007). She sees child protection referrals turned into 'concerns', as if somehow using a softer word or classification insulates the social work service from the seriousness and the suffering.

The solution to demand cannot, in the current climate, be to seek more social workers, but to use their skills to better effect. This requires clarity on what interventions are effective, how these can be accessed, and how social workers can work alongside these, rather than blindly referring on or delegating work. To continue mass screening through assessments leading to few accessing services, raising eligibility criteria, invites the referers to give up calling, to raise the stakes, or to make the referral anyway and to walk away. Social work underestimates the contribution it can make in helping colleagues explore, understand and directly help complex and risky situations. Working with universal services in a mode of consultation and advice does not mean inviting more referrals in; it enables more situations to be 'held' within those services, and also enables those services to be more effective in their own terms. This demands confidence and credibility, attributes in social workers that are not always welcomed in the workplace, which requires them to process systems, not to display or develop practice wisdom. These are certainly part of the leadership skills social workers require early in their career, and call for recognition of the value of work beyond the individual case.

The re-emergence of interest in community-focused practice and co-production of community resources in adult services could be positive, if the space can be cleared and efficacy assured. In the hard-nosed climate of research in health services that compete for the same resources in services for adults, rigour is required (Huxley et al, 2012b) to help avoid this being a passing phase or fashion in social work (Barclay, 1982; Hadley and McGrath, 1984). The essence of a community-orientated approach is the recognition of the potential resources available within communities, universal services and families. It is an aspiration that social work has the capacity and energy to foster, to enhance and, if necessary, to build these resources, mobilising them for the benefit of isolated, excluded and marginalised people who form the majority of social work's clientele. These resources, by their very nature, rebuild social networks and social participation; they have the capacity to improve quality of life and a sense of wellbeing as well as being sources of direct formal and informal help. It was notable that during the early years of UK Labour government from 1997 to 2010 there was a substantial investment in urban regeneration, such as the New Deal for Communities (Batty et al, 2010), with a significant economic regeneration remit. This was marked with a strong community partnership ethos, and had three people-related outcomes – on education, health and worklessness. They were judged to be successful in these terms, but the links to mainstream social care were weak, and the growing focus on providing or funding services for those in greatest need was difficult to moderate with preventative, medium-term positive improvements for whole populations. For social work to re-engage and work positively with communities, this may yield dividends if skills are renewed and time can be found to invest.

It requires lifting the horizon of practice above the individual case or the incident that triggers a referral. Each social worker engaged in community-focused work needs to be ready to demonstrate the benefits of that investment, or risks finding themselves having been diverted into an area of work that is not valued or cannot be shown to be effective.

Self-leadership of professional development

For social work, the domination of a culture of procedure-driven process, with very limited recognition of judgement and evidence from practice, and a focus on general management, remains a persistent challenge. It is a conflict now so longstanding that it could be considered part of the enduring history, no end or resolution in sight. The adaptive engagement required is the development of practice expertise and confidence in practice combined with assured and assertive behaviours. While the so-called leadership development activities supported and organised by employers focus on what is essentially an administrative and managerial agenda, there is both the responsibility and opportunities in direct practice, leading practice, teaching and in research, to continue to build and expound at every opportunity, practice wisdom and evidence-informed practice. This, coupled with an internalised ownership of the benefits of high-quality reflective supervision and objectively validated continuous professional development, requires a determination to both receive and to deliver. While these standards are allocated to employers or employer organisations in England, even though woefully and inadequately upheld (Wiseman and Davies, 2013), and sometimes pursued by inspectors and regulators, they can be treated as external, to be ignored at will, by isolates, bystanders and passive participants. When they become intrinsic to the social work identity, internalised and demanded as rights, required in order to provide a good service, they cease to be an imposition, or a benefit to be conferred by employers at their will. Followers, who seek to go faster than those who hold leadership positions as managers, have real authority through their capability, competence, skills in practice and research awareness. One of the potential hindrances of the *Professional capabilities framework* (Social Work Reform Board, 2010; College of Social Work, 2013b) is that progression is to be assessed and overseen by employers. There *is* the opportunity to grasp, to sustain and rebuild the network of post-qualifying awards, accessed by social workers, through support from their employers if they are willing, and through individual initiative and investment, which are objectively validated with higher education academic credits. The advantages of this approach are that it gives each social worker the opportunity to progress their own professional development without the restraints or sanction of individual managers, employer interest or their current post position in their levels on the capabilities framework.

It gives and builds capacity for practitioners, and their supervisors, to participate in research and evaluation of both practice and services (Shaw and Norton, 2007). The involvement of both the post-qualifying award candidate and their supervisor gives two higher-level university experiences for the price of one. The benefits of fastening post-qualifying development to university assessments, as well as of practice, are the enduring value of such education and development through external validation, the portability throughout career, credibility beyond an individual employer, credibility beyond the profession, and the opportunity to achieve higher degrees through a modular route. Finally, it binds the service to education and to the access of the latest research knowledge *and* it binds the universities to the latest service needs and current demands in social work practice. These awards, originally validated by professional associations, later by CCETSW and subsequently by the GSCC, benefited from sporadic government grants, although a substantial proportion of post-qualifying awards were achieved through candidates funding themselves and using their own time as part of their personal ownership of their professional development and professional identity. Whatever the funding source, these awards require the personal commitment by social workers of energy and their own time. Developing advanced practitioners requires investment, and if it is to be linked to evidence-informed practice, an emphasis on research skills and research evaluation is required (Webber, 2013). Employers and individual managers may not have the money or the interest in the professional development of enthusiastic social workers, ambitious to learn and to enhance their practice skills, but they can, with some flexibility, as part of their own ambitions for the leadership of social work, support post-qualifying awards. The benefits for the service of an influx of the most up-to-date research, the presence of thoughtfulness, critical reflection and reflexivity, intellectual stimulation, hunger for new ways of working, and the long-term asset of a knowledgeable, analytical, thoughtful, articulate and confident social worker are immense. These enduring benefits outweigh those from 'sheep-dip' short courses with no validation of learning or transfer to specific social work practice expertise.

Building learning into the service organisation as an integral part of ordinary work, valued as a necessary part of assuring good and improving services, requires the personal engagement of senior managers, in terms of interest, commitment of finance and staff time, and above all, respecting the benefits of learning. Equally, or even more important, is the personal commitment and personal investment of each and every social worker to focus on their own continuing professional development and for those with responsibilities as supervisors. It is too important to be dependent on specially allocated funds; it is integral to the identity and values of social work. The challenges for social work, placed within a far larger workforce of social care staff and an even larger milieu of multi-agency and multi-disciplinary working, are balancing the benefits of shared learning with the specific learning, development of practice skills and knowledge requisite for social work. The context of local government will often drive a focus on corporate performance and collaboration, leaving specific service learning to the service or individual professions or professionals. While most learning and development resources are managed centrally at a corporate level in local government in England, with the exception of shared inter-agency training for safeguarding children and adults, the specific needs of social work can be lost. Avowedly 'learning organisations' can be overwhelmed or overshadowed: 'Power relationships in organisations are a major threat to the democratic and participative approach required for the learning organisation' (Gould and Baldwin, 2004, p 172). Social work within local government has both benefited and been restrained by specific government grants for training and professional development. This funding has enabled a degree of ring-fencing and protection, despite local government's longstanding resistance to restraints on how it spends money allocated by central government. However, it is always short-term, sporadic and driven by current or recent central government priorities or initiatives, and often channelled through third party employer organisations. It is also complex to access for organisations that employ social workers outside local government. Welcome though this national funding is, coming from an external source it lifts the sense of responsibility for social work professional development from the individual social worker, from the employer, and from the social work profession.

Returning to the internalisation of continuous learning and development, including active reflective supervision, these become part of ordinary working, part of the routine, a way of life. The ways of accessing these include maintaining regular reading of research and practice development in journals, knowledge websites and university libraries. Bringing this knowledge and the attendant critical reflection into practice, citing research in case discussions, formal reports, team discussions and sharing reading are all activities of the leadership of practice carried out by all, not the exclusive domain of managers, supervisors and educators. They are the imperatives of practice, not the responsibility of managers.

Shifting and taking responsibility for leadership

Recognising and owning leadership as an integral part of all social work endeavour is a challenge to the culture of local government which is essentially hierarchical and reluctant to accept another profession into a designated position of authority. It is antithetical to the managerialist culture (Ayre and Preston-Shoot, 2010), which requires great courage, confidence and ultimately competence to combat. It is ironic that as social work became an all-graduate profession, practice was becoming progressively circumscribed by procedure and process. Equally, despite all the efforts and enthusiasm behind the Social Work Task Force, university post-qualifying awards are now excluded from national policy, and a widespread aspiration for qualification at Master's level and a first year after qualification prior to full registration have been lost. All is suggestive, if not indicative, of a government and employer preference for a less ambitious, less well-prepared, less assertive and less authoritative social work workforce:

> It sometimes seems to me that we are caught up in a dreadful whirlpool of happenings, crises and instant communication; this includes, but goes far beyond, our own share of child care alarms and excursions. There is a loss of collective wisdom, of a sense of continuity which

gives us a framework to understand current behaviour.
(Stevenson, 2013, p 97)

In retrospect, the enormous investment in social work reforms in England from 2008 to 2013 can be seen to have been largely spent in re-learning lessons from the past, and failing to begin to address the restrictions on social work practice and learning. A greater sense of continuity and respect was required for the experience of social work practice and learning, which had started in universities over a hundred years before. For the future, self-leadership, both in practice and from within each social worker, is required to militate against change being led by managers and governments, and by organisations whose future will be challenged by more capable, confident and assertive social workers.

Casting experienced and senior social workers as executives in the capabilities framework suggests separation, and potentially feeds any latent sense of self-importance that is 'the enemy of collegiality' (Grundy, 2011, p 74). The isolation within hierarchies and the separation, even to a group of similarly ranked peers, segregates from shared learning, shared reflection and critical analysis, identity becoming fixed by titular position, rather than values, skills and an enduring vocation. The distancing of titular leaders and strategic managers from their own identity as social workers, while to an extent understandable if they have responsibilities for wider services, for example, integrated services for children and families or for adult social care and provision integrated with health, denies the opportunity for modelling professional practice, and disclaims the respect to be accorded to any profession to be represented at a senior level. In avowing and retaining active membership of their professional status, the manager social worker is showing solidarity with fellow social workers, and showing respect for other occupations that they manage. By holding fast to and retaining their knowledge, skills and research awareness, constantly updating and refreshing these, they are equipped to lead and work *with* their colleagues, rather than becoming administrators and managers of an organisation. It may be harder to retain a rights-based perspective across the full range of work, in direct practice, service development and in policy advocacy and in activism. Public sector priorities will not always align with social work values or even what works best. This deserves and requires open questioning and debate. Policies, priorities and statutory guidance are open to discourse and challenge. Creative implementation can nuance otherwise rigid central edicts to accommodate complexity and social justice. It can be a mechanism for avoiding the dual loyalty that social work inevitably has to hold at a personal and community level:

> We need to be strategic as social workers – a combination of heart and mind. Above all we must remain idealistic and creative and impart the social change quest to practitioners who are caught up in micro-practice and the mundanity of bureaucratic procedure. (Briskman, 2013, p 62)

Social worker managers remain active practitioners, although many may not recognise or acknowledge this. They deputise for those they supervise, co-working complex and difficult cases, chairing and leading case conferences and reviews, and making case decisions. In addition, their professional, reflective supervision and shared critical analysis within supervision necessitates a continuing expertise and knowledge and high levels of skills as educators. Consequently their own development and the enhancement of these requires continuous activity, over and above any development they may need as a manager. The lacuna in much of the leadership literature, particularly in social care, in both the adult and the children and families fields, is any emphasis on practice knowledge or anything specific to the content or efficacy of services. Values, principles and personal qualities (The National Skills Academy Social Care and DH, 2013) are important, and are self-evidently universal human qualities to be valued and enhanced if possible. Ensuring service quality, personalised care and support, addressing risk and safety, collaboration and partnership working, co-production and building capacity are universal managerial activities, not unique to social care or social work. These fail to address practice skills and current research on 'what works'. For the energetic, enthusiastic social worker who retains and regularly enhances their practice skills and research awareness this may not matter, because they are doing this for themselves. For those who are not, leadership is a term being used for generic, general management or administration.

The confidence and assuredness for self-leadership (Manttz and Neck, 2009) can be captured in the concept of self-efficacy, a belief in one's own ability to succeed, to view challenges as something to be conquered rather than avoided, and in one's own power to affect situations (Bandura, 1992). The top five traits of leadership identified by Kouzes and Posner (2002) are being honest, inspiring, forward looking, competent and intelligent, all desirable and requisites for effective social work. No social worker should feel they cannot own and demonstrate these qualities. No human being would not aspire to these. It rather blows the myth of leadership being an activity, a set of skills or attributes reserved for people in titular positions. The discomfort of the organisational working environment and the emotional impact of the pain and disadvantage faced by many of the people who are receiving the service is challenging. It is important to recognise the origin of these challenges, to address them as such, and not locate them as personal failing or lack of capability. Internal resilience (Pransky and McMillen, 2013) or emotional resilience is strength-based, focusing on the potential for all to enhance and develop these qualities.

What to do and what to change

Social work can take its own lead – we cannot delegate it upwards or leave it to organisations. A research-aware social worker who demonstrably uses this knowledge and these insights explicitly in their day-to-day practice, in case recording, reports and in discussions at case conferences and panels, will not only be more effective, but also more credible and able to lead within their peer groups, teams and services. Equally, personally investing in progressive, validated professional development, post-registration training and learning ensures both individually and collectively that the quantum changes required can be made, both in the quality and effectiveness of the service provided and in filling the current vacuum in leadership.

Current opportunities for leadership in social work and the leadership skills and approaches required for social work practice lie firmly within the ambit and personal responsibility of each and every member of the profession. Concentrated attention to the energetic development of practice as well as analysis skills and knowledge, with an emphasis on learning and developing leadership qualities and capabilities, make social work practice more authoritative and more effective. A passive social worker who approaches their work as a bureaucrat, procedure and process-driven, with no hunger to refresh and renew their therapeutic skills and research knowledge, will achieve little, and will have scant respect from their employers, and most important of all, from the people with whom they work. A respected and valued professional takes responsibility for their own progressive and validated continuing professional development in which they personally invest, whether or not their employer or manager shares that interest. Social workers in senior management and designated leadership positions can own and demonstrate their professional responsibilities in grounding service design in knowledge of research-based effective practice, and in ensuring good reflective supervision and progressive professional development are in place. In acknowledging and demonstrating their own use of their professional skills and knowledge when making decisions on individual cases, as opposed to presenting these as management decisions, they have a critical role in building, modelling and promoting effective social work practice.

There can be no leadership without a confident and clearly articulated account of what is being done, what is aimed to be achieved, an explicit evidence base for interventions, and making a specialist, expert contribution in multi-disciplinary and multi-agency work. Any vagueness or lack of clarity demonstrates an absence of an ambition to be a professional or to be a member of a profession. Ultimately it profoundly denigrates what each social worker brings to their work and to the whole services in which they work. It belittles the people who they claim to serve, denying them clarity on what is being offered, and denies the complexity and scale of their needs.

References

Ahmad, B. (1990) *Black perspectives in social work*, Birmingham: Venture Press.

Armstrong, D. (2007) 'Professionalism, indeterminacy and the evidence-based medicine project', *BioSocieties*, no 2, pp 73-84, London: London School of Economics and Political Science.

Ash, A. (2013) 'A cognitive mask? Camouflaging dilemmas in street-level policy implementation to safeguard older people from abuse', *British Journal of Social Work*, vol 43, no 1, pp 99-115.

Asquith, S., Clark, C. and Waterhouse, L. (2005) *The role of the social worker in the 21st century: A literature review*, Insight Report 25, Edinburgh: Scottish Executive Education Department.

ASW (Association of Social Workers) (1966) *New thinking about administration*, London: ASW.

Atwal, A. and Caldwell, K. (2005) 'Do all health and social care professionals interact equally?', *Scandinavian Journal of Caring Science*, vol 19, no 3, pp 268-73.

Audit Commission (2012) *Reducing the cost of assessments and reviews*, London: Audit Commission.

Ayre, P. and Calder, M. (2010) 'The de-professionalisation of child protection: regaining our bearings', in P. Ayre and M. Preston-Shoot (eds) *Children's services at the crossroads: A critical evaluation of contemporary policy for practice*, Lyme Regis: Russell House Publishing.

Ayre, P. and Preston-Shoot, M. (eds) (2010) *Children's services at the crossroads: A critical evaluation of contemporary policy for practice*, Lyme Regis: Russell House Publishing.

Bandura, A. (1992) 'Exercise of personal agency through the self-efficacy mechanisms', in R. Schwarzer (ed) *Self-efficacy: Thought control of action,* Washington, DC: Hemisphere.

Barclay, P. (1982) *Social workers: Their roles and tasks*, London: Bedford Square Press.

Barker, C., Martin, B. and Zournazi, M. (2008) 'Emotional self-management for activists', *Reflective Practice*, vol 9, no 4, pp 423-35.

Barry, M. (2007) *Risk assessments in social work: An international literature review*, Edinburgh: Scottish Executive Social Research.

Barth, R., Lee, B., Lindsey, M., Collins, K., Strieder, F., Chorpita, B., Becker, K. and Sparks, J. (2012) 'Evidence-based practice at a crossroads: the timely emergence of common elements and common factors', *Research on Social Work Practice*, vol 22, pp 109-19.

Bass, B. and Alvilio, B. (1994) *Improving organisational effectiveness through transformational leadership*, London: Sage.

BASW (British Association of Social Workers) (2012) *Code of ethics for social work*, Birmingham: BASW.

Batmanghelidjh, C. (2007) *Shattered lives: Children who live with courage and dignity*, London: Jessica Kingsley Publishers.

Batty, E., Beatty, C., Foden, M., Lawless, P., Pearson, S. and Wilson, I. (2010) *The New Deal for Communities experience: A final assessment*, Sheffield and London: Sheffield Hallam University and Department for Communities and Local Government.

Bazalgette, L., Hahn, B. and Morris, M. (2012) *Ageing across Europe*, London: Women's Royal Voluntary Service.

Becket, F. (2010) *What did the baby boomers ever do for us?*, London: Biteback Publishing.

Beddoe, L., Davys, A. and Adamson, C. (2014) 'Never trust anyone who says "I don't need supervision": practitioners' beliefs about social worker resilience', *Practice: Social Work in Action*, vol 26, no 26, April, pp 113-30.

Bennett, N., Wise, C., Woods, P. and Harvey, J. (2003) *Distributed leadership: A review of literature*, Nottingham: National College for School Leadership.

Bennis, W. (1989) *On becoming a leader*, New York: Basic Books.

Beresford, P., Fleming, J., Glynn, M., Bewley, C., Croft, S., Branfield, F. and Postle, K. (2011) *Supporting people: Towards a person-centred approach*, Bristol: Policy Press.

Biesteck, F. (1957) *The casework relationship*, Chicago, IL: Loyola University Press.

Bilton, K. (2010) *The proposed college of social work: Some historical reflections*, London: Social Work History Network.

Birch, S. (1976) *Working party on manpower and training for the social services*, London: HMSO.

Black, J. (2002) *Decentring regulation: Developing strategies of self-regulation*, Oxford: Oxford University Press.

Blewett, J. and Boaz, A. (2010) 'Providing objective, impartial evidence for decision making: public accountability', in K. Briar-Lawson, J. Orme, R. Ruckdeschel and I. Shaw (eds) *The Sage book of social work research*, London: Sage.

Boddy, J. and Statham, J. (2009) *European perspectives on social work: Models of education and professional roles*, London: Thomas Coram Research Unit.

Borrego, M. and Newswander, L. (2008) 'Characteristics of successful cross-disciplinary engineering education collaboration', *Journal of Engineering Education*, vol 97, no 1, pp 123-34.

Boyatzis, R.E. and McKee, A. (2005) *Resonant leadership: Renewing yourself and connecting with others through mindfulness, hope, and compassion*, Boston, MA: Harvard Business School Press.

Bowyer, S. (2008) *Multi-professional working: Distinct professional identities in multi-professional teams*, Dartington: Research in Practice.

Bradford, D. and Cohen, A. (2008) *Power up: Transforming organisations through shared leadership*, New York: John Wiley.

Brand, D., Reith, T. and Statham, D. (2005) 'The need for social work intervention: A discussion paper for the 21st century', *Social Work Review*, Edinburgh: Scottish Executive.

Brandon, D. and Jordan, B. (1979) *Creative social work*, Oxford: Blackwell.

Brandon, M., Bedderson, P., Warren, C., Howe, D., Gardner, R., Dodsworth, J. and Black, J. (2008) *Analysing child deaths and serious injury through abuse or neglect: What can we learn? Biennial analysis of serious case reviews 2003-05*, Research Briefing, DCSF RR03, London: Department for Education.

Brandon, M., Sidebotham, P., Bailey, S., Belderson, P., Hawley, C., Ellis, C. and Megson, M. (2012*) New learning from serious case reviews: A two year report for 2009-2011*, London: Department for Education.

Brewer, C. and Lait, J. (1980) *Can social work survive?*, London: Temple Smith.

Brilliant, E. (1986) 'Social work leadership: a missing ingredient?', *Social Work*, September-October, pp 325-31.

Briskman, L. (2013) 'Courageous ethnographers or agents of the state: challenges for social work', *Critical and Radical Social Work*, vol 1, no 3, pp 51-66.

Brown, G. and Harris, T. (1978) *Social origins of depression: A study of psychiatric disorder in women*, London: Tavistock.

Burnham, D. (2011) 'Selective memory: a note on social work historiography', *British Journal of Social Work*, vol 41, no 1, pp 5-21.

Burnham, D. (2012) *The social worker speaks*, Aldershot: Ashgate.

Burnham, J. (1941) *The managerial revolution*, New York: John Day.

Cambridge Education and Children's Workforce Development Council (2009) *Report on findings from initial employer support visits – Newly qualified social workers pilot programme*, Leeds: Cambridge Education and Children's Workforce Development Council.

Cameron, A., Lart, R., Bostock, L. and Coomber, C. (2012) *Factors that promote and hinder joint and integrated working between health and social care services*, London: Social Care Institute for Excellence.

Cameron, A., Lart, R., Bostock, L. and Coomber, C. (2014) 'Factors that promote and hinder joint and integrated working between health and social care services: a review of research literature', *Health and Social Care in the Community*, vol 22, no 3, pp 225-33.

Carpenter, J., Patsios, D., Wood, M., Platt, D., Shardlow, S., Scholar, H., Haines, C., Wong, C. and Blewett, J. (2012) *Newly Qualified Social Worker programme: Final evaluation report (2008-2011)*, London: Department for Education.

Carr, S. (2008) *Personalisation: A rough guide,* London: SCIE.

CCETSW (Central Council for Education and Training in Social Work) (1995) *Assuring quality in the Diploma in Social Work: Rules and requirements for the Diploma in Social Work*, London: CCETSW.

Chaleff, I. (2009) *The courageous follower: Standing up to and for our leaders*, San Francisco, CA: Berrett-Koehler.

Chamberlain, C. and Ward, D. (2013) *Looked-after children in London: An analysis of changes in the numbers of looked-after children in London*, London: London Councils.

Changing Lives User and Carers Forum (2008) *Principles and standards of citizenship leadership*, Edinburgh: Scottish Government.

Chartered Society of Physiotherapy, RCSLT (Royal College of Speech and Language Therapists), BDA (British Dietetic Association) and RCN (Royal College of Nursing) (2006) *Supervision, accountability and delegation of activities: A guide for registered practitioners and support workers*, London: Chartered Society of Physiotherapy, RCSLT, BDA and RCN.

Children's Commissioner for England (2009) *Children and young people's views on safeguarding: Research findings*, London: Children's Commissioner for England.

Clarke, J. and Newman, J. (1997) *The managerial state*, London: Sage.

Coats, D. and Passmore, E. (2008) *Public value: The next steps in public service reform*, London: Work Foundation.

Cole, C. (1846) 'The strength of tyranny', *The Northern Star and National Trades Journal*, 9 May.

College of Social Work (2012) *The business case for social work with adults: A discussion paper*, London: College of Social Work.

College of Social Work (2013a) *Roles and tasks requiring social workers*, Advice Note, London: College of Social Work.

College of Social Work (2013b) *Professional capabilities framework*, London: College of Social Work.

College of Social Work (2014) *Roles and functions of social workers in England*, Advice Note, London: College of Social Work.

College of Social Work, Nirmala Niketan Institute, University of Mumbai (2013) www.cswnn.edu.in

Commission on the Future Funding of Health and Social Care in England (2014) *A new settlement for health and social care*, London: The King's Fund.

Conservative Party (2010) *Invitation to join the government of Britain,* London: Conservative Party.

Cousins, C. (1987) *Controlling social welfare*, Brighton: Wheatsheaf.

Cree, V. (ed) (2003) *Becoming a social worker*, London: Routledge.

Croisdale-Appleby, D. (2014) *Re-visioning social work education: An independent review*, London: Department of Health.

Crompton, R. (1927) *William in trouble*, London: Newnes.

Cullen, A. (2012) '"Leaders in our own lives": suggested implications for social work leadership from a study of social work practice in a palliative care setting', *British Journal of Social Work*, vol 43, no 8, pp 1527-44.

Cutler, T. and Waine, B. (1997) *Managing the welfare state*, Oxford: Berg.

Darzi, A. (2008) *High quality care for all: NHS next stage review: Final report*, London: Department of Health.

Davies, B. and Challis, D. (1986) *Matching needs to resources*, Aldershot: Gower.

Davies, M. (1994) *The essential social work: An introduction to professional practice in the 1990s*, Aldershot: Ashgate.

DCSF (Department for Children, Schools and Families) (2003) *Every child matters*, London: DCSF.

Department for Children, Schools and Families and Department of Health (2009) *Letter of invitation for College of Social Work, First Steps meeting*, 11 December 2009.

Derber, C. (1983) 'Managing professionals: ideological proletarianization and post-industrial labor', *Theory and Society*, vol 12, no 3, pp 309-41.

DfE (Department for Education) (2011a) *Social work standards for employers and supervision framework*, London: DfE.

DfE (2011b) *An action plan for adoption: Tackling delay*, London: DfE.

DfE (2013) *Working together to safeguard children: A guide to interagency working to safeguard and promote the welfare of children*, London: DfE.

DfE (2014a) *Characteristics of children in need in England, 2013–14*, London: DfE.

DfE (2014b) *Knowledge and skills for child and family social work*, London:DfE.

DfE (2014c) *Consultation on knowledge and skills for child and family social workers, Government response*, London, DfE.

DH (Department of Health) (1969) *Report of the Committee of Inquiry, Ely Hospital*, Cmnd 3975, London: HMSO.

DH (1971) *Report of the Committee of Inquiry, Farleigh Hospital,* Cmnd 4757, London, HMSO.

DH (1974) *Report of the Committee of Inquiry, South Ockendon Hospital*, London, HMSO.

DH (1978) *Report of the Committee of Inquiry, Normansfield Hospital*, Cmnd 7357, London: HMSO.

DH (1990) *Community care in the next decade and beyond: Policy guidance*, London: DH.

DH (2002) *Requirements for social work training*, London: DH.

DH (2008) *Transforming adult social care*, LAC(DH)(2008)1, London: DH.

DH (2012) *Transforming care: A national response to Winterbourne Hospital, Department of Health review final report,* London: DH.

DH (2013) *Winterborne View: transforming care one year on,* London, DH.

DH (2014) *Adult social care outcomes framework 2014/15*, London: DH.

DH and DCSF (2009) *Facing up to the task: The interim report of the Social Work Task Force,* London: DH and DCSF.

DHSSPS (Department of Health, Social Services and Personal Safety) (2011) *Transforming your care: A review of health and social care in Northern Ireland*, Belfast: DHSSPS.

Dillow, C. (2007) *The end of politics: New Labour and the folly of managerialism*, Petersfield: Harriman House.

Dilnot, A. (2011) *Commission on funding of care and support: Fairer care funding*, London: Department of Health.

Donnellan, H. and Jack, G. (2010) *The survival guide for newly qualified child and family social workers: Hitting the ground running*, London: Jessica Kingsley

Donzelot, J. (1997) *The policing of families*, London: Hutchinson.

Dolman, E. and Bond, D. (2011) 'Mindful leadership', *The Ashridge Journal*, Spring, pp 36-43.

Dworkin, R. (1997) *Taking rights seriously*, Cambridge, MA: Duckworth Press.

Ellis, K. (2007) 'Direct payments and social work practice: the significance of "street-level bureaucracy" in determining eligibility', *British Journal of Social Work*, vol 37, no 3, pp 405-22.

Emilsson, U.M. (2013) 'The role of social work in cross-professional teamwork: examples from an older people's team in England', *British Journal of Social Work*, vol 43, no 1, pp 116-34.

Evans, T. and Harris, J. (2004) 'Street-level bureaucracy, social work and the (exaggerated) death of discretion', *British Journal of Social Work*, vol 34, no 6, pp 871-95.

Fairhurst, G. (2007) *Discursive leadership: In conversation with leadership psychology*, Thousand Oaks, CA: Sage.

Farmer, E. and Lutman, E. (2012) *Effective working with neglected children and their families: Linking interventions to long-term outcomes*, London: Jessica Kingsley Publishers.

Farmer, E. and Wijedasa, D. (2013) 'The re-unification of looked-after children with their parents: what contributes to return stability', *British Journal of Social Work*, vol 43, no 8, pp 1611-29.

Fauth, R., Jelicic, H., Hart, D., Burton, S. and Shemmings, D. (2010) *Effective practice to protect children living in 'highly resistant' families*, London: Centre for Excellence and Outcomes in Children and Young People's Services.

Featherstone, B., White, S. and Morris, K. (2014) *Re-imagining child protection: Towards humane social work with families*, Bristol: Policy Press.

Ferguson, H. (2011) *Child protection practice*, London: Palgrave Macmillan.

Ferguson, H. (2014) 'What social workers do in performing child protection work: evidence from research into face-to-face practice', *Child and Family Social Work*, March.

Ferguson, I. (2007) 'Increasing user choice or privatizing risk: the antinomies of personalisation', *British Journal of Social Work*, vol 37, no 3, pp 387-403.

Ferguson, I. (2008) *Reclaiming social work, challenging neo-liberalism and promoting social justice*, London: Sage.

Ferguson, I. and Woodward, R. (2009) *Radical social work in practice: Making a difference*, Bristol: Policy Press.

Flynn, M. (1992) 'We can change the future: self and citizen advocacy', in S. Segal and V. Varma (eds) *Prospects for people with learning difficulties*, London: David Fulton.

Flynn, M. (2012) *Winterbourne View: A serious case review*, Thornbury: South Gloucestershire Safeguarding Adults Board.

Folgheraiter, F. (2012) *The mystery of social work,* Trento, Italy: Erickson.

Forrester, D. and Harwin, J. (2011) *Parents who misuse drugs and alcohol: Effective interventions in social work and child protection*, Chichester: Wiley & Sons Ltd.

Fukuyama, F. (1992) *The end of history and the last man*, London: Hamish Hamilton.

Galpin, D., Bigmore, J. and Parker, J. (2012) *The survival guide for newly qualified social workers in adult and mental health services*, London: Jessica Kingsley Publishers.

Gilbert, P. (2005) *Leadership: Being effective and remaining human*, Lyme Regis: Russell House.

Glasby, J. (2014) 'The controversies of choice and control: why some people might be hostile to English social care reforms', *British Journal of Social Work*, vol 44, no 2, pp 252-66.

Glendinning, C., Jones, K., Baxter, K., Rabiee, P., Curtis, L., Wilde, A., Arksey, H. and Forder, J. (2010) *Home care re-ablement services: Investigating the longer-term impacts (prospective longitudinal study)*, York: Social Policy Research Unit, University of York.

Glastonbury, B., Cooper, D. and Hawkins, P. (1982) *Social work in conflict: The practitioner and the bureaucrat*, Birmingham: British Association of Social Workers.

GMC (General Medical Council) (2009) *Tomorrow's doctors*, London: GMC.

GMC (2012) *Leadership and management for all doctors*, London: GMC.

Godden, J. (2011) *Supervision in social work, with particular reference to supervision practice in multidisciplinary teams*, Birmingham: British Association of Social Workers, College of Social Work.

Goldberg, E. (1967) *The families of schizophrenic patients*, London: National Institute for Social Work Training.

Goleman, D. (1998) *Working with emotional intelligence*, New York: Bantam Books.

Goleman, D. (2000) 'Leadership that gets results', *Harvard Business Review*, Boston, MA: Harvard Business School.

Goodall, A. (2011) 'Physician-leaders and hospital performance: is there an association?', *Social Science & Medicine*, vol 73, no 4, pp 535-9.

Goodall, A. and Pogrebna, G. (2012) *Expert leaders in a fast-moving environment*, Discussion paper 6715, Bonn, Germany: Institute for the Study of Labor (IZA).

Goodman, S. and Trowler, I. (eds) (2011) *Social work reclaimed: Innovative frameworks for child and family social work practice*, London: Jessica Kingsley Publishers.

Gould, N. and Baldwin, M. (eds) (2004) *Social work, critical reflection and the learning organisation*, Aldershot: Ashgate.

Grant, L. and Kinman, G. (2013) 'Bouncing back? Personal representations of resilience of student and experienced social workers', *Practice: Social Work in Action*, vol 25, no 5, pp 349-66.

Greenleaf, R.K. (2002) *Servant leadership: A journey into the nature of legitimate power and greatness*, Mahwah, NJ: Paulist Press.

Griffiths, R. (1988) *Community care: Agenda for action*, London: HMSO.

Grundy, M. (2011) *Leadership and oversight: New models for episcopal oversight*, London: Mowbray.

GSCC (General Social Care Council) (2008) *Statement on the roles and tasks of social workers*, London: GSCC.

Hadley, R. and McGrath, M. (1984) *When social services are local: The Normanton experience*, London: George Allen & Unwin.

Hafford-Letchfield, T., Leonard, K., Begum, N. and Chick, N. (2008) *Leadership and management in social care*, London: Sage.

Halfpenny, N. (2011) 'Discretion and control at the front line: rationalities of practice in child and youth services', PhD, Bentley, WA, Australia: Curtin University of Technology, Faculty of Humanities.

Hall, C., Parton, N., Peckover, S. and White, S. (2010) 'Child-centric information and communications technology (ICT) and the fragmentation of child welfare practice in England', *Journal of Social Policy*, vol 39, no 3, pp 393-413.

Hallett, C. and Stevenson, O. (1980) *Child abuse: Aspects of interprofessional co-operation*, London: George Allen & Unwin.

Halmos, P. (1965) *The faith of the counsellors*, London: Constable

Halmos, P. (1978) *The personal and the political*, London: Hutchinson.

Hamer, M. (2006) *The barefoot helper*, Lyme Regis: Russell House Publishing.

Harkness, D. and Hensley, H. (1991) 'Changing the focus of social work supervision: effects on client satisfaction and generalised contentment', *Social Work*, vol 36, no 6, pp 506-12.

Harris, J. and White, V. (eds) (2009) *Modernising social work: Critical considerations*, Bristol: Policy Press.

Harris, N. (2012) 'Assessment: when does it help and when does it hinder? Parents' experience of the assessment process', *Child and Family Social Work*, vol 17, pp 180-91.

Hatton, C., Waters, J. and Routledge, M. (2013) *National personal budgets survey 2013*, London: Think Local Act Personal.

HCPC (Health and Care Professions Council) (2012a) *Standards of conduct, performance and ethics*, London: HCPC.

HCPC (2012b) *Standards of continuing professional development*, London: HCPC.

Hegel, G. (1977) *Phenomenology of spirit* (translated by A.V. Miller), Oxford: Clarendon Press.

Herod, J. and Lymbury, M. (2002) 'The social work role in multidisciplinary teams', *Practice, Social Work in Action*, vol 14, no 4, pp 17-27.

Hill, C. (1970) *God's Englishman: Oliver Cromwell and the English revolution*, London: Weidenfield & Nicholson.

Hill, C. (1993) *The English Bible and the seventeenth-century revolution*, London: Allen Lane.

Hodson, R. and Cooke, E. (2007) *Leading evidence-informed practice: A handbook*, Dartington: Research in Practice.

Hoggett, P. and Hambleton, R. (1987) *Decentralisation and democracy: Localising public services*, Bristol: School for Advanced Urban Studies, University of Bristol.

Holden, G., Meenaghan, T., Anastas, J. and Metrey, G. (2002) 'Outcomes of social work education: the case for social work self-efficacy', *Journal of Social Work Education*, vol 38, pp 115-33.

Holmes, E., Miscampbell, G. and Robin, B. (2013) *Reforming social work: Improving social worker recruitment, training and retention and child development*, London: Policy Exchange.

Holroyd, J. and Brown, K. (2011) *Leadership and management development for social work and social care*, Bournemouth: Learn to Care.

Honey, P. (2001) *Teams and teamwork*, Maidenhead: Peter Honey Publications.

Honey, P. and Mumford, A. (2000) *The learning styles helpers guide*, Maidenhead: Peter Honey Publications.

Horne, M. and Shirley, T. (2009) *Co-production in public services: A new partnership with citizens*, London: Cabinet Office Strategy Unit.

Host Policy Research (2013) *Concepts to reality: Implementation of the AYSE with social workers in adult services*, Leeds: Skills for Care.

Houghton Committee Report (1972) *Report of the Departmental Committee on the adoption of Children*, London and Edinburgh: Home Office and Scottish Education Department.

House of Commons Education Committee (2011a) Transcript of evidence, The College of Social Work 8 November 2011, (HC 1630-i).

House of Commons Education Committee (2011b) Letter from the Chair Graham Stuart MP to Tim Loughton MP, Parliamentary Under-Secretary of State for Education, 9 November.

House of Commons Education Select Committee (2011) *Correspondence and written evidence on the College of Social Work*, 25 November (www.parliament.uk/education-committee).

HSCIC (Health and Social Care Information Centre) (2014) *Learning disabilities census report – Further analysis*, London: HSCIC.

Huby, G., Warner, P., Harries, J., Donaghy, E., Lee, R., Williams, L., Huxley, P., Evans, S., Baker, C., White, J. and Philpin, S. (2010) *Supporting reconfiguration of social care roles in integrated settings in the UK: A comparative study across three health and social care economies*, Swansea and Edinburgh: University of Swansea and University of Edinburgh.

Hudson, B. (1993) *The busy person's guide to care management*, Sheffield: Joint Unit for Social Services Research, University of Sheffield.

Hugman, R. (1991) *Power in the caring professions*, Basingstoke: Macmillan.

Huxley, P., Baker, C., Madge, S., White, J., Onyett, S. and Gould, N. (2012a) 'The social care component of multidisciplinary mental health teams: a review and national survey', *Journal of Health Services Research & Policy*, vol 17 (Supplement 2), pp 23-9.

Huxley, P., Evans, S., Madge, S., Webber, M., Burchardt, T., McDaid, D. and Knapp, M. (2012b) 'Development of a social inclusion index to capture subjective and objective life domains (Phase II): psychometric development study', *Health Technology Assessment*, vol 16, no 1.

Huzzard, T. and Spoelstra, S. (2011) 'Leaders as gardeners: leadership through facilitating growth', in M. Alvesson and A. Spicer (eds) *Metaphors we lead by: Understanding leadership in the real world*, London: Routledge, pp 76-95.

Ioakimidis, V. (2013) 'Beyond the dichotomies of cultural and political relativism: arguing the case for a social justice-based "global social work" definition', *Critical and Radical Social Work*, vol 1, no 2, pp 183-99.

IFSW (International Federation of Social Workers) (2000) *Global definition of social work*, Berne: IFSW.

IFSW (2014) *Global definition of social work*, Berne: IFSW.

Ingram, R. (2013) 'Locating emotional intelligence at the heart of social work practice', *British Journal of Social Work*, vol 43, no 5, pp 987-1004.

Jackson, A. (1999) *Ireland*, Oxford: Blackwell.

Jay, A. (2014) *Independent inquiry into child sexual exploitation in Rotherham*, Rotherham: Rotherham Metropolitan Council.

Johnson, T. (1972) *Professions and power*, London: Macmillan.

Jones, C. and Pound, L. (2008) *Leadership and management in early years*, Maidenhead: Open University Press.

Jones, C., Ferguson, I., Lavelette, M. and Penketh, L. (2004) *Social work and social justice: A manifesto for a new engaged practice,* Social Work Action Network (SWAN) website: www.socialworkfuture.org

Jones, R. (2012) 'The leadership journey', *The International Journal of Leadership in Public Services*, vol 8, no 2, pp 77-82.

Jordan, B. (1972) *The social work in family situations*, London: Routledge & Kegan Paul.

Jordan, B. (1983) *Invitation to social work*, Oxford: Martin Robertson.

Jordan, B. with Jordan, C. (2000) *Social work and the third way: Tough love as social policy*, London: Sage.

Kadushin, A. (1976) *Supervision in social work*, New York: Columbia University Press.

Kagan, S. and Hallmark, L. (2001) 'Cultivating leadership in early care and education', *Child Care Information Exchange*, vol 140, pp 7–10.

Keith-Lucas, A. (1957) *Some casework concepts for the public welfare worker*, Chapel Hill, NC: University of North Carolina Press.

Kelley, R. (1988) 'In praise of followers', *Harvard Business Review*, vol 66, no 6, pp 142-8.

Kellerman, B. (2012) *The end of leadership*, New York: HarperCollins.

Kemshall, H., Parton, N., Walsh, M. and Waterson, J. (1997) 'Concepts of risk in relation to organizational structure and functioning within the personal social services and probation', *Social Policy & Administration*, vol 31, no 3, pp 213-32.

Kerr, B., Gordon, J., MacDonald, C. and Stalker, K. (2005) *Effective social work with older people*, Edinburgh: Scottish Executive Social Research.

King's Fund, The (2011) *The future of leadership and management in the National Health Service: No more heroes*, London: The King's Fund.

King's Fund, The (2013) *Patient-centred leadership: Rediscovering our purpose*, London: The King's Fund.

Kirkman, E. and Melrose, K. (2014) *Clinical judgements and decision-making in children's social work: An analysis of the 'front door' system*, London: Department for Education.

Kotter, J.P. (1996) *Leading change*, Boston, MA: Harvard Business School Press.

Kouzes, J. and Posner, B. (2002) *The leadership challenge*, San Francisco, CA: Jossey-Bass.

Laming, Lord (2003) *The Victoria Climbié Inquiry: Report of an inquiry by Lord Laming*, Cm 5730, London: HMSO.

Langan, J. and Lindow, V. (2006) *Living with risk: Mental health service users and their involvement in risk assessment and management*, Bristol: Policy Press.

Leadbeater, C. and Lownsbrough, H. (2005) *Personalisation and participation: The future of social care in Scotland*, London: Demos.

Lefevre, M. (2013) 'Becoming effective communicators with children: developing practice capability through social work education', *British Journal of Social Work*, vol 43, no 4, pp 1-21.

Leff, J. (1976) 'Schizophrenia and sensitivity to the family environment', *Schizophrenia Bulletin*, vol 2, no 4, pp 566-74.

Leslie, C. (2013) *Towards a Royal College of Teaching: Raising the status of the profession*, London: Royal College of Surgeons in England.

LGA (Local Government Association) (2013) *Joint Improvement Programme: A framework for individual care reviews*, London: LGA.

LGA (Local Government Association) (2014) *The standards for employers of social workers in England*, London: LGA.

Lipsky, M. (1980) *Street-level bureaucracy: The dilemmas of individuals in public service*, New York: Russell Sage Foundation.

Lister, R. (1998) 'Citizenship on the margins. Citizenship, social work and social action', *European Journal of Social Work*, vol 1, pp 5-18.

Littlechild, B. (2008) 'Social work with involuntary clients in child protection work', in M. Calder (ed) *The carrot or the stick? Towards effective practice with involuntary clients in safeguarding children work*, Lyme Regis: Russell House Publishing, pp 141-51.

Lloyd, J. (2012) *The roadmap: England's choices for the social care crisis*, London: The Strategic Society Centre.

London County Council (1947) *Handbook on mental health social work*, London: Public Health Department, London County Council.

Lorenz, W. (2008) 'Paradigms and politics: understanding methods paradigms in an historical context: the case for social pedagogy', *British Journal of Social Work*, vol 38, no 4, pp 625-44.

Lymbery, M. (2013) 'Reconciling radicalism, relationship and role: priorities for social work with adults in England', *Critical and Radical Social Work*, vol 1, no 2 pp 201-15.

McAuliffe, C. (2009) 'Experiences of social workers within an interdisciplinary team in the intellectual disability sector', *Critical Social Thinking: Policy and Practice*, vol 1, pp 125-43.

McCrae, N., Murray, J., Huxley, P. and Evans, S. (2005) 'The research potential of mental health social workers: a qualitative study of the views of senior mental health service managers', *British Journal of Social Work*, vol 35, no 1, pp 55-71.

McDonald, C. and Chenoweth, L. (2009) 'Leadership: a crucial ingredient in unstable times', *Social Work and Society*, vol 7, no 1 (www.socwork.net/sws/article/viewFile/47/104).

McGregor, K. (2013) 'The state of social work supervision in 2013,' *Community Care,* 18 June.

McKitterick. W. (2008) 'Being constantly suspicious is part of the territory', *The Times,* 13 November.

McKitterick, W. (2012a) *Supervision,* Maidenhead: Open University Press and McGraw-Hill.

McKitterick, W. (2012b) 'Recruiting, retaining and making the best use of social workers in adult social care', *Journal of Social Care and Neurodisability,* vol 3, no 3, pp 116-21.

McKitterick, W. (2012c) *Social care needs and funding issues,* Care Knowledge Special Report 68, Hove: Pavilion.

Macdonald, G. (2001) *Effective interventions in child abuse and neglect: An evidence-based approach to evaluating and planning interventions,* Chichester: John Wiley.

McNeil, F., Batchelor, S., Burnett, R. and Knox, J. (2005) *Reducing re-offending: Key practice skills,* Edinburgh: Social Work Inspection Agency, Glasgow School of Social Work, Scottish Executive.

Maguire, L., Miller, S. and MacDonald, G., (2012) 'Home-based child development interventions for pre-school children from socially disadvantaged families', in T. Long, *Evaluation of the Action for Children UK Neglect Project,* Campbell Systematic Reviews 8, 1, Manchester: University of Salford.

Manthorpe, J. and Martineau, S. (2011) 'Serious case reviews in adult safeguarding in England: an analysis of a sample of reports', *British Journal of Social Work,* vol 41, no 2, pp 224-41.

Manthorpe, J., Goodman, C., Drenna, V., Davies, S., Masey, H., Gage, H., Scott, C., Brearley, S. and Iliffe, S. (2012) 'Nurse-led care management in the NHS: bridging clinical and social worlds', *Primary Health Care Research and Development,* vol 13, no 2, pp 153-64.

Manz, C. and Neck, C. (2009) *Mastering self-leadership: Empowering yourself for personal excellence,* Englewood Cliffs, NJ: Prentice Hall.

Martin, P, (2007) 'The times they are a changing: the challenges facing social work in Northern Ireland', *Child Care in Practice,* vol 13, no 3, pp 261-9.

Marturano, A. and Gosling, J. (eds) (2007) *Leadership: The key concepts,* London: Routledge.

Mattinson, J. (1975) *The reflection process in casework supervision,* London: Institute of Marital Studies, Tavistock Institute of Human Relations.

Meyerson, D. (1995) *Tempered radical: How everyday leaders inspire change at work*, Watertown, MA: Harvard Business Press.

Milburn, N.L., Lynch, M. and Jackson, J. (2008) 'Early identification of mental health needs for children in care: a therapeutic assessment programme for statutory clients of child protection', *Clinical Child Psychology and Psychiatry*, vol 13, no 1, pp 31-47.

Milne, M., Sullivan, M., Tanner, D., Richards, S., Ray, M., Lloyd, L., Beech, C. and Phillips, J. (2014) *Social work with older people: A vision for the future*, Birmingham, Bristol, Uxbridge, Keele, Canterbury, Oxford, Swansea and London: Universities of Birmingham, Bristol, Brunel, Keele, Kent, Oxford Brookes, Swansea and The College of Social Work.

Morley, R. (2007) *The analysand's tale*, London: Karnac.

Morris, P. (1969) *Put away: A sociological study of institutions for the mentally retarded*, London: Routledge & Kegan Paul.

Morrison, T. (2008) 'Emotional intelligence, emotion and social work: characteristics, complications and contribution', *British Journal of Social Work*, vol 38, no 2, pp 245-63.

Morrison, T. (2010) 'The role of the scholar-facilitator in generating practice knowledge to inform and enhance the quality of relationship-based social work practice with children and families', Submission for PhD by publication, University of Huddersfield (eprints.hud.ac.uk).

Munro, E. (2010) *The Munro review of child protection: Part One: A systems analysis*, London: Department for Education.

Munro, E. (2011) *The Munro review of child protection: Final report – A child-centred system*, London: Department for Education.

Narey, M. (2011) *Adoption and Permanence Taskforce report*, London: Department for Education.

Narey, M. (2014) *Making the education of social workers consistently effective*, London: Department of Health.

National Skills Academy for Social Care, The, and DH (Department of Health) (2013) *Leadership starts with me: The why, what and how of leadership in adult social care*, London: The National Skills Academy for Social Care and DH.

Neck, C. and Manz, C. (2013) *Mastering self-leadership: Empowering yourself for personal excellence* (3rd edn), Upper Saddle River, NJ: Prentice-Hall.

Needham, C. and Carr, S. (2009) *Co-production: An emerging evidence base for adult social care*, London: Social Care Institute for Excellence.

Newman, M., Bangpan, M., Brunton, J., Tripney, J., Williams, T., Thieba, A., Lorenc, T., Fletcher, A. and Bazan, C. (2007) *Methods and study characteristics in the Systematic Rapid Evidence Assessment: Interventions to improve the co-ordination of service delivery for high cost high harm household units (HCHHHU)*, London: EPPI-Centre, Social Science Research Unit, Institute of Education, University of London.

Newman, S. (ed) (2009) *Personalisation: Practical thoughts and ideas from people making it happen*, Brighton: Pavilion Publishing.

Newman, T., Moseley, A., Tierney, S. and Ellis, A. (2005) *Evidence-based social work: A guide for the perplexed*, Lyme Regis: Russell House Publishing.

NHS (National Health Service) Institute for Innovation and Improvement and the Academy of Medical Royal Colleges (2009) *Medical leadership competencies framework* (2nd edn), Coventry: NHS Institute for Innovation and Improvement.

NHS Leadership Academy (2014) *Healthcare leadership model*, Leeds: NHS Leadership Academy.

North, M. (1972) *The secular priests: Psychotherapists in contemporary society*, London: Allen & Unwin.

NSPCC (2012) *What can I do? Protecting your child from sexual abuse*, London: NSPCC.

Nuttall, K. (1985) *The place of family therapy in social work: A critical review*, Norwich: University of East Anglia.

Ofsted (Office for Standards in Education, Children's Services and Skills) (2012) *High expectations, high support and high challenge: Protecting children more effectively through better support for front line social work practice*, London: Ofsted.

Okitikpi, T. (ed) (2011) *Social control and the use of power in social work with children and families*, Lyme Regis: Russell House Publishing.

Oliver, D. (2008) '"Acopia" and "social admission" are not diagnoses: why older people deserve better', *Journal of the Royal Society of Medicine*, vol 101, pp 168-74.

Oliver, J., Bridges, K., Huxley, P. and Mohamed, H. (1996) *Quality of life and mental health services*, London: Routledge.

O'Sullivan T. (2005) 'Some theoretical propositions on the nature of practice wisdom', *Journal of Social Work*, vol 5, no 7, pp 221-43.

Page, R. (2007) *Revisiting the welfare state*, Maidenhead: McGraw-Hill and Open University Press.

Parker, G. (2014) *Intermediate care, reablement or something else? A research note about the challenges of defining services*, York: Social Policy Research Unit, University of York.

Parker, M. (2002) *Against management: Organization in the age of managerialism*, Cambridge: Polity Press.

Parton, D. (2014) 'How soon is now?', *Learning Disability Today*, Jul/ Aug.

Parton, N. (2000) 'Some thoughts on the relationship between theory and practice', *British Journal of Social Work*, vol 30, no 4, pp 449-63.

Payne, M. (2006) *What is professional social work?*, Bristol: Policy Press.

Pearson, G. (1975) *The deviant imagination,* London: Macmillan.

Perkin, H. (1996) *The third revolution: Professional elites in the modern world*, London: Routledge.

Petrie, P., Boddy, J., Cameron, C., Heptinstall, E., McQuail, S., Simon, A. and Wigfall, V. (2005) *Pedagogy – A holistic, personal approach to work with children and young people across services. European models for practice, training, education and qualification*, London: Thomas Coram Research Unit.

Philp, A. (1963) *Family failure: A study of 129 families with multiple problems*, London: Faber & Faber.

Pithouse, A., Hall, C., Peckover, S. and White, S. (2009) 'A tale of two CAFs: The impact of the electronic common assessment framework', *British Journal of Social Work,* vol 39, no 4, pp 599-612.

Platt, D. (2008) 'Care or control? The effects of investigations and initial assessments on the social worker–parent relationship', *Journal of Social Work Practice: Psychotherapeutic Approaches in Health, Welfare and the Community*, vol 22, no 3, pp 301-15.

Plomin, J. (2013) 'The abuse of vulnerable adults at Winterbourne View Hospital: the lessons to be learned', *The Journal of Adult Protection,* vol 15, issue 4, pp 182-91.

Pransky, J. and McMillen, D. (2013) 'Exploring the true nature of internal resilience: a view from the inside out', in D. Saleeby (ed) *The strengths perspective in social work practice* (6th edn), Upper Saddle River, NJ: Pearson.

Pritchard, C. (2006) *Mental health social work: Evidence-based practice*, London: Routledge.

Pullen-Sansfaçon, A. and Ward, D. (2012) 'Making interprofessional working work: introducing a groupwork perspective', *British Journal of Social Work*, 30 December, pp 1-17.

Purcell, M., Christian, M. and Frost, N. (2012) 'Addressing the challenges of leading children's services in England: leadership in a changing environment', *Journal of Children's Services*, vol 7, no 2, pp 86-100.

Purkis, J. (2001) *Leadership cultures: The problem of authority in a radical environmental group, in leadership and social movements*, Manchester: Manchester University Press

QAA (Quality Assurance Agency) for Higher Education (2011) *The framework for higher education qualifications in England, Wales and Northern Ireland*, Mansfield: QAA for Higher Education.

Rao, P., Ali, A. and Vostanis, P. (2010) 'Looked-after and adopted children: how should specialist CAMHS be involved?', *Adoption and Fostering*, vol 34, no 2, pp 58-72.

Rawson, J. (2002) 'The practice-research relationship: a case of ambivalent attachment?', *Journal of Social Work*, vol 2, pp 105-22.

Ray, M. and Phillips, J. (2012) *Social work with older people*, Basingstoke: Palgrave Macmillan.

Ray, M., Pugh, R., Roberts, D. and Beech, B. (2008) *Mental health and social work*, Research Briefing, London: Social Care Institute for Excellence.

Raynes, N., Clark, H. and Beecham, J. (eds) (2006) *The report of the Older People's Inquiry into "That bit of help"*, York: Joseph Rowntree Foundation.

Rein, M. and White, S. (1981) 'Knowledge for practice', *Social Service Review*, vol 55, pp 1-41.

Reynolds, J. (2007) 'Discourses of interprofessionalism', *British Journal of Social Work*, vol 37, no 3, pp 441-57.

Richmond, M. (1917) *Social diagnosis*, New York: Russell Sage Foundation.

Riddell, R. (2003) *Schools for our cities: Urban learning in the 21st century*, Stoke on Trent: Trentham Books.

Rintal, D., Hanover, E., Alexander, J., Robert, W., Sanson-Fisher, R., Willems, E. and Halstead, L. (1986) 'Team care: an analysis of verbal behaviour during patient rounds in a rehabilitation hospital', *Archives of Physical Medical Rehabilitation*, vol 1086, no 121, pp 118-22.

Robinson, V. (2001) 'Embedding leadership in task performance', in K. Wong and C. Evers (eds) *Leadership for quality schooling: International perspectives*, London: Falmer, pp 90-102.

Rodd, J. (1998) *Leadership in early childhood*, Maidenhead: Open University Press.

Royal College of Psychiatrists (2013) *Leadership and management in psychiatry: A position statement from the Royal College of Psychiatrists*, London: Royal College of Psychiatrists.

Rubin, A. and Babbie, E. (2011) *Research methods for social work*, Belmont, CA: Brooks/Cole.

Ruch, G. (2012) 'Where have all the feelings gone? Developing reflective and relationship-based management in child-care social work', *British Journal of Social Work*, vol 42, no 7, pp 1315-32.

Ruch, G., Turney, D. and Ward, A. (2010) *Relationship-based social work: Getting to the heart of practice*, London: Jessica Kingsley Publishers.

Ryan, T. and Walker, R. (2007) *Life story work*, London: British Association for Adoption and Fostering.

Sainsbury, E. (1970) *Social diagnosis in casework*, London: Routledge.

SCIE (Social Care Institute for Excellence) (2011) *Safeguarding adults at risk of harm: A legal guide for practitioners*, London: SCIE.

SCIE (2013) *Maximising the potential of re-ablement*, Guide 49, London: SCIE.

SCIE and University of Bristol (2013) *Social work practice pilots and pioneers in social work for adults*, London: SCIE.

SCLD (Scottish Consortium for Learning Disability) (2008) *The principles and standards of citizen leadership*, Glasgow: User and Carer Forum (www.scld.org.uk/scld-projects/citizen-leadership/principles-and-standards).

Scott, J. (1971) *Internalisation of norms: A sociological theory of moral commitment*, Upper Saddle River, NJ: Prentice-Hall.

SCSN (Social Care Strategic Network) for Mental Health (2010) *Positive future of adult mental health social work*, London: SCSN (scsnmh.com).

Seabrook, J. (2013) *Pauperland: Poverty and the poor in Britain*, London: C. Hurst & Co.

Searing, H. (2006) *Illusion and disillusion* (www.radical.org.uk/barefoot).

Searle, R. and Patent, V. (2013) 'Recruitment and retention and role slumping in child protection: the evaluation of in-service training initiatives', *British Journal of Social Work*, vol 43, no 6, pp 1111-29.

Seebohm Report (1968) *Report of the Committee on Local Authority and Allied Personal Social Services*, Cmnd 3707, London: HMSO.

Sellick, C., Thoburn, J. and Philpot, T. (2004) *What works in adoption and foster care*, London: Jessica Kingsley Publishers.

Selwyn, J., Sturgess, W., Quinton, D. and Baxter, C (2006) *Costs and outcomes of non-infant adoptions*, London: British Association for Adoption and Fostering.

Senge, P. (1990) *The fifth discipline: The art and practice of the learning organisation*, New York: Doubleday & Co.

Sergiovanni, T. (1990) *Value-added leadership: How to get extraordinary performance in schools*, Orlando, FL: Jovanovich Publishing.

Shaping Our Lives, National User Network (2013) (www. shapingourlives.org.uk).

Sharman, C. (2007) *Leading by example*, Boston, MA: Harvard Business School Press.

Shaw, G. (1911) *The doctor's dilemma: Preface on doctors*, New York: Harmondsworth.

Shaw, I. (2004) 'Evaluation for a learning organisation', in N. Gould and M. Baldwin (eds) *Social work, critical reflection and the learning organisation*, Aldershot: Ashgate.

Shaw, I. and Norton, M. (2007) *The kinds and quality of social work research in UK universities*, London: Social Care Institute for Excellence.

Sheldon, B. and Chilvers, R. (2000) *Evidence-based social care: A study of prospects and problems*, Lyme Regis: Russell House Publishing.

Sheldon, B. and Macdonald, G. (2009) *A textbook of social work*, London: Routledge.

Sheppard, M. (1995) 'Social work, social science and practice wisdom', *British Journal of Social Work*, vol 25, no 3, pp 265-93.

Sheppard, M. (1998) 'Practice validity, reflexivity and knowledge for social work', *British Journal of Social Work*, vol 28, no 5, pp 763-81.

Simon, B.L. (1994) *The empowerment tradition in American social work*, New York: Columbia University Press.

Skills for Care and Development (2012) *Leadership and management in care services*, National Occupational Standards, Leeds: Skills for Care and Development.

Skills for Care and Development (2013) *Developing social workers' practice: Core principles for employers providing opportunities for social workers continuing professional development*, Leeds: Skills for Care.

Smale, G., Tuson, G., Cooper, M., Wardle, M. and Crosbie, D. (1988) *Community social work: A paradigm for change*, London: National Institute for Social Work.

Smith, P. (1995) 'On the unintended consequences of publishing performance data in the public sector', *International Journal of Public Administration*, vol 18, nos 2 and 3, pp 277-310.

Social Work Task Force (2009) *Building a safe, confident future*, London: Department for Health and Department for Children, Families and Schools.

Social Work Reform Board (2010) *Building a safe and confident future: Implementing the recommendations of the Social Work Task Force*, London: Department for Education and Department of Health.

Social Work Reform Board (2012) *Building a safe and confident future: Maintaining the momentum*, London: Department for Education and Department of Health.

Stanley, N., Austerberry, H., Bilson, A., Farrelly, N., Hargreaves, K., Hollingworth, K., Hussein, S., Ingold, A., Larkins, C., Manthorpe, J., Ridley, J. and Strange, V. (2012) *Social work practices: Report of the national evaluation*, London: Department for Education.

Stevens, A., MacClellan, J. and Sergeant, T. (1996) *Diploma in Social Work pathways: Adult services particular pathways to the Diploma in Social Work*, London: Central Council for Education and Training in Social Work.

Stevenson, O. (2013) *Reflections on a life in social work*, Buckingham: Hinton House.

Steventon, A., Bardsley, M., Billings, J., Georghiou, T. and Lewis, G. (2011) *An evaluation of the impact of community-based interventions on hospital use*, London: Nuffield Trust.

SWAN (Social Work Action Network) (2004) *Social work and social justice: A manifesto for a new engaged practice*, Paisley, SWAN (www.socialworkfuture.org).

Sydanmaanlakka, P. (2002) *Intelligent organisations, integrating performance, competence and knowledge management*, London: Capstone.

Tadd, W., Hillman, A., Calnan, M., Calnan, S., Read, S. and Bayer, A. (2012) *Dignity in practice: An exploration of the care of older people in acute NHS trusts, A research summary*, Cardiff: Cardiff University.

Tarren-Sweeney, M. (2010) 'It's time to re-think mental health services for children in care, and those adopted from care', *Clinical Child Psychology and Psychiatry*, vol 15, no 4, pp 613-26.

Taylor, B. and Campbell, B. (2011) 'Quality, risk and governance: social workers perspectives', *The International Journal of Leadership in Public Services*, vol 7, no 4, pp 256-72.

Taylor, I. and Bogo, M. (2013) 'Perfect opportunity – perfect storm? Raising the standards of social work education in England', *British Journal of Social Work*, 2 May.

Tenkasi, R. and Hay, G. (2004) 'Actionable knowledge and scholar practitioners: a process model of theory practice linkage', *Systemic Practice and Action Research*, vol 17, no 3, pp 177-205.

Thoburn, J., with Making Research Count Consortium (2009) *Effective interventions for complex families where there are concerns about or evidence of a child suffering significant harm,* London, Centre for Excellence and Outcomes in Children and Young People's Services.

Thomas, S. and Wolfensberger, W. (1999) 'An overview of social role valorization', in R.J. Flynn and R.A. Lemay, *A quarter century of normalization and social role valorization: Evolution and impact,* Ottawa: University of Ottawa Press.

Thompson, L. and West, D. (2013) 'Professional development in the contemporary education context: encouraging practice wisdom', *Social Work Education*, vol 32, no 1, pp 118-33.

Thompson, S. and Thompson, N. (2008) *The critically reflective practitioner,* London: Macmillan.

Trevithick, P. (2003) 'Effective relationship-based practice: a theoretical exploration', *Journal of Social Work Practice*, vol 17, no 2, pp 163-76.

Trevithick, P. (2008) 'Revisiting the knowledge base of social work: a framework for practice', *British Journal of Social Work*, vol 38, no 6, pp 1212-37.

Trevithick, P. (2012) *Practice skills and knowledge: A practice handbook,* Maidenhead: Open University Press.

Triseliotis, J., Feast, J. and Kyle, F. (2005) *The adoption triangle revisited: A study of adoption, search and reunion experiences,* London: British Association for Adoption and Fostering.

Tsui, C. (2008) 'The nature of practice wisdom in social work revisited', *International Social Work*, vol 51, pp 47-54.

Unrau, Y., Gabor, P. and Grinnell, R. (2007) *Evaluation in social work: The art and science of practice* (4th edn), New York: Oxford University Press.

van Zwanenberg, Z. (ed) (2010) *Leadership in social care,* Research Highlights in Social Work No 51, London: Jessica Kingsley Publishers.

Walker, P. (2002) 'Co-production' in E. Mayo and H. Moore (eds) *Building the mutual state,* London: New Economics Foundation.

Wanless, D. (2006) *Securing good care for older people: Taking a long-term view*, London: The King's Fund.

Ward, H., Brown, R., Westlake, D. and Munro, E.R. (2010) *Infants suffering, or likely to suffer, significant harm: A prospective longitudinal study*, Research Brief, DfE-RB053, London: Department for Education.

Wastell, D. and White, S. (2010) 'Technology as magic: fetish and folly in the IT-enabled reform of children's services', in P. Ayre and M. Preston-Shoot (eds) *Children's services at the crossroads: A critical evaluation of contemporary policy for practice*, Lyme Regis: Russell House Publishing, pp 107-14.

Wastell, D., White, S., Broadhurst, K., Hall, C., Peckover, S. and Pithouse, A. (2010) 'Children's services in the iron cage of performance management: street level bureaucracy and the spectre of Svejism', *International Journal of Social Welfare*, vol 19, pp 310-20.

Webber, M. (2013) 'Developing advanced practitioners in mental health social work: pedagogical considerations', *Social Work Education*, vol 31, no 7, pp 944-55.

Webber, M., Huxley, P. and Harris, T. (2011) 'Social capital and the course of depression: six month prospective cohort study', *Journal of Affective Disorders*, vol 129, pp 149-57.

Welsh Assembly (2011) *Sustainable social services for Wales: A framework for action*, Cardiff: Welsh Assembly.

White, S. (2002) 'Accomplishing "the case" in paediatrics and child health: medicine and morality in inter-professional talk', *Sociology of Health and Illness*, vol 24, no 4, pp 409-35.

White, V. (2009) 'Quiet challenges? Professional practice in modernised social work', in J. Harris and V. White (eds) *Modernising social work: Critical considerations*, Bristol: Policy Press.

Wilde, A. and Glendinning, C. (2012) '"If they're helping me then how can I be independent?" The perceptions and experience of users of home-care re-ablement services', *Health and Social Care in the Community*, vol 20, no 6, pp 583-90.

Wilkinson, D. (2007) *Distributed leadership*, Briefing Paper, Leeds: Northern Leadership Academy.

Wilson, V. and Pirrie, A. (2000) *Multidisciplinary teamwork. Beyond the barriers? A review of the issues*, Glasgow: University of Glasgow.

Windle, K., Wagland, R., Forder, J., d'Amico, F., Janssen, D. and Wistow, G. (2009) *National evaluation of partnerships for older people*, Canterbury: Personal Social Services Research Unit, University of Kent.

Wiseman, J. and Davies, E. (2013) *Response to the Social Worker Employers Standards*, Research Report, Birmingham: Bostock.

Wood, C. and Salter, J. (2012) *The home cure*, London: Demos.

Woodcock, G. and Avakumovic, I. (1950) *The anarchist prince: A biographical study of Peter Kropotkin*, London: Boardman.

Wootton, B. (1959) *Social science and social pathology*, London: George Allen & Unwin.

Young, P. (1965) 'Supervision of staff' in P. Young, B. Warham and D. Pettes, *Administration and staff supervision in the child care services*, London: Association of Child Care Officers.

Younghusband, E. (1959) *Report of the working party on social workers in the local authority health and welfare services*, London: Department of Health.

Younghusband, E. (1978) *Social work in Britain: 1950-1975: A follow-up study*, London: George Allen & Unwin.

Zucchelli, F. (2013) 'Taking the right approach', *Mental Health Today*, July/August, pp 8-9.

Index

A

accountability and social work 24, 38, 72, 82, 101, 103, 127-8
Adoption and Permanence Taskforce 36
adoption policies 36-7
adult social services 39-44
  guiding and navigating roles of social workers 121-2
  and personalisation trends 79-81
  promoting independence and empowerment 136-41
  promoting the psychosocial 141-4
anti-professionalism approaches 46
Armstrong, D 52
Ash, A 12, 43
Asquith, S et al 46, 53
assessment and social work practice 39-43
  electronic 70
  see also proceduralisation of practice
Association of Social Workers (ASW) 152
ASYE (assessed and supported year in employment) 45, 79, 110, 153
Atwal, A and Caldwell, K 141
Audit Commission 40, 52
authoritarian leadership 20, 22
  and Dworkin's 'doughnut of discretion' 23
autonomy 21-4, 102-5
  and funding constraints 16, 45, 60-1
  see also discretion; judgement
Ayre, P and Calder, M 151
Ayre, P and Preston-Shoot, M 82, 165

B

Bandura, A 167-8
Barclay Report (1982) 90, 145, 161
Barker, C et al 17

Barry, M 98
Barth, R et al 51, 151
Bass, B and Alvilio, B 6
BASW *see* British Association of Social Workers (BASW)
Batmanghelidjh, C 160
Batty, E et al 161
Bazalgette, L et al 34
Beckett, F 150
'bed-blocking' 140-1
Beddoe, L et al 17
Bennett, N et al 57
Bennis, W 3
Beresford, P et al 157
Biesteck, F 114, 116, 157
'Big Society' 115-16
Bilton, K 32, 63
Black, J 22
Blewett, J and Boaz, A 46
Boddy, J and Statham, J 119
'bonfire of the quangos' 59
Borrego, M and Newswander, L 132-3, 139
Bowyer, S 131
Boyatzis, RE and McKee, A 7
Bradford, D and Cohen, A 29
Brand, D et al 76, 86-7
Brandon, D and Jordan, B 118
Brandon, M et al 116-17, 131
Brewer, C and Lait, J 89, 156
Brilliant, E 153
Briskman, L 19, 31, 38, 167
British Association of Social Workers (BASW) 59-67, 79, 120, 125
  background and history of 63-6
  and the Children Act-1989 37
  relationship with the College of Social Work 63-7
  relationship with Social Care Institute for Excellence (SCIE) 61

Brown, G and Harris, T 143
Burnham, D 77
Burnham, J 53

C
Cambridge Education and Children's
 Workforce Development Council
 78, 110
Cameron, A et al 131-2
campaigning work 71-2
capabilities framework see Professional
 capabilities framework
Care Council for Wales 59
care management, in adult services
 39-44
Care Programme Approach (CPA)
 41-2
Carpenter, J et al 45, 78-9, 94, 96,
 110, 153
Carr, S 79
CCETSW 40, 109
Centre for Excellence and Outcomes
 in Children and Young People's
 Services 58
Chaleff, I 160
Chamberlain, C and Ward, D 102
Chartered Society of Physiotherapy
 128
Chief Social Worker for Adults/
 Children and Families 32, 72
child development training 48
child and family services
 leadership roles in social work
 practice 116-22
 see also child protection
Child Poverty Action Group (CPAG)
 37
child protection 82-4
 legal definition 38
 performance indicators 37-8
 research skills 46
Children Act 1989 37-8, 40, 82
Children's Commissioner for England
 14
citizen / servant leadership 10-12,
 13-15, 21
Clarke, J and Newman, J 53, 151
clerical leadership 27
clinical leadership competency
 framework 29
co-production 115, 151, 161
Coats, D and Passmore, E 33
code of ethics (BASW) 125
Cole, C 138
collaborative working models 10-12,
 25-6
collective responsibility 25-6
College of Social Work 2, 15, 40-2,
 49-50, 59-67, 89-90, 104, 106,
 109, 123, 125, 145, 154, 162

characteristics and roles 59-67
development of capabilities
 framework 44-5
establishment 60-2
funding and autonomy 16, 45, 61
identification of reserved duties
 89-90
lack of elections and open
 collaborations 49
roles and functions of social workers
 50
collegiate patronage 49, 64-5
Commission on the Future Funding
 of Health and Social Care in
 England 81
commissioning 122, 144, 152
community-focused practice 7-8, 26,
 130, 145, 161-2
competence 108
consciousness-raising 119-21
Conservative Party 115
continuing professional development
 45-6
 demonstrating responsibility for
 learning 103
 and self-leadership 162-5
core skills of social work 15
Cousins, C 49, 64
creativity 4-5, 20
Cree, V 91
Croisdale-Appleby, D 5, 31-2, 47, 69,
 72, 77, 80, 107-8, 159-60
Crompton, R 24-5
Cromwell, Oliver 25
Cullen, A 56, 130
Cutler, T and Waine, B 35

D
Darzi, A 29
Davies, B and Challis, D 79, 137
Davies, M 75
DCSF 61, 82
defensive practices 101
demands on services 100-2, 160-1
democratisation and follower power
 53-4
Derber, C 50
DfE 36, 38-40, 62, 78, 82-4, 97, 107,
 131, 149-50, 152
DH 41-3, 48, 51, 61, 79-80, 106, 144
DH and DfE 86
DHSSPS 79
Dillow, C 151
Dilnot, A 81
discretion 21-4, 52-3, 102-5
 see also judgement
distributed leadership 56-8
 and cross-boundary working 122-8
Dolman, E and Bond, D 16, 55
Donnellan, H 94

Donnellan, H and Jack, G 105
Donzelot, J 130
Dworkin, R 22-3, 52, 103

E

early childhood services 27-8
education of social workers *see* social
    work education and training
educational services and leadership 28
    and distributed leadership 57
elder abuse 43
eligibility criteria 52-3
elitism 32, 45-6, 53
Ellis, K 52
Emilsson, UM 139
emotional intelligence 16
employer partnership professional
    development initiatives 45, 68-72,
    79, 110, 153
empowerment 119-21
    promotion of 136-41
English Civil War 25
Evans, T and Harris, J 102
evidence-informed practice
    arguments for 68-72, 83-4, 149,
    162-4
    and social justice 67-8
    and social work education 45-8,
    67-8
    vs. intuition 83

F

Fairhurst, G 6
family therapy 115
Farmer, E and Lutman, E 134, 154
Farmer, E and Wijedasa, D 82
Fauth, R et al 117
Featherstone, B et al 2, 11, 47, 78,
    117
Ferguson, H 11, 35, 114
Ferguson, I 71
Ferguson, I and Woodward, R 71
Flynn, M 41-2, 120, 144
Folgheraiter, F 76-7
'followership' 14, 53-4, 55-6, 157-60
Formula One, leadership and success
    26
Forrester, D and Harwin, J 46
Frontline 69
Fukuyama, F 159
funding of organisational structures
    58-61
    and education 16, 45, 60-1
    reliance on 65-7

G

Galpin, D et al 123
'gardener' metaphors 12-13
General Medical Council (GMC) 95,
    107, 124

General Social Care Council (GSCC)
    86
Gilbert, P 3, 17-18
Glasby, J 81
Glastonbury, B et al 96
Glendinning, C et al 80, 136
Godden, J 94
Goldberg, E 143
Goleman, D 16, 55
Goodall, A 26
Goodall, A and Pogrebna, G 26
Goodman, S and Trowler, I 115
Gould, N and Baldwin, M 28, 164
Grant, L and Kinman, G 17
Greenleaf, RK 13, 152-3
Griffiths Report 90
Grundy, M 3, 27, 166

H

Hadley, R and McGrath, M 26, 161
Hafford-Letchfield, T et al 57-8
Halfpenny, N 38
Hall, C et al 101
Hallett, C and Stevenson, O 131
Halmos, P 89-90, 156
Hamer, M 156
Harkness, D and Hensley, H 94
Harris, J and White, V 1, 49
Harris, N 114
Hatton, C et al 81
Health and Care Professions Council
    (HCPC) 95, 108-9
healthcare
    and NHS leadership 28-30
    and state mediation 52
    working with social workers 130-4,
    135-6, 139-41
Healthcare leadership model 29
Hegel, G 38
Herod, J and Lymbury, M 143
Hill, C 13, 25
Hodson, R and Cooke, E 74
Hoggett, P and Hambleton, R 26
Holden, G et al 153
Holmes, E et al 48, 62, 68, 103-6
Holroyd, J and Brown, K 17
Honey, P 98
Horne, M and Shirley, T 115
hospital discharges 136-41
Host Policy Research 45
Houghton Committee 36
HSCIC 42-3
Huby, G et al 136
Hudson, B 137
Hugman, R 96
Huxley, P et al 142, 143, 161
Huzzard, T and Spoelstra, S 12

I

identity crisis in the profession 46

IFSW 52, 74, 114
independence, promotion of 136-41
independent practices 51-2
informal leaders 26
Ingram, R 16
integrated working 129-47
inter-disciplinary working 129-47
internalisation of values 100
intuition, vs. evidence-based practice 83
Ioakimidis, V 77

J
Jack, Gordon 94
Jackson, A 159
Jay, A 9
Johnson, T 31, 49, 64
Jones, C and Pound, L 27
Jones, C et al 46, 75
Jones, R 26
Jordan, B 46, 115
Jordan, B with Jordan, C 46
'joyful activism' 17
    see also positivity and positive approaches
judgement 20, 83-4, 93-4, 102-3, 107, 162
    and empowerment 120
    vs. proceduralisation 100-2, 151
    see also discretion
Just William (Crompton) 24-5

K
Kadushin, A 94
Kagan, S and Hallmark, L 27
Keith-Lucas, A 157
Kellerman, B 53-4, 55, 69, 158-9
Kelley, R 158
Kemshall, H et al 98
Kerr, B et al 40, 81
King's Fund 57, 124
Kirkman, E and Melrose, K 83
Kotter, JP 4-5
Kouzes, J and Posner, B 168

L
lack of esteem 46
Laming, Lord 117, 156
Langan, J and Lindow, V 11
Leadbeater, C and Lownsbrough, H 79
'leaderless-ness' 25-6
leaders
    attributes 48-9
    and proactive approaches 49
leadership
    benefits and value 4
    core qualities and components 5, 6
    descriptions and purpose of 3-6

    alternative views and practice examples 6-10
    and citizen leadership 10-12, 13-15
    leader as 'gardener' 12-13
    as 'process' 6
    and transformational leadership 6-9
    in direct social work practice 114-22
        empowerment 119-21
        guiding and navigating 121-2
        social pedagogy 119
        working with children and families 116-19
    essential aspects of 17-18
    lack of in social work profession 31-54
        background policy contexts 33-5
        causes 33-4, 45-6
        externally driven agendas 36-9
        filling the vacuum 54
        therapeutic work vs. 'assessment' in adult services 39-44
    need for 1-3
    other services and professions 27-30
    potential demise of 53-4
    public policy contexts
        externally driven agendas 36-9
        subordination of social work profession 50-3
    sources 55-72
    styles and theories, spectrum and overview 19-21
    taking responsibility for 165-8
    vs. democratisation and follower power 53-4
    ways of taking a lead 48-54, 149-69
        dealing with service demands 160-2
        promoting self-leadership 162-5
        taking responsibility 165-8
        through followership 157-60
        through relationship-based practice 156-7
    see also self-leadership
leadership practice, principles of 54
learning disability
    challenges for adult social care services 41-3
    promoting psychosocial perspectives 144
Lefevre, M 15
Leff, J 143
legal frameworks and regulations
    taking precedence over social work profession 9-10, 50
    vs discretion 22
Leslie, C 65
LGA (Local Government Association) 42, 44-5

Lipsky, M 34, 52, 102
Lister, R 14
Littlechild, B 11, 117
Lloyd, J 81
Local Government Association (LGA) 42, 44-5, 108
Local Safeguarding Children's Board 83
London County Council 145
Lorenz, W 119
Lymbery, M 80

M

McAuliffe, C 130
McCrae, N et al 136
McDonald, C and Chenoweth, L 153-4
Macdonald, G 46, 82
McGregor, K 94
McKitterick, W 34, 53, 103, 117, 128, 146
McNeil, F et al 120
Making Research Count 67, 69
management and leadership (general) 4-6
see also social work managers
managerialism 31, 33-5, 53, 84
Manthorpe, J et al 139
Manthorpe, J and Martineau, S 131
Mantz, C and Neck, C 16, 167-8
Maquire, I et al 67
Martin, P 60-1
Marturano, A and Gosling, J 6
Mattinson, J 94
measurable outcomes 50-1
see also performance measurement
medical profession
    management capabilities 107
    standards of practice 95
membership and social work organisations 61-2
mental capacity 12
mental health services, promoting psychosocial perspectives 141-4
Meyerson, D 48-9
Milburn, NL et al 135
Milne, M et al 80
mindfulness 16-17
mission statements 22-4
models of leadership 20-1
    SCLD User and Carer Forum 13-14
Morley, R 156
Morrison, T 16, 71
Morris, P 42
multi-disciplinary working 129-47
    characteristics 129-34
    evidence base for 131-2
    key issues 131-2
    leadership roles 122-8

promoting independence and re-ablement 136-41
promoting the psychosocial model 141-4
social workers as lead professionals 134-6
Munro Review (2010/2011) 19-20, 31, 82-4, 102, 152

N

Narey, M 9, 20, 31-2, 36, 47, 69, 75, 159-60
national campaigning 71-2
National Children's Bureau 58
National Skills Academy for Social Care 58-9
National Skills Academy for Social Care and DH 54, 155, 167
Neck, C and Manz, C 55
Needham, C and Carr, S 115
negativity 17
New Deal for Communities 161
'New Right' 53
Newman, M et al 51
Newman, S 10
Newman, T et al 46, 67, 133
NHS Institute for Clinical Innovation and Improvement and the Academy of Medical Royal Colleges 54, 56
NHS Institute for Innovation and Improvement 29
NHS and leadership 28-30
see also healthcare
NHS Leadership Academy 29
Normansfield Hospital 42-3
Northern Ireland Social Care Council 59
North, M 89-90, 156
NSPCC 122
nurse-led case management 139
Nuttall, K 115

O

Ofsted 94, 100, 102, 117
Okitikpi, T 115
older people, and bed-blocking 140-1
Oliver, D 140
Oliver, J et al 143
organisational leadership 22-4
organisational learning, need for 2
organisational structures in social care 58-67
    funding 60-1, 65-7
    history of 63-5
    membership challenges 61-2
    setting standards 62-3
O'Sullivan, T 46

P
pace-setting leadership 20-1
Page, R 37
paperwork burden 20
Parker, G 136-7
Parker, M 24, 151
Parton, D 43
Parton, N 67
passive leadership 24-5
Payne, M 120-1
Pearson, G 67
peer working
    essential aspects of self-leadership 18
    leadership roles 122-8
performance measurement 34-5, 38-9
    vs personal accountability 38
Perkin, H 53
personal accountability
    and child protection work 38
    need for 72
'personalisation agenda' 35, 79-81
Petrie, P et al 119
Philp, A 114
Pithouse, A et al 70
Platt, D 114
Plomin, J 42-3
positivity and positive approaches 17,
    34, 41, 48-9, 53-4, 77-8, 91-2,
    102, 115
power relations within professions 49,
    53-4, 164-5
    and democratisation 53-4
power-based leadership concepts 7
Pransky, J and McMillen, D 168
principal social worker 7, 32
principles of leadership practice 54
Pritchard, C 136
probation service 60
proceduralisation of practice 38-9,
    70-1
    as response to management demands
        100-2
    vs. judgement 101-2, 151
Professional capabilities framework
    (SWRB; CSW)
    citations 15, 44, 99, 104-11, 123-7,
        154, 162-3, 166
    development of 44-5
professional development *see*
    continuing professional
    development
professional education and training *see*
    social work education and training
professional elite 53
professional identity crisis 46, 50-3
professional judgement *see* judgement
professional standards *see* standards of
    practice
professionalism
    constraints 20

recognition and valuing 33-4
    see also self-leadership
professions
    an analysis of power 49
    standards of practice 95
psychosocial perspectives in practice
    141-4
public policy, and marginalisation of
    social work 50-3
Pullen-Sanfacon, A and Ward, D 130
Purcell, M et al 146, 154
Purkis, J 26

Q
QAA for Higher Education 123

R
Rao, P et al 135
Rawson, J 70
Ray, M and Phillips, J 133
Ray, M et al 135-6
re-ablement services 136-41
recruitment of social workers 103
referral rates 160
reflective supervision 94-7
Reform Board *see* Social Work
    Reform Board
registration bodies 95
Rein, M and White, S 153
relationship-based practice 11, 14-15,
    41, 43, 56, 114-20, 134, 143, 149-
    51, 156-7
research and evaluation skills 45-8
Research in Practice / (Adults) 58
reserved duties 88-90
resilience, internal / emotional 17,
    168
resonance 7
responsibility and ownership of roles
    165-8
Reynolds, J 62
Richmond, M 40
Riddell, R 28
Rintal, D et al 141
risk avoidance 98, 140
Robinson, V 6
Rodd, J 27
Rotherham child sexual exploitation
    scandals 9-10
Royal College of Psychiatrists 56-7,
    124
Rubin, A and Babbie, E 2
Ruch, G 100
Ruch, G et al 114
Ryan, T and Walker, R 15

S
safeguarding 82-4
    see also child protection
Sainsbury, E 40

'scholar-practitioner' 70-1
SCIE (Social Care Institute for
    Excellence) 12, 58, 61-2, 136-7
SCIE and University of Bristol 21
SCLD User and Carer Forum 13-14
Scottish Consortium for Learning
    Disability (SCLD) User and Carer
    Forum 13
Scottish Social Services Council 59
Scott, J 100
SCSN for Mental Health 130
Seabrook, J 1
Searing, H 91-2
Searle, R and Patent, V 103, 106, 118
Seebohm Implementation Action
    Group 37
Seebohm Report (1968) 44, 156
self-leadership
    concepts and descriptions 16-18
    and continuing professional
        development 162-5
    and distributed leadership 56-8
    with peers 15-19
    practical tasks in social work practice
        18
    as responsibility of all 18
    and self-management 17
self-management 17
Sellick, C et al 37
Selwyn, J et al 37
Senge, P 28
Sergiovanni, T 28
servant leadership 10-12, 13, 21, 153
Shaping Our Lives, National User
    Network 156
shared leadership models 29
    and cross-agency working 122-8
Sharman, C 12-13
Shaw, G 46
Shaw, I and Norton, M 2, 163
Sheldon, B and Chilvers, R 46
Sheldon, B and Macdonald, G 75,
    153
Sheppard, M 5, 14, 46, 67
Simon, BL 120
Skills for Care and Development 4,
    58-9, 108-9
skills in practice
    capabilities framework 15, 44-5, 99,
        104-11, 123-6, 154, 162-3, 166
    and flexible decision making 104-5
    procedure-based vs. therapeutic
        relationship-based work 39-44
    see also social work practice;
        supervision
Smale, G et al 26
Smith, P 39
Social Care Institute for Excellence
    (SCIE) 12, 58
    relationship with BASW 61

'social diagnosis' 40
social justice 34
    and evidence-informed practice
        67-8
    vs. state-mediated professions 50
social pedagogy 119
Social Work Action Network
    (SWAN) 34, 67-8
social work with adults see adult social
    services
social work education and training
    challenges 44-8
    development and history of 44-5,
        60-1, 110-11
    funding of 16, 45, 60-1
    key reforms post-2000 48
    partnerships with employers 68-72,
        103-4
    places for 'social justice and the
        personal' 67-8
    professional capabilities framework
        15, 44, 99, 104-11, 123-7, 154,
        162-3, 166
    research capacities 69-72
    research skills 45-8
    self-leadership in 162-5
    trust in 103-4
    see also continuing professional
        development
social work managers 97-100
    key roles 98-9
    as educators 105-11
    internalisation of values 100
    managing demands 100-2
    modelling good practice 99
    segregation and isolation of 166
    see also leadership; self-leadership
social work organisations see
    organisational structures in social
    care
social work practice
    demands on services 100-2, 160-1
    leadership with colleagues and across
        services 122-8
    leadership in direct social work
        114-22
        with children and families 116-19
        empowerment 119-21
        guiding and navigating 121-2
        in social pedagogy 119
    modelling of good practice 99
    roles and responsibilities 74-9
        child protection and safeguarding
            82-4
        community-focused practice 7-8,
            26, 130, 145, 161-2
        extent of remits 84-8
        personalisation trends in adult
            services 79-81

relationship-based work 11, 14-15, 41, 43, 56, 114-20, 134, 143, 149-51, 156-7
reserved duties 88-90
skills and capability frameworks 15, 44, 99, 104-11, 123-7, 154, 162-3, 166
standards for 62-3
uncertainty discourses 90-2
Social Work Reform Board 15, 31, 44, 62, 83, 106, 109, 154, 159-60, 162
social work supervision 94-7
Social Work Task Force 16, 31-2, 44, 47, 60-1, 83, 85
social workers
as 'all things to all men' 84-8
as 'gardener' 12-13
as 'lead professionals' 134-6
as 'servant' 10, 13
standards of practice
application and take up 62-3
development of 62
registration bodies 95
and supervision 94-7
Stanley, N et al 21, 51, 103
'state-mediated professions' 49-50, 52, 64
Step Up to Social Work 69
Stevens, A et al 40
Stevenson, O 73, 156-7, 165-6
Steventon, A et al 139
'street-level bureaucrats' 34-5
styles of leadership 19-21
supervision 94-7
SWAN see Social Work Action Network (SWAN)
Sydanmaanlakka, P 55

T
Tadd, W et al 140
target-driven managerialism 33-5, 38-9
Tarren-Sweeney, M 135
Taylor, B and Campbell, B 152
Taylor, I and Bogo, M 108
teaching and leadership 28
team leaders 5-6
team managers 99
'tempered radical' professionals 48
Tenkasi, R and Hay, G 70
'therapeutic imperative' of positive change 34
therapeutic work, vs. procedural work 39-44
Third Way 46-7
Thoburn, J et al 118
Thomas, S and Wolfensberger, W 138
Thompson, S and Thompson, N 49
trade unions 63-4, 66

training and education see social work education and training
transactional leadership 20-1
transformational leadership 21
core components 6-7
and discretion 22
and Dworkin's 'doughnut of discretion' 23
practice examples 7-9
Trevithick, P 114, 116, 156-7
Triseliotis, J et al 37
trust 20
and distributed leadership 57-8, 103-4
Tsui, C 45-6

U
uncertainty and social work practice 90-2
Unison 64, 66
Unrau, Y et al 51
urban regeneration 161-2

V
van Zwanenberg, Z 13
vulnerability factors 142-3

W
Walker, P 115
Wanless, D 81
Ward, H et al 48
Wastell, D and White, S 38
Wastell, D et al 52
Webber, M 163
Webber, M et al 142-3
Welsh Assembly 79
White, S 101, 145
White, V 39, 50
Wilkinson, D 154-5
Wilson, V and Pirrie, A 131-2
Windle, K et al 139, 146
Winterbourne View Hospital 41-4, 144
Wiseman, J and Davies, E 45, 94, 97, 162
Wood, C and Salter, J 140-1
Woodcock, G and Avakumovic, I 53
Wootton, B 40, 89, 156

Y
young people, need for better listening skills 14
Younghusband, E 37, 44, 46, 50, 52, 91, 109
Young, P 94

Z
Zucchelli, F 145